First World War
and Army of Occupation
War Diary
France, Belgium and Germany

37 DIVISION
Headquarters, Branches and Services
Adjutant and Quarter-Master General
1 August 1915 - 30 June 1918

WO95/2516/1

The Naval & Military Press Ltd
www.nmarchive.com
Published in association with The National Archives

Published by

The Naval & Military Press Ltd

Unit 10 Ridgewood Industrial Park,

Uckfield, East Sussex,

TN22 5QE England

Tel: +44 (0) 1825 749494

www.naval-military-press.com

www.nmarchive.com

This diary has been reprinted in facsimile from the original. Any imperfections are inevitably reproduced and the quality may fall short of modern type and cartographic standards.

Contents

Document type	Place/Title	Date From	Date To
Heading	WO95/2516/1		
Miscellaneous	Public Record Office		
Heading	37th Division 'A' & 'Q' Branch Aug 1915-Sep 1918		
Heading	37th Division H.Q. 37th Div. "A" Vol 1.2.3. August 15 To October 1915		
Heading	War Diary Of Administrative Staff, Headquarters 37th Division From 1st August 1915 To 31st August 1915 (Volume 1)		
War Diary	Tilques	01/08/1915	03/08/1915
War Diary	Renescure	04/08/1915	04/08/1915
War Diary	Caestre	05/08/1915	08/08/1915
War Diary	In Trench Warfare	08/08/1915	08/08/1915
War Diary	Caestre	09/08/1915	24/08/1915
War Diary	Doullens	25/08/1915	31/08/1915
Heading	War Diary Of Administrative Staff, Headquarters 37th Division From 1st September 1915 To 30th September 1915 (Volume 2)		
War Diary	Doullens	01/09/1915	05/09/1915
War Diary	Pas	06/09/1915	30/09/1915
Heading	War Diary of Administrative Staff, Headquarters 37th Division from 1st October 1915 to 31st October 1915 Volume 3		
War Diary	Pas	01/10/1915	31/10/1915
Heading	HQ 37 Division A&Q 1915 Nov		
Heading	Gap X Temp Edward For W.D. 154/66 1915 Nov		
Heading	H.Q. 37th Div. "A" Vol 4 Nov. 15		
Heading	War Diary of Administrative Staff 37th Division From 1st November 1915 To 30th November 1915		
War Diary	Pas	01/11/1915	30/11/1915
Miscellaneous	Statement Shewing Material From Enemy-Ended 19th Nov. 1916	27/11/1916	27/11/1916
Heading	A Branch 37th Div. Vol 5		
Heading	War Diary Of Administrative Staff, 37th Division From 1st December 1915 To 31st December 1915		
War Diary	Pas	01/12/1915	31/12/1915
Heading	A.&.Q 37th Div. Vol 6		
Heading	War Diary of Administrative Staff, 37th Division From 1st January 1916 to 31st January 1916		
War Diary	Pas	01/01/1916	31/01/1916
Heading	War Diary of Administrative Staff 37th Division From 1st February 1916 To 29th February 1916		
Heading	A. & Q 37th Div. Vol 7		
War Diary	Pas	01/02/1916	21/02/1916
War Diary	Bavincourt	21/02/1916	29/02/1916
Heading	War Diary of Administrative Staff, 37th Division from March 1 1916 to March 31 1916		
War Diary	Bavincourt	01/03/1916	19/03/1916
War Diary	Lucheux	20/03/1916	31/03/1916

Heading	War Diary of Administrative Staff 37th Divisional Headquarters From 1st April, 1916 to 30th April 1916 (Volume 9)		
War Diary	Lucheux	01/04/1916	30/04/1916
Heading	War Diary of Administrative Staff, 37th Division From 1st May, 1916 to 31st May 1916 (Volume 10)		
War Diary	Lucheux	01/05/1916	02/05/1916
War Diary	Bavincourt	03/05/1916	31/05/1916
Heading	War Diary of Administrative Staff, 37th Division from 1st June 1916 to 30th June 1916 Vol 11		
Miscellaneous	D.A.G. G.H.Q. 3rd Echelon	02/07/1916	02/07/1916
War Diary	Bavincourt	01/06/1916	30/06/1916
Heading	War Diary of Administrative Staff 37th Division from 1st to 31st July 1916		
Miscellaneous	D.A.G. G.H.Q. 3rd Echelon	01/08/1916	01/08/1916
War Diary	Bavincourt	01/07/1916	04/07/1916
War Diary	Pas	05/07/1916	15/07/1916
War Diary	Lignereuil	15/07/1916	16/07/1916
War Diary	Bryas	17/07/1916	20/07/1916
War Diary	Orton	21/07/1916	27/07/1916
War Diary	Camblain L'Abbe	28/07/1916	31/07/1916
Heading	War Diary Administrative Staff 37th Divn Aug/16 Vol 13		
War Diary	Camblain L'Abbe	01/08/1916	14/08/1916
War Diary	Bruay	15/08/1916	31/08/1916
Heading	War Diary H.Q. 37th Divn. Sept 1916 Vol 14		
War Diary	Bruay	01/09/1916	18/09/1916
War Diary	Barlin	19/09/1916	30/09/1916
Heading	W.D.		
War Diary	Barlin	01/10/1916	17/10/1916
War Diary	Roellecourt	18/10/1916	20/10/1916
War Diary	Lecauroy	21/10/1916	21/10/1916
War Diary	Marieux	22/10/1916	31/10/1916
Miscellaneous	Administrative Arrangement (Reference 37th Divl. Operation Order no. 40 of 13/10/16). Appendix I	13/10/1916	13/10/1916
Miscellaneous	Administrative Arrangements (Reference 37th Divl. Operation Order No. 40 of 13/10/16).	14/10/1916	14/10/1916
Miscellaneous	Billeting And Supply Arrangement 20th Oct. 1916 Appendix II	19/10/1916	19/10/1916
Miscellaneous	Billeting Arrangements For 21st October 1916 Appendix III	20/10/1916	20/10/1916
Miscellaneous	Billeting and Supply Arrangements 22nd October 1916 Appendix IV	21/10/1916	21/10/1916
War Diary	Marieux	01/11/1916	15/11/1916
War Diary	Hedauville	16/11/1916	17/11/1916
War Diary	Forceville	18/11/1916	25/11/1916
War Diary	Marieux	26/11/1916	30/11/1916
War Diary	Officers Or		
Miscellaneous	Statement of Stores Salved On The Battlefield Appendix II	18/11/1916	18/11/1916
Miscellaneous	Casualties Appendix I 13th-24th Novr. 1916		
Heading	War Diary A. & Q. H.Q. 37th Division Month of December 1916 Vol 17		
War Diary	Marieux	01/12/1916	13/12/1916
War Diary	Frohen-Le-Grand	14/12/1916	14/12/1916
War Diary	Flers	15/12/1916	15/12/1916

War Diary	Monchy Cayeux	16/12/1916	16/12/1916
War Diary	Norrent Fontes	17/12/1916	17/12/1916
War Diary	St-Venant	18/12/1916	20/12/1916
War Diary	Lestrem	21/12/1916	31/12/1916
Miscellaneous	Fifth Army "A" V Corps "A" Appendix II	13/12/1916	13/12/1916
Miscellaneous	Administrative Arrangements Reference 37th Divn Order No. 58 d/18/12/16 Appendix I	21/12/1916	21/12/1916
Miscellaneous	Tabulated Results of The March of 37th Division From Fifth to First Army Area Dec. 14-18 1916 Appendix III		
Heading	War Diary HQ 37th Div January 1917 Vol 18		
War Diary	Lestrem	01/01/1917	12/02/1917
War Diary	Noeux-Les-Mines	13/02/1917	28/02/1917
Heading	War Diary Mar 1917 Headquarters 37th Divn Vol 20 Administrative Branch		
War Diary	Noeux Les Mines	01/03/1917	03/03/1917
War Diary	Norrent Fontes	04/03/1917	08/03/1917
War Diary	Roellecourt	09/03/1917	31/03/1917
Heading	War Diary Feb 1917 Administrative Staff 37 Divn Vol 21		
War Diary	Roellecourt	01/04/1917	04/04/1917
War Diary	Agnez-Les-Duisans	05/04/1917	13/04/1917
War Diary	Lignereuil	14/04/1917	20/04/1917
War Diary	Etrun	21/04/1917	25/04/1917
War Diary	Arras	26/04/1917	29/04/1917
War Diary	Lignereuil	30/04/1917	30/04/1917
Miscellaneous	37th Division	15/04/1917	15/04/1917
Miscellaneous	Estimated Casualties Up to 12 Noon 13th April 1917 Appendix A		
Miscellaneous	Officer Casualties Appendix B		
Miscellaneous	37th Division Officers Casualties.		
Miscellaneous	Third Army "A" VIth Corps "A" XVIII Corps "A"	16/04/1917	16/04/1917
Miscellaneous	Estimated Casualties 25/4/17 up to Noon Appendix D		
Miscellaneous	37th Division Appendix C	16/04/1917	16/04/1917
Miscellaneous	37th Division List no. 2	18/04/1917	18/04/1917
Miscellaneous	37th Division List No. 3	19/04/1917	19/04/1917
Miscellaneous	37th Division List No. 4	21/04/1917	21/04/1917
Miscellaneous	37th Division Total estimated Casualties (o.r. to nearest 50 excluding M.C. Cos.) of Infantry Battalion and Machine Gun Companies from 22nd-30th April 1917		
Miscellaneous	37th Division Appendix A		
War Diary	Lignereuil	01/05/1917	18/05/1917
War Diary	Warlus	19/05/1917	20/05/1917
War Diary	Arras	21/05/1917	31/05/1917
War Diary	Lignereuil	01/05/1917	03/05/1917
Heading	H.Q. Administrative Staff 37th Division June 1917 Vol 23		
War Diary	Arras	01/06/1917	01/06/1917
War Diary	Lignereuil	02/06/1917	07/06/1917
War Diary	Bomy	08/06/1917	22/06/1917
War Diary	Steenbecque	23/06/1917	23/06/1917
War Diary	Locre	24/06/1917	29/06/1917
War Diary	Dranoutre	30/06/1917	30/06/1917
Heading	War Diary Administrative Staff 37th Divl. Vol 24		
War Diary	Dranoutre	01/07/1917	31/07/1917
Heading	War Diary Administrative Staff 37th Divn. Vol 25		
War Diary	Dranoutre	01/08/1917	07/08/1917

War Diary	Scherpenberg Camp Near Locre	08/08/1917	31/08/1917
Heading	War Diary Sept. 1917 H.Q. Administrative Staff 37th Division Vol 26		
War Diary	Scherpenberg Camp Nr Locre	01/09/1917	11/09/1917
War Diary	St Jans Cappel	12/09/1917	27/09/1917
War Diary	Zevecoten	28/09/1917	30/09/1917
Heading	War Diary H.Q. Administrative Staff 37th Divn. Oct 1917 Vol 27		
War Diary	De Zon Camp Near La Clytte	01/10/1917	15/10/1917
War Diary	St Jans Cappel	16/10/1917	09/11/1917
War Diary	Scherpenberg Near La Clytte	10/11/1917	11/01/1918
War Diary	Blaringhem	12/01/1918	16/02/1918
War Diary	Westoutre	17/02/1918	24/02/1918
War Diary	Chateau-Segard	25/02/1918	28/03/1918
War Diary	Toutencourt	29/03/1918	29/03/1918
War Diary	Pas	30/03/1918	31/03/1918
Heading	Administrative Staff 37th Division April 1918		
War Diary	Souastre	01/04/1918	02/04/1918
War Diary	Couin	03/04/1918	15/04/1918
War Diary	Authie	16/04/1918	23/04/1918
War Diary	Henu	24/04/1918	16/05/1918
War Diary	Authie	17/05/1918	05/06/1918
War Diary	Cavillon	06/06/1918	09/06/1918
War Diary	Wailly	10/06/1918	20/06/1918
War Diary	Pas	21/06/1918	25/06/1918
War Diary	Henu	26/06/1918	30/06/1918
Heading	37th Division Administrative Staff War Diary July 1918 Volume XXXVI		
Miscellaneous			
Miscellaneous		22/08/1918	22/08/1918
Miscellaneous	37th Division Strength Return made up to 12 noon Saturday July 27th 1918	27/07/1918	27/07/1918
Miscellaneous	37th Division Strength Return made up to 12 noon Saturday July 20th 1918	20/07/1918	20/07/1918
Miscellaneous	37th Division Strength Return made up to 12 noon Saturday July 6th 1918 Appendix III	06/07/1918	06/07/1918
Miscellaneous	37th Division Strength Return made up to 12 noon Saturday July 13th 1918	13/07/1918	13/07/1918
Miscellaneous	Accommodation Allotted To 37th Division In Iv Corps Area Appendix A		
Heading	War Diary Administrative Branch 37th Division August Vol 37		
Miscellaneous			
Miscellaneous	August 1st-31st 1918 37th Division Appendix I		
Miscellaneous	37th Division Strength Return made up to 12 noon Saturday August 3rd 1918 Appendix II	03/08/1918	03/08/1918
Miscellaneous	37th Division Strength Return made up to 12 noon Saturday August 10th 1918	10/08/1918	10/08/1918
Miscellaneous	37th Division Strength Return made up to 12 noon Saturday August 17th 1918	17/08/1918	17/08/1918
Miscellaneous	37th Division Weekly Fighting Strength Return up to 18 Noon Saturday 24/8/18	24/08/1918	24/08/1918
Miscellaneous	37th Division Strength Return Made up to 12 noon Saturday August 24th 1918	24/08/1918	24/08/1918
Miscellaneous	37th Division Strength Return made up to 12 noon Saturday August 31st 1918	31/08/1918	31/08/1918

Heading	War Diary Administrative Branch 37th Division September 1918 Vol 38		
Miscellaneous			
Miscellaneous	Sept. 1st-30th 1918. 37th Division Appendix I		
Miscellaneous	37th Division Strength Return Made up to noon Saturday September 7th 1918 Appendix II	07/09/1918	07/09/1918
Miscellaneous	37th Division Strength Return Made up to noon Saturday September 14t6h. 1918	14/09/1918	14/09/1918
Miscellaneous	37th Division Strength Return Made up to noon Saturday September 21st 1918	21/09/1918	21/09/1918
Miscellaneous	37th Division Strength Return Made up to noon Saturday September 28th 1918	28/09/1918	28/09/1918

PUBLIC RECORD OFFICE.

One Document, being 37 DIVISION. Adjutant and Quartermaster General: Appendix VI to Diaries 1918 July.
List of Courts Martial Cases to be closed for 100 years
W/O 95/2516

has been removed to W.O. 154/58

March 1965

J.H. Adams p.p.
P. McCaffrey

(12517) Wt. 10696/324 3,000 9/32 Hw. G.620

37TH DIVISION

'A' & 'Q' BRANCH

AUG 1915-~~DEC~~ SEP 1918

37th Division

121/7595

L

H.Q. 37th Div. "A"

Vols 1, 2, 3.

August 15

to

October 1915

C O N F I D E N T I A L .

W A R D I A R Y.

o f

Administrative Staff, Headquarters 37th Division.

From 1st August 1915 to 31st August 1915.

(VOLUME / .)

Instructions regarding War Diaries and Intelligence Summaries are contained in F. S. Regs., Part II. and the Staff Manual respectively. Title pages will be prepared in manuscript.

WAR DIARY
or
INTELLIGENCE SUMMARY.
(Erase heading not required.)

Army Form C. 2118.

Place	Date	Hour	Summary of Events and Information	Remarks and references to Appendices
TILQUES	Sun. Aug. 1		Move of Division continues. Personnel of 111th Infy. Brigade ~~continued~~ arriving during early hours. Divn. is billeted in the area TILQUES — MOULLE — SERQUES — RUMINGHEM — POLINCOVE — ZUTKERQUE — NIELLES LES ARDRES — ZOUAFQUES — BONNINGUES — MENTQUE — NORTLEULINGHEM	
"	Mo. — 2		Move of Division continued. Personnel of 112th Infy. Brigade arriving in ~~small hours~~ forenoon.	
"	Tues. — 3		Concentration of Division completed during night of 2nd/3rd. Orders received 3 p.m. for Division to move tomorrow to billets between ARQUES and HAZEBROUCK on the ST. OMER — HAZEBROUCK road.	
RENESCURE	Wed. — 4		Division moved to billets as above. Average distance of march about 11 or 12 miles. Divl. H.Q. at RENESCURE. R.A. Area nearest to HAZEBROUCK. In 110th Brigade area are: — 289 Co. A.S.C. 152nd Fd. Co. R.E. + 48th Fd. Ambulance. In 111th Brigade area: — 290 Co. A.S.C. 153rd Fd. Co. R.E. + 49th Fd. Ambulance. In 112th Brigade area: — 291 Co. A.S.C. 154th Fd. Co. R.E. + 50th Fd. Ambul. In H.Q. area, all Divnl. troops (but ~~today~~ for tonight Pioneer Battn. attd. to 110th Brigade.	
CAESTRE	Thurs. — 5		Divn. moved from billets as above to billets in the area HAZEBROUCK — HONDEGHEM — CASSEL — ST. SYLVESTRE — EECKE — CAESTRE — ROUGE CROIX. Divnl. H.Q. in CAESTRE. H.Q. Divnl. R.A. at HONDEGHEM.	
"	Fri. — 6		Orders received as to distribution of Divn. for purposes of instruction. Divn. is attd. to 2nd Corps (H.Q. BAILLEUL) in 2nd Army (H.Q. CASSEL)	
"	Sat. — 7		NIL	
"	Sun. — 8		110th Infantry Brigade moved by road from the Eecke area via CAESTRE to LOCRE for duty in trenches (under instruction*) attd. to 28th Division. Also working party of 2000 (500 from each Battn.) for trench digging from 111th Brigade under Col. White marched to BAILLEUL + billetted there for the night. Gen. Sir Herbert Plumer, Comdg. 2nd Army, visited Divnl. H.Q. at 9.30 am + saw 110th Brigade [illegible] through, then inspected 111th + 112th Brdes.	
* in trench warfare				

Personnel of Arty. moved forward by train: 123 Bde + 1 How. Batt. to 28th Divn. 124 Bde + 1 How. to 12th Divn. 125 Bde + 126 Bde [illegible]

2353 Wt. W2514/1454 700,000 5/15 D. D. & L. A.D.S.S./Forms/C. 2118.

Instructions regarding War Diaries and Intelligence Summaries are contained in F. S. Regs., Part II. and the Staff Manual respectively. Title pages will be prepared in manuscript.

WAR DIARY
or
INTELLIGENCE SUMMARY.
(Erase heading not required.)

Army Form C. 2118.

Place	Date	Hour	Summary of Events and Information	Remarks and references to Appendices
CAESTRE	Mon. Aug. 9		Working party (2000) of 111th Infy Brigade moved on from BAILLEUL to ARMENTIERES. 152nd Co. R.E. + Pioneer Battn. to N.W. of NIEPPE to work under C.R.E. 37th Divn. on 2nd line (GHQ line). 153 Co. R.E. to NEUVE EGLISE + 154 Co. to LOCRE.	
"	Tues. — 10		Working party (2000) of 112th Brigade moved from HAZEBROUCK to near LOCRE (Cameronians).	
"	Wed. — 11		Exhibition of gas (as used by Germans) given by Capt. Barley, Gas Expert 2nd Army, for 111th Brigade near Quaestraete (just E. of CASSEL).	
"	Thurs. — 12			
"	Fri. — 13			
"	Sat. — 14		Lecture by Lt. Col. Wroughton, A.A.G. 2nd Army, on F.G.C.M.'s + Mily. Law at present.	
"	Sun. — 15			
"	Mon. — 16		111th Brigade (H.Q. + balance of each Battn.) marched through CAESTRE to BAILLEUL where they billetted.	
"	Tues. — 17		110th Brigade returned to billets in EECKE area sending working party of 2000 to ARMENTIERES (to work on subsidiary line). 111th Brigade arrived at ARMENTIERES, attd. for training to 12th Divn (in trench warfare).	

(3350) W. [illegible] 1915 D. D. & L. A.D.S.S./Forms/C. 2118.

Army Form C. 2118.

Instructions regarding War Diaries and Intelligence Summaries are contained in F. S. Regs., Part II. and the Staff Manual respectively. Title pages will be prepared in manuscript.

WAR DIARY
or
INTELLIGENCE SUMMARY.
(Erase heading not required.)

Place	Date	Hour	Summary of Events and Information	Remarks and references to Appendices
CAESTRE	Wed. Aug. 18		G.C.M. at St. MARIE CAPELL on Officer of 123rd Brigade R.F.A. Ammtn. Col. Finding: "Not guilty."	
"	Thurs. – 19			
"	Fri. – 20			
"	Sat. – 21			
"	Sun. – 22		Reinforcements for Battns. arrived as follows: — 8/Leicester Regt 90; 13/Royal Fusiliers 100; 9/N. Stafford Regt. 75; 11/R. Warwick Regt. 60; 6/Bedford Regt. 60	
"	Mon. – 23		Orders received for Divn. to move South to neighbourhood of DOULLENS to join 3rd Army.	
"	Tues. – 24		D.A.A.&Q.M.G. & Staff Capts. of Infy. Brigades & Divnl. Arty & ~~Adn~~ St. André (Chief Interpreter) & Liaison Officer proceeded by motor via BAILLEUL, ARMENTIERES & BETHUNE to H.Q. 7th Corps at MARIEUX where orders were received as to area assigned to 37th Divn. Divnl. H.Q. to be at DOULLENS.	
DOULLENS	Wed. 25th		Divn. began to entrain at CASSEL & GODEWAERSVELDE, detraining stations MONDICOURT and DOULLENS respectively. Divnl. H.Q. established at DOULLENS.	
"	Thurs. 26th		Movement by rail continued. Corps Comdr. visited troops of 112th Brig. in billets.	

Army Form C. 2118.

Instructions regarding War Diaries and Intelligence Summaries are contained in F. S. Regs., Part II. and the Staff Manual respectively. Title pages will be prepared in manuscript.

WAR DIARY
or
INTELLIGENCE SUMMARY.
(Erase heading not required.)

Place	Date	Hour	Summary of Events and Information	Remarks and references to Appendices
	Aug.			
DOULLENS	Fri. 27th		H.Q. 112th Brig. & 8/E. Lancs. Regt. moved to MAILLY + MAILLET, 11/R. Warwick Regt. to HEBUTERNE + 10/Loyal N. Lanc. Regt. to ENGLEBELMER, all for instruction ~~[illegible]~~ in trench warfare under 4th + 48th Divns. 6/Bedford Regt. remaining at ORVILLE. Movement by rail continued.	
"	Sat. 28th		Detrainment of Divn. completed in afternoon.	
"	Sun. 29th		Gen. Sir Charles C. Monro, G.O.C. 3rd Army visited Divnl. H.Q. + saw all Divnl. Staff + Brigadiers + ~~Staff~~ Brig. Majors of 110th + 112th Brigades + R.A.	
"	Mon. 30th		Corps Comdr. inspected 110th + 111th Brigades + Divnl. Troops near their billets. Drafts for 6/Leicesters (37), 7/Leic. (40) + 8/Leic. (30) + 10/Royal Fus. (20) + 13/Rifle Brig. (16) arrive.	
"	Tues. 31st		NIL	

2353 Wt. W2514/1454 700,000 5/15 D. D. & L. A.D.S.S./Forms/C. 2118.

C O N F I D E N T I A L.

W A R   D I A R Y.

o f

Administrative Staff, Headquarters 37th Division.

From 1st September 1915, to 30th September 1915.

(VOLUME 2 .)

Instructions regarding War Diaries and Intelligence Summaries are contained in F. S. Regs., Part II. and the Staff Manual respectively. Title pages will be prepared in manuscript.

WAR DIARY
or
INTELLIGENCE SUMMARY.
(Erase heading not required.)

Army Form C. 2118.

Place	Date Sept.	Hour	Summary of Events and Information	Remarks and references to Appendices
DOULLENS	Wed. 1st		6/Leic. Regt. moved to POMMIER & 13/R. Brig. to ST. AMAND. Orders issued regarding the move of units into the new area & relieving the French.	
"	Thurs. 2nd		8/Leic. Regt. moved to POMMIER, [illegible] & 9/ to HUMBERCAMP, 7/ to HUMBERCAMP & POMMIER. 10th & 13th Royal Fus. to ST. AMAND. H.Q. 111th Brig. to ST. AMAND. Reconnaissance carried out by other Bns. prior to taking over.	
"	Fri. 3rd		6/Leic. Regt. arrived at BERLES-AU-BOIS at 1 am. & relieved 65th Chasseurs in the BERLES Sector of the 1st Line trenches. 13th Bn. Rifle Brig. arrd. BIENVILLERS 12.30 am. & relieved HANNESCAMPS Sector of 1st Line. Enemy did not hinder these reliefs in any way. Relief of artillery proceeding gradually, British guns being placed alongside French guns. Pioneer Bn. moved to POMMIER.	
"	Sat. 4th		8/Leic. Regt. relieved French in the Supporting point of BERLES at 2.30 am. 9/Leic. Regt. relieved French in BIENVILLERS section of front line at 1 am. 7/Leic. Regt. relieved BIENVILLERS village supporting point at 2.30 am. 10/R. Fus. relieved ESSARTS Sector of 1st Line at 1 am. 13/R.F. relieved the HANNESCAMPS & BIENVILLERS supporting points at 2 am. 123rd & 124th Bdes. R.F.A. moved up to LA CAUCHIE & LA BAZÈQUE respectively & Div. Amm. Col. to GRENAS. Reliefs unhindered by enemy. 22nd Divn. detraining at FLESSELLES.	
"	Sun. 5th		French Artillery between BERLES & POMMIER & W. of FONQUEVILLERS was relieved by 124th & 125th Bdes. R.F.A. respectively. Div. H.Q. moved to PAS & Divnl. Troops into new area.	
~~PAS~~	~~Mon~~		37th Div. area now entirely clear of French troops (56th Divn.) which consisted (Infy.) of 111th & 112th Infy. Brigades, curiously enough. All trenches & emplacements now occupied by 37th Divn. 6/Bedfords moved to FONQUEVILLERS to be attd. to 143rd Infy. Brig. (48th — S. Midland Territorial — Divn.). French Arty. W. & N.W. of BERLES & S. of BIENVILLERS relieved by 123rd + 124th Bdes. R.F.A. respec.	
PAS	Mon. 6th		12th Corps being formed, with H.Q. at DOULLENS.	
"	Tues. 7th		Went to H.Q. 22nd Divn. at FLESSELLES & saw F.G.	
"	Wed. 8th		1 Sectn. 19th Heavy Batty. (60 Pr.) arrived at BIENVILLERS.	

2353 Wt. W 3344/454 700,000 3/15 D.D.&L. A.D.S.S./Forms/C. 2118.

Instructions regarding War Diaries and Intelligence Summaries are contained in F. S. Regs., Part II. and the Staff Manual respectively. Title pages will be prepared in manuscript.

WAR DIARY
or
INTELLIGENCE SUMMARY.
(Erase heading not required.)

Army Form C. 2118.

Place	Date	Hour	Summary of Events and Information	Remarks and references to Appendices
	Sept.			
PAS	Thurs 9th		8/Leic. Regt. relieved 6/Leic. Regt. in trenches in BERLES section at right.	
"	Fri. 10th		13/K.R.R. relieved 13/R.B. in ESSART section of the line & 7/Leic. relieved 9/Leic. in BERLES section at right. 20th Heavy Batty. R.G.A. (60 Pr.) arrived & took up positions (S.E. & S.) at POMMIER, their waggon lines at GAUDIEMPRE	
"	Sat. 11th		Following drafts arrived during the week: 13/K.R.R. 28, 13/R.B. 40, 8/E. Lancs. 56, 10/Loyal N. Lancs 60. 6/Bedfords 70 6/Bedfords returned to 112th Bde. & billetted in HUMBERCAMPS. Casualties: 1 Off. & 1 other ranks wounded	
"	Sun. 12th		Casualties: 7 O.R. wounded (1 accidentally). 15th Siege Batty. R.G.A. (6" Howitzers) drawn by mechanical transport arrived & took up positions at BERLES, the Mech. Transport at POMMIER	
"	MON. 13th		Casualties: 8 O.R. wounded (1 accidentally).	
"	Thurs. 14th		Brig. Gen. P.M. Robinson assumed command of 112th Brigade vice Brig. Gen. Marriott. Draft of 20 men for 13/R.B. arrived. Casualties: 2 O.R. wounded.	
"	Wed. 15th		In evening 112th Brigade relieve 111th Brig. in HANNESCAMPS—FONQUEVILLERS section of our line: 8/E. Lancs. ½ Bn. in trenches on right, ½ Bn. in Fonquevillers, 10/L. N. Lancs. in centre (whole Bn. in trenches), 11/R. War. Regt. on left ½ Bn. in trenches, ½ Bn. in support in HANNESCAMPS, 6/Bedford Regt. in BIENVILLERS. 111th Bde. went into reserve as: Bde. H.Q. & 2 Bns. at ST. AMAND, 2 Bns. HUMBERCAMPS. Relief carried out quietly. Draft of 30 men for Bedford Regt. arrived. No. 4 Entrenching Battn. (these battns. are composed of drafts from various regts. waiting at Base Depots to join their regts. & are used for work on defences in the 2nd or 3rd Lines) strength: 25 Offs. & 1005 other ranks, & also ½ 141st Co. R.E. (Army Troops, previously with 4th Divn.) 2 Offs. & 60 o.r. sent to be attd. to 37th Divn. & billetted in GAUDIEMPRE. Casualties: 5 o.r. wounded (1 slightly, at duty).	

Instructions regarding War Diaries and Intelligence Summaries are contained in F. S. Regs., Part II. and the Staff Manual respectively. Title pages will be prepared in manuscript.

WAR DIARY
or
INTELLIGENCE SUMMARY.
(Erase heading not required.)

Army Form C. 2118.

Place	Date Sept.	Hour	Summary of Events and Information	Remarks and references to Appendices
PAS	Thurs. 16th		Casualties: 2 off. wounded (1 accidentally), other ranks: 3 killed, 10 wounded.	
"	Fri. 17th		Casualties: Other ranks: 1 killed 3 wounded ~~Brig~~ Brig. Gen. F. Potts C.M.S. from Meerut Divnl. Arty, assumed command of 37th Divisional ~~assumed~~ Arty. vice Brig. Gen. S. Lushington.	
"	Sat. 18th		Casualties: ~~O.r.~~ O.r. 3 wounded. Fighting strength of ~~Divn.~~ (calculated according to 3rd Army instructions, ~~exclud~~ including details) of Yeomanry Squadron, Cyclist Co., 3 Infy. Brigades & Pioneer Battn.: 385 offs. 13,109 other ranks, of which 10 off. 230 o.r. are details. Field State: 601 offs. 18,796 other ranks 1479 riding horses 4146 draught & pack horses & mules 64 guns 60 machine guns 15,186 rifles 593 tool, technical etc Carts. Branch of Expeditionary Force Canteen opened at GAUDIEMPRÉ.	
"	Sun. 19th		Casualties: other ranks 4 wounded. Major A.C. Edwards (from 130th Bde. R.F.A., 28th Divn.) assumed command of 123rd Brig. R.F.A. vice Lieut. Col. J. W. Reid.	
"	Mon. 20th		Casualties: other ranks, 3 wounded. Preparations being made for possible advance.	
"	Tues 21st		Casualties: 1 off. killed + 1 wounded, other ranks 4 killed (1 died of wounds), 5 wounded. Enemy shelled BERLES.	
"	Wed. 22nd		Casualties: other ranks, 1 killed, 4 wounded. 16th Heavy Battery, R.G.A., arrived at GAUDIEMPRÉ. Enemy shelled BERLES & POMMIER in afternoon, ~~but~~ without doing much damage. One of the guns was a 15 cm. 12th Corps is now South of the R. SOMME (27th, 22nd & 26th Divns.)	
"	Thurs. 23rd		10/R. Fus.rs moved from ST. AMAND to LA CAUCHIE + 13/K.R.R. from ST. AMAND to HUMBERCAMP where it was mostly accommodated in tents. Germans shelled POMMIER again in afternoon after fire from our 60 Prs. Capt. G. W. Ainsworth, 10/Loyal North Lancashire Regt. arrived to be attd. to Divnl. H.Q. for instruction in D.A.Q.M.G.'s duties. Casualties: other ranks, ~~killed~~ 2 killed, 4 wounded.	

2353 Wt. W2544/1454 700,000 5/15 D. D. & L. A.D.S.S./Forms/C. 2118.

Army Form C. 2118.

WAR DIARY
or
INTELLIGENCE SUMMARY.
(Erase heading not required.)

Instructions regarding War Diaries and Intelligence Summaries are contained in F. S. Regs., Part II. and the Staff Manual respectively. Title pages will be prepared in manuscript.

Place	Date Sept.	Hour	Summary of Events and Information	Remarks and references to Appendices
PAS	Fri. 24th		Casualties: 2 offs. wounded (1 accidentally), other ranks 2 killed, 8 wounded. 16th Heavy Batty. left GAUDIÈMPRÉ, returning to 4th & 48th Divns. The local representatives (H Section, Hedauville) of the Graves Registration Commission called & stated that cemeteries arrangements satisfactory. Raining in the early morning & late afternoon. ~~SOUASTRE handed over~~ Accommodation for 1 Battn. in SOUASTRE handed over to 48th Divn. Our Arty. cut some of the wire in front of the enemy's trenches.	
"	Sat. 25th	11 am.	Information received that our 1st Army attacked at 6.30 a.m. today & made considerable progress.	
		2.30 p.m.	French ~~artillery~~ on our left have advanced & gained some ground. RANSART (about 2½ miles N.E. of BERLES) reported to be in flames.	
		4 p.m.	Information received that ~~the~~ whole of German 1st line trenches "in Champagne" have been captured & that French Cavalry have broken through there.	
		later	During the day the French 9th Corps on our immediate left took the WAILLY ridge between FICHEUX & BLAIREVILLE with their right Brigade. Our howitzers assisted by firing on the German guns. Unfortunately the remainder of the French 9th Corps could not advance in face of the German artillery fire & the right Brigade had to retire to its original line. All quiet in our immediate front.	
"	Sun. 26th		~~News~~ Favourable news received as to the French advance in Champagne.	
"	Mon. 27th		Stated that French have made an advance of 4 kilometres on a front of 10 kilometres in Champagne getting through the 3 lines of trenches of the German 1st line and that they are now held up in front of ~~the~~ the German 2nd line which has a belt of wire in front of it 50 to 60 yds. wide & sunk below the level of the ground so that it is difficult for French arty. to destroy.	

Army Form C. 2118.

Instructions regarding War Diaries and Intelligence Summaries are contained in F. S. Regs., Part II. and the Staff Manual respectively. Title pages will be prepared in manuscript.

WAR DIARY
or
INTELLIGENCE SUMMARY.
(Erase heading not required.)

Place	Date	Hour	Summary of Events and Information	Remarks and references to Appendices
	Sept.			
PAS	Tues. 28th		Announced that British Army captures amount to:— 53 officers, 2800 other ranks, 18 guns & 32 machine guns. We ~~hold~~ have captured (on 25th) LOOS (close to LENS) & part of Quarries near HULLUCH but not HULLUCH itself.	
			French captures stated to be 23,000 prisoners & at least 30 guns.	
"	Wed. 29		Capt. Barrett, 8th Leic. Regt. arrived & attached to 37th Divl. Cyclist Co. pending investigations by Court of Inquiry.	
"	Thurs. 30		Major W. Drysdale DSO G.S.O. (2) to 7/Leic. Regt. & assumed command (dating from tomorrow. Colonel Carleton 7/Leic. Regt. to England.	
			Major W. Pitt-Taylor DSO Rifle Brigade arrived to take up appointment of G.S.O. 2	
			Capt. Buckley, D.C.L.I., arrived to take up appointment of G.S.O. 3 vice Major Stourton to Brig. Major 112th Bde	
			A German aeroplane dropped 4 bombs at MONDICOURT about midday ~~killed~~ wounding a woman & killing her child but doing no military damage.	

C O N F I D E N T I A L.

W A R D I A R Y.

o f

Administrative Staff, Headquarters 37th Division.

From 1st October 1915 to 31st October 1915.

(VOLUME 3.)

Instructions regarding War Diaries and Intelligence Summaries are contained in F. S. Regs., Part II. and the Staff Manual respectively. Title pages will be prepared in manuscript.

WAR DIARY
or
INTELLIGENCE SUMMARY.
October 1915 *(Erase heading not required.)*

Army Form C. 2118.

Place	Date Oct.	Hour	Summary of Events and Information	Remarks and references to Appendices
PAS	Fri 1st		Major Pollok-Morris H.L.I. late Brig. Major 112th Brigade left for England. Lt. Colonel J.D. Mackay, Hampshire Regt, assumed command of 8th E. Lancs. Regt. Col. Melville late O.C. 8/E. Lancs. Regt. to England.	
"	Sat. 2nd		NIL	
"	Sun. 3rd		NIL	
"	Mon. 4th		Draft of 50 arrived for 8/E. Lancs. Regt. Advance party of 36th (Ulster) Div. arrive at FLESSELLES.	
"	Tues. 5th		NIL	
"	Wed. 6th		NIL	
"	Thurs. 7th		NIL	
"	Fri. 8th		Drafts arrived as follows:— 6/Leic. Regt. 1 off. + 56, 8/E. Lancs. 19, 13/Rifle Brig. 1 off. (2/Lt. W.W. Nothard) + 52 men, of the 13/R.B. draft the officer + 19 O.R. came from PORT ELIZABETH, South Africa, + belong to the Prince Alfred's Guard, an infantry batt. of the S.A. Defence Force which was in the Cape Peninsula from Aug. 1914. The men of this party have paid their own way to England.	
"	Sat. 9th		147th Army Troops Co. R.E. arrived 11 p.m. at MONDICOURT (Strength 4 Offrs. + 145) + billetted in MONDICOURT.	
"	Sun. 10th		NIL	

2353 Wt. W2544/1454 700,000 5/15 D. D. & L. A.D.S.S./Forms/C. 2118.

Instructions regarding War Diaries and Intelligence Summaries are contained in F. S. Regs., Part II. and the Staff Manual respectively. Title pages will be prepared in manuscript.

WAR DIARY
or
INTELLIGENCE SUMMARY.
(Erase heading not required.)

Army Form C. 2118.

Place	Date Oct. 1915	Hour	Summary of Events and Information	Remarks and references to Appendices
PAS	Mon. 11th		NIL	
"	Tues. 12th		NIL	
"	Wed. 13th		NIL	
"	Thurs. 14th		NIL	
"	Fri. 15th		NIL	
"	Sat. 16th		NIL	
"	Sun. 17th		Major C.H. Haig Leic. Regt. arrived & assumed command of 9th Leic. Regt. Col. H.R. Mead 9/Leic. left for England	
"	Mon. 18th		NIL	
"	Tues. 19th		NIL	
"	Wed. 20th		NIL	
"	Thurs. 21st		NIL	
"	Fri. 22nd		NIL	
"	Sat. 23rd		During the week the following drafts have been received: 7/Leic. Regt. 20, 8th Leic Regt. 60, 9th Leic. 30, 13th Royal Fus. 47, 12th Rifle Brigade 20, 11th R. Warwick Regt. 50, 6th Bedford Regt. 30, 10th Loyal N. Lancs. Regt. 14.	
"	Sun. 24th		NIL	

2353 Wt. W2544/1454 700,000 5/15 D. D. & L. A.D.S.S./Forms/C. 2118.

Instructions regarding War Diaries and Intelligence Summaries are contained in F. S. Regs., Part II. and the Staff Manual respectively. Title pages will be prepared in manuscript.

WAR DIARY
or
INTELLIGENCE SUMMARY.

(Erase heading not required.)

Army Form C. 2118.

Place	Date	Hour	Summary of Events and Information	Remarks and references to Appendices
	Oct. 1915			
PAS	Mon. 25th		H.M. The KING + PRESIDENT POINCARÉ visit 3rd Army Area. Parade at Acheux for them of units from various Divisions. 11th Royal Warwickshire Regt. present from 37th Division, Guard of Honour furnished at H.Q. 7th Corps MARIEUX for the KING by the 10th Loyal N. Lancs. Regt.	
"	Tues. 26		NIL	
"	Wed. 27		NIL	
"	Thurs. 28		NIL	
"	Fri. 29		Following drafts arrived: 6th Leic. Regt. 40, 6th Bedford Regt. 20.	
"	Sat. 30		NIL	
"	Sun. 31		NIL	

2353 Wt. W2544/1454 700,000 5/15 D. D. & L. A.D.S.S./Forms/C. 2118.

154/57

PA

HQ 37 DIVISION

A + Q

1915 NOV

Box 2516.

154/57

GAP ×

Temp Extracts for

WO 154 | 66

1915 NOV

H.Q. 37th Div:
"A"
Vol: 4

121
7724

Nov. 15

L

nil
Cu.

Bot 2516

C O N F I D E N T I A L .

W a r   D i a r y

of

Administrative Staff 37th D i v i s i o n,

From 1st November 1915 To 30th November 1915.

Instructions regarding War Diaries and Intelligence Summaries are contained in F. S. Regs., Part II. and the Staff Manual respectively. Title pages will be prepared in manuscript.

WAR DIARY

~~or~~

~~INTELLIGENCE SUMMARY.~~

(Erase heading not required.)

Army Form C. 2118.

November 1915.

Place	Date	Hour	Summary of Events and Information	Remarks and references to Appendices
PAS	Nov. Mon. 1st		Leave commenced for the Division. 25 leaves per day allotted for the whole Division. & 1 Section (2 guns) 46th Siege Battery (9.2" Howitzers) moved into the Divl. Area & took up position at ST. AMAND. Section 50th Siege Batty. (6" Mark VII guns) is also in position near SOUASTRE.	
"	Tues. 2nd			
"	Wed. 3rd			
"	Thurs. 4th			
"	Fri. 5th		16th Heavy Brigade R.G.A. consisting of 9th & 14th Heavy Batteries (47th H.B. which belongs to the Bde. having been detached elsewhere in the 7th Corps), arrived at GAUDIEMPRÉ from ARMENTIÈRES.	
"	Sat. 6th		Guns of 16th Heavy Brigade R.G.A. moved up into position, ~~[illegible]~~ 9th Batty. at POMMIER, 14th Batty. at BIENVILLERS. ~~[illegible]~~ Waggon lines & Bde. Ammtn. Column remain at GAUDIEMPRÉ. Exchange carried out by tonight of the complete personnel of 1 section in each of 8 18 Pr. Batteries & 2 Howitzer Batteries between the Divisional Artillery of the 37th & 4th Divisions.	
"	Sun. 7th		10th Anti-Aircraft Section (2 13 Prs.) arrived from the 5th Corps & billeted in SOUASTRE.	
"	Mon. 8th			
"	Tues. 9th			
"	Wed. 10th			

Original Removed to
w/o 154/57

Instructions regarding War Diaries and Intelligence Summaries are contained in F. S. Regs., Part II. and the Staff Manual respectively. Title pages will be prepared in manuscript.

WAR DIARY
or
INTELLIGENCE SUMMARY.
(Erase heading not required.)

Army Form C. 2118.

Place	Date	Hour	Summary of Events and Information	Remarks and references to Appendices
	Nov.			
PAS	Thurs. 11th			
"	Fri. 12th			
"	Sat. 13th			
"	Sun. 14th		~~Hara~~	
"	Mon. 15th		Hard frost began.	
"	Tues. 16th		4" to 6" of snow fell during the ~~day~~ early morning.	
			1st Cambridgeshire Regt. (Terr.) less 1 Co., detached from 27th Div. on the departure of that Div. for the Mediterranean & now Army Troops, attd to 37th Div. for work on Corps Line, arrived at HALLOY	& billeted for the night.
"	Wed. 17th		1/Cambridge Regt. moved into Divl. Area & billeted in LAHERLIÈRE.	
"	Thurs. 18th		1 Co. 1/1 Camb. Regt. from FLESSELLES. billeted in HALLOY for night.	
			G.C.M. No. of leaves for Divn. increased to 49 (to be reduced to 45 on arrival of 7th Divn.	
"	Fri. 19th		1 Co. 1/Camb. Regt. joined its Battn. in LAHERLIÈRE.	
			Following drafts arrived:—	
			7/Leic. Regt. 40 — 8/Leic. Regt. 20 — 13/R.B. 1 off. — 8/E. Lancs 1 off.	
			10/R.F. 40 — 6/Bedford Regt. 20	

Instructions regarding War Diaries and Intelligence Summaries are contained in F. S. Regs., Part II. and the Staff Manual respectively. Title pages will be prepared in manuscript.

WAR DIARY

or

~~INTELLIGENCE SUMMARY.~~

(Erase heading not required.)

Army Form C. 2118.

Place	Date	Hour	Summary of Events and Information	Remarks and references to Appendices
	Nov.			
PAS	Sat. 20th		Capt. Barrett, 8/E. Lancs. Regt. for England & also Lt. & Qmr. Sandilands (to give evidence)	
"	Sun. 21st			
"	Mon. 22nd			
"	Tues. 23rd		H.Q. & 1 Battn. (24th Manchester Regt.) 91st Brigade & 201st Fd. Co., all of 30th Divn. to be attd. to the Divn.	
"	Wed. 24th		Orders for 1/Cambs. Regt. to go to FLIXECOURT shortly, in place of Princess Patricia's Canadian L.I.	
"	Thurs. 25th		Following officers arrd.:- 7/Leic. 3, 8/Leic. 3, 9/Leic. 2, 13/K.R.R. 2, 6/Bedfords 2, 8/E. Lancs. 1, 11/R. Warwick Regt. 1, 13/R.F. draft of 30 other ranks.	
"	Fri. 26th		24/Manchester Regt. arrived at HALLOY. Adv. party of 100 1/Cambs. Regt. to FLIXECOURT.	
"	Sat. 27th		24/Manch. Regt. marched from HALLOY to BERLES. 201st Fd. Co. R.E. arrived at HALLOY	
"	Sun. 28th		201st Fd. Co. R.E. marched from HALLOY to ~~[illegible]~~ POMMIER	
"	Mon. 29th		20/Liverpool Regt. arrived at HALLOY. At 6 a.m. ~~a~~ complete thaw began.	
"	Tues. 30th		20/Liverpool Regt. marched from HALLOY to LAHERLIÈRE. 1/Cambs. Regt. left LAHERLIÈRE at 10.30 a.m. in buses for FLIXECOURT. Roads very bad.	
				L.W.f.

1577 Wt. W10791/1773 500,000 1/15 D. D. & L. A.D.S.S./Forms/C. 2118.

Appendix II

STATEMENT SHEWING MATERIAL CAPTURED FROM ENEMY - Week ended 19th Nov. 1916.

UNIT	Nature of material taken.		Date of Capture.	How disposed of.	R E M A R K S.
190th Inf. Brigade.	Machine Guns complete	3.	13-11-16.	Dumped at MESNIL pending transmission to Railhead.	190th Infantry Brigade were placed at the disposal of 37th Division for one day for salvage work on 16th November 1916.
	-do- mountings	2	13-11-16.		
	-do- belts full	9	-do-		
	Ammunition, boxes of.	39	-do-		
	-do- pouches, full	40	-do-		
	Guns, Pineapple.	8	-do-		
	Pineapples.	14	-do-		
	Pistols, very light.	2	-do-		
	Rifles.	477	-do-		
	Bayonets	207	-do-		
	Helmets.	30	-do-		
	Bombs, various	70	-do-		
	-do- Sticks	1500	-do-		
	Star Shells.	100	-do-		
	Blankets.	3	-do-		
	Overcoats	3	-do-		
	Packs	12	-do-		
	Smoke helmets	12	-do-		
	Saw large	1	-do-		
	Hatchet	1	-do-		

sgd. D. Duncan, Captain.
D.A.A. & Q.M.G. for

Major General.
Commanding 37th Division.

27th November. 1916.

"A" Branch 37th Div:

Vol: 5

121
7931

C o n f i d e n t i a l.

W a r D i a r y

of

Administrative Staff, 37th D i v i s i o n.

From 1st December 1915 to 31st December 1915.

Instructions regarding War Diaries and Intelligence Summaries are contained in F. S. Regs., Part II. and the Staff Manual respectively. Title pages will be prepared in manuscript.

Administrative Staff 37th Division

WAR DIARY
or
INTELLIGENCE SUMMARY.
(Erase heading not required.)

December 1915

Army Form C. 2118.

Place	Date	Hour	Summary of Events and Information	Remarks and references to Appendices
	Dec.			
PAS	Wed. 1st		NIL	
"	Thurs. 2		Drafts arrived: 8/E. Lancs Regt. 14, 13/K.R.R. 20, 6/Bedford Regt. 14, 9/North Stafford Regt. 20.	
"	Fri. — 3		NIL	
"	Sat. — 4		NIL	
"	Sun. — 5		24th Manchester Regt. left BERLES for HALLOY.	
"	Mon. — 6		NIL	
"	Tues. — 7		NIL	
"	Wed. — 8		Section 46th Siege Battery (9.2" Howitzers) left ST. AMAND, moving to TOUTENCOURT first.	
"	Thurs. — 9		19th Manchester Regt. arrived at BERLES for attachment to the Division. 5 officers of Special Reserve Battns. at Home — Lord Ampthill, Lt. Col. Austin, Major Hall, Lt. Col. Brownlow & Lt. Col. Sir A. Griffiths-Boscawen — arrive to be attached to the Division.	
"	Fri. — 10		NIL	
"	Sat. — 11		201st Field Co. R.E. (30th Division) left the Division on conclusion of period of attachment	
"	Sun. — 12		NIL	

1577 Wt. W10791/1773 500,000 1/15 D. D. & L. A.D.S.S./Forms/C. 2118.

Instructions regarding War Diaries and Intelligence Summaries are contained in F. S. Regs., Part II. and the Staff Manual respectively. Title pages will be prepared in manuscript.

WAR DIARY
or
INTELLIGENCE SUMMARY.
(Erase heading not required.)

Army Form C. 2118.

December 1915

Place	Date	Hour	Summary of Events and Information	Remarks and references to Appendices
	Dec.			
PAS	Mon. – 13		Attached Special Reserve Officers left the Division.	
"	Tues. – 14		Draft of 30 for 8/Leicester Regt. arrived.	
"	Wed. – 15		NIL	
"	Thurs. – 16		Major Heyworth-Savage G.S.O.2 59th (Terr.) Division arrived for attachment to Divnl. H.Q. Major Raymond & Colonel Turner, a Brigade Major & Brigadier respectively also arrived for attachment to Brigades	
"	~~Fri~~			
"	Fri. – 17		NIL	
"	Sat. – 18		NIL	
"	Sun. – 19		Attached Officers left.	
"	Mon. – 20		NIL	
"	Tues. – 21		NIL	
"	Wed. – 22		NIL	
"	Thurs. – 23		NIL	
"	Fri. – 24		19th Manchester Regt. ~~left the~~ (30th Divn.) left the Division on conclusion of period of attachment.	
"	Sat. – 25		20th Liverpool Regt. (30th Division) left the Divn. ditto	

1577 Wt. W10791/1773 500,000 1/15 D. D. & L. A.D.S.S./Forms/C. 2118.

Instructions regarding War Diaries and Intelligence Summaries are contained in F. S. Regs., Part II. and the Staff Manual respectively. Title pages will be prepared in manuscript.

WAR DIARY
or
INTELLIGENCE SUMMARY.
(*Erase heading not required.*)

Army Form C. 2118.

December 1915

Place	Date	Hour	Summary of Events and Information	Remarks and references to Appendices
	Dec.			
PAS	Sun.-26		200th Field Co. R.E. (~~30th Divn.~~) left the Division. Following drafts arrived: 8/Leic. Regt 20 13/Royal Fus. 30 6/Bedford Regt. 30.	
"	Mon-27		NIL	
"	Tues.-28		NIL	
"	Wed.-29		NIL	
"	Thurs.-30		Following drafts arrived: 7/Leic. Regt. 11 13/K.R.R. 11 11/R. Warwick Regt. 15 13/Rifle Brigade 50 10/Loyal N. Lancs. Regt. 12	
"	Fri-31		Draft of 96 for 8/E. Lancs. Regt. arrived. Notification received that Lt. Col. L. F. Green-Wilkinson, A.A. & Q.M.G. of the Division, has been appointed to command the 166th Infantry Brigade, 55th Division, also that Capt. E. O. Collison, A.O.D., D.A.D.O.S., has been appointed D.A.D.O.S. of the 55th Division.	
			E.I.D.G.	

C o n f i d e n t i a l .

W A R   D I A R Y

of

Administrative Staff, 37th D i v i s i o n.

From 1st January 1916 to 31st January 1916.

Instructions regarding War Diaries and Intelligence Summaries are contained in F. S. Regs., Part II. and the Staff Manual respectively. Title pages will be prepared in manuscript.

Army Form C. 2118.

WAR DIARY or INTELLIGENCE SUMMARY.

Administrative Staff Hdqrs. 37th Division (Erase heading not required.) JANUARY 1916.

Place	Date	Hour	Summary of Events and Information	Remarks and references to Appendices
	Jan. 1916			
PAS	Sat. 1st		NIL	
"	Sun. 2nd		Draft of 30 men for 13th K.R.R. arrived.	
"	Mon. 3rd		Lieut. Colonel L. F. Green-Wilkinson, A.A. & Q.M.G. 37th Division, left to take up command of 166th Infantry Brigade (55th Division) with temporary rank of Brig. Gen. Capt. E. O. Collinson, A.O.D., D.A.D.O.S. left to take up D.A.D.O.S. 55th Divn. Temp. Lieut. W.D. HARBINSON, A.O.D., took up duties of D.A.D.O.S. 37th Divn.	
"	Tues. 4th		NIL	
"	Wed. 5th		2nd Essex Regt. (from 12th Brig., 36th Divn.) attd to the Divn. for work on the Divnl Line arrived at HALLOY. Draft of 20 men for 7th Leic. Regt. arrived	
"	Thurs. 6th		2nd Essex Regt. arrived in Divnl. Area, attd to 110th Infy. Bde. & billetted in BERLES.	
"	Fri. 7th		Drafts of 30 men for 6th Leic. Regt. + 12 for 13/R. Fus. arrived.	
"	Sat. 8th			
"	Sun. 9th		NIL	
"	Mon. 10th			
"	Tues. 11th			
"	Wed. 12th			

Instructions regarding War Diaries and Intelligence Summaries are contained in F. S. Regs., Part II. and the Staff Manual respectively. Title pages will be prepared in manuscript.

WAR DIARY
or
INTELLIGENCE SUMMARY.
(Erase heading not required.)

Army Form C. 2118.

Place	Date	Hour	Summary of Events and Information	Remarks and references to Appendices
	1916 Jan.			
PAS	Thurs. 13th			
[illegible] "	Fri. 14th			
"	Sat. 15th		Following drafts arrived:— 9/Leic. Regt. 30 men, 13th Royal Fus. 40.	
"	Sun. 16th			
"	Mon. 17th		Wire received stating that C-in-C. has awarded a D.C.M. to No 17192	
x			Sergt CYRIL MELLORS 7th Leic. Regt.	
"	Tues. 18th		Major Gen. J.C. Young, Comdg. 67th Divn. with 3 staff officers arrived to be attd for instruction	
"	Wed. 19th			
"	Thurs. 20th			
"	Fri. 21st			
"	Sat. 22nd		The machine gun section (with guns) of 2/Essex Regt. leave to proceed to AILLY to ~~pass~~ join 12th Brigade Machine Gun Coy. now in course of formation	
			Gen. Young & attd officers left for England.	
			48th Siege Battery arrived at ST AMAND & HENU.	

Instructions regarding War Diaries and Intelligence Summaries are contained in F. S. Regs., Part II. and the Staff Manual respectively. Title pages will be prepared in manuscript.

WAR DIARY
or
INTELLIGENCE SUMMARY.
(Erase heading not required.)

Army Form C. 2118.

Place	Date	Hour	Summary of Events and Information	Remarks and references to Appendices
	1916 Jan.			
PAS	Sun. 23rd		NIL	
"	Mon. 24		NIL	
"	Tues. 25		NIL	
"	Wed. 26		Capt. F. Russell Roberts 10th R. Fus. awarded Mily. Cross & Pte. Mappiniades 10/R.F. the D.C.M.	
"	Thurs. 27		36th Siege Batty. arrived at LA CAUCHIE	
"	Fri. 28		Major Sir Alex. Bannerman Bart. R.E. left for England, ordered Home to train a Corps Signal Co.	
			Capt. Edwards, from ~~48th~~ 48th (N. Midland) Divnl Signal Co. took over command of the 37th Divnl. Signal Co.	
			Orders received to give up part of the Divnl. Area viz., MONDICOURT, GRENAS, & FAMECHON.	
"	Sat. 29th			[initials]
"	Sun. 30th			
"	Mon. 31st		Following drafts arrived:— 8th Leic. Regt. 34, 13th R. Fus. 20, 13/R.B. 12, 11/R. War. R. 13, 8/S. Lancs. Regt. 9, 10/ L. North Lancs. 13.	
			Composite Ind Cav. regt. (dismounted) consisting of 1 Brit. Off. 1 Ind. Off. + 55 other ranks from each of the 12 Ind. Cav. regts in the Ind. Cav. Corps, strength ~~[illegible]~~ 14 B.O.s, 14 I.O.s + 690 O.R. arrived + billeted in LA HERLIÈRE (for work on the Corps line).	

Confidential.

War Diary.

of

Administrative Staff 37th Division.

From 1st February 1916 To 29th February 1916.

A.Q. 37th Div:

Vol: 7

Instructions regarding War Diaries and Intelligence Summaries are contained in F. S. Regs., Part II. and the Staff Manual respectively. Title pages will be prepared in manuscript.

WAR DIARY
or
INTELLIGENCE SUMMARY.
(Erase heading not required.)

Feb. 1916.

Army Form C. 2118.

Place	Date	Hour	Summary of Events and Information	Remarks and references to Appendices
	1916 Feb.			
PAS	Tues. 1st		Draft of 40 for 6th Leic. Regt. from 4th Entrenching Battn.	
"	Wed. 2		FAMECHON & GRENAS + MONDICOURT evacuated by this Divn. D.A.C. moving to WARLINCOURT (from GRENAS), Yorkshire Dragoons from FAMECHON to WARLINCOURT, Motor Machine Gun Batty. & Cyclist Co. from MONDICOURT to PAS. Also 2 Cos. Pioneers moved from POMMIER + GRINCOURT to HALLOY, SARTON + AUTHIEULE to work on roads	
	Thurs 3		Orders received for Major PITT-TAYLOR to go as G.S.O. 4th Army + Major FULLER from G.S.O. 3 7th Corps to succeed him	
	Fri. 4		2/Essex Regt. left BERLES for COLINCAMPS to rejoin 12th Bde. Draft of 32 men arrd. for 9th Leic. Regt.	
	Sat. 5		Major Pitt Taylor left	
	Sun. 6		33 men arrd for D.A.C.	
	Mon. 7		NIL	
	Tues 8		Brig. Gen. Lord St. Levan (Comdg. 3/1 Wessex Divn. T.F.) & 3 Staff Offs. arrived to be attached.	
	Wed 9		Major Fuller arrd. ~~NIL~~	
	Thurs. 10		NIL	
	Fri. 11		Lord St. Levan and 3 other attd. officers left	

Instructions regarding War Diaries and Intelligence Summaries are contained in F. S. Regs., Part II. and the Staff Manual respectively. Title pages will be prepared in manuscript.

WAR DIARY
or
INTELLIGENCE SUMMARY.
(Erase heading not required.)

Army Form C. 2118.

Place	Date	Hour	Summary of Events and Information	Remarks and references to Appendices
	1916 Feb.			
PAS	Sat. 12		111th Infy. Bde. take over BERLES—BELLACOURT sector from French Cav. Divns.	
			Draft of 76 arrived for R.F.A.	
"	Sun. 13		112th Infy. Bde. handed over FONQUEVILLERS—HANNESCAMPS sector to 144th Infy. Bde. 48th Divn.	
"			27 officers arrd. for Battns. in the Divn. also 20 men for 6/Bedford Regt. + 33 for 13/R. Bde.	
"	Mon. 14			
"	Tues. 15			
"	Wed. 16			
"	Thurs. 17			
"	Fri. 18			
"	Sat. 19			
"	Sun. 20			
"	Mon 21		Divnl. H.Q. moved to BAVINCOURT.	
BAVINCOURT	Tues. 22		LARBRET ~~now our~~ railhead in place of MONDICOURT	
	Wed. 23			
	~~Thurs. 24~~			

1577 Wt. W10791/1773 500,000 1/15 D. D. & L. A.D.S.S./Forms/C. 2118.

Instructions regarding War Diaries and Intelligence Summaries are contained in F. S. Regs., Part II. and the Staff Manual respectively. Title pages will be prepared in manuscript.

WAR DIARY
or
INTELLIGENCE SUMMARY.
(Erase heading not required.)

Army Form C. 2118.

Place	Date	Hour	Summary of Events and Information	Remarks and references to Appendices
	Feb.			
BAVINCOURT	Thurs. 24		Leave stopped. Draft of 39 for 8/8. Lancs. arrd. Snow fell to about 4 or 5 inches. Orders received for most of the billetting accommodation in BAVINCOURT to be given to 55th Divn. who are losing BARLY + FOSSEUX (placed at disposal of 6th Corps now moving North to take over from the French round ARRAS)	
"	Fri. 25		Liverpool Irish (1/5? King's Liv.) billetted in BAVINCOURT for night. Frost at night.	
"	Sat. 26		1/5 K.O. (Lanc.) Regt. billetted in BAVINCOURT for night in place of Liverpool Irish. Frost	
"	Sun. 27		Ind. Cav. Corps Composite (Digging) Regt. left ~~LARBRET~~ LAHERLIERE (from LARBRET 8th Sig.) 1/5 K.O. Lanc. Regt., 1/2 West Lancs. Heavy Batty. R.G.A. + 55th Divl. Cyclist Co. moved to LAHERLIÈRE + billetted. & Waggon Lines of 11 Batteries 55th Divl. Arty. billetted in BAVINCOURT, 3 batteries W. Lines in LARBRET. Partial thaw.	
"	Mon. 28		Thaw commenced. Traffic restrictions — no lorries or horse transport to be allowed on roads except for supplies, ammunition + road metal — imposed last night late + taken off again 8.30 a.m. today (frost during night)	
"	Tues. 29		Thaw. Traffic restrictions imposed until further orders.	

1577 Wt. W10791/1773 500,000 1/15 D. D. & L. A.D.S.S./Forms/C. 2118.

WO 95/37/1 Vol 8

CONFIDENTIAL.

War Diary

of

Administrative Staff, 37th Division

from March 1. 1916 to March 31, 1916

Instructions regarding War Diaries and Intelligence Summaries are contained in F. S. Regs., Part II. and the Staff Manual respectively. Title pages will be prepared in manuscript.

WAR DIARY
or
INTELLIGENCE SUMMARY.
(Erase heading not required.)

Army Form C. 2118.

Administrative Staff
37th Division
March 1916.

Place	Date	Hour	Summary of Events and Information	Remarks and references to Appendices
	March 1916			
BAVINCOURT	Wed. 1st		37th Divnl. Cyclist Co. moved to LUCHEUX.	
"	Thurs. 2nd		Draft of 68 for 10th Royal Fus. arrived from 5th Entrenching Battn.	
"	Fri. 3rd		Snow nearly all gone in morning.	
"	Sat. 4th		Snow fell in early morning. 110th, 111th & 112th Infy. Brigade Machine Gun Cos. arrived at DOULLENS during the night & marched up to their Brigades in the course of the day. Drafts arrd. 13/R.B. 23, 6/Beds. 25.	
"	Sun. 5th		Snow fell last night. LARBRET to be handed over to 55th Divn. and LA HERLIERE to be given back to 37th Divn.	
"	Mon. 6th		Snow fell heavily in early morning & a good deal during day.	
"	Tues. 7th		Some snow at night.	
"	Wed. 8th		NIL	
"	Thurs. 9th		NIL	
"	Fri. 10th		Drafts arrd. 6th Leic. Regt 25 - 8th Leic. 40 - Snow last night	
"	Sat. 11th		Definite orders received for 37th Divn. to move out of the line & go into Reserve being relieved by the 4th Divn.	G.D.T.

Instructions regarding War Diaries and Intelligence Summaries are contained in F. S. Regs., Part II. and the Staff Manual respectively. Title pages will be prepared in manuscript.

WAR DIARY
or
INTELLIGENCE SUMMARY.
(Erase heading not required.)

Army Form C. 2118.

Administrative Staff
37th Division
March 1916

Place	Date	Hour	Summary of Events and Information	Remarks and references to Appendices
	March 1916			
BAVINCOURT				
"	Sat. 11th		NIL	
"	Sun. 12		Thaw.	
"	Mon. 13		Fine day & mild	
"	Tues. 14		Fine, quite warm Distribution of Div. in new area now settled viz., 111th Bde. W. of DOULLENS—FREVENT road, ~~110th Bde~~ (OCCOCHES, MEZEROLLES, BARLY & NEUVILLETTE), 110th Bde. at SUS (2 Bns.) LE SOUICH, & WARLUZEL (E. of DOULLENS—FREVENT road) & 112th Bde. at ST AMAND, HUMBERCAMP & MONDICOURT as Reserve Bde. to 4th Div. Divnl. H.Q. at LUCHEUX.	
"	Wed. 15th		~~Nil~~ 37th Divl. Arty. to remain in the line for the present.	
"	Thurs. 16		~~Nil~~ Draft of 40 for 9th North Stafford Regt. arr. from 5th Entrenchg. Bn	
"	Fri. 17		Move of the 2 Divns. began, 2 Bns. (10/R.F. & 13/R.B.) of 111th Bde. moving from BAILLEULVAL & BAILLEULMONT to ~~H.Q.~~ hutments at HALLOY (for 1 night) on way to new area & being replaced by 2 Bns. of 12th Bde. 4th Div.	E.H.S.

1577 Wt. W10791/1773 500,000 1/15 D. D. & L. A.D.S.S./Forms/C. 2118.

Instructions regarding War Diaries and Intelligence Summaries are contained in F. S. Regs., Part II. and the Staff Manual respectively. Title pages will be prepared in manuscript.

WAR DIARY
or
INTELLIGENCE SUMMARY.
(Erase heading not required.)

Army Form C. 2118.

Administrative Staff
37th Division
March 1916

Place	Date	Hour	Summary of Events and Information	Remarks and references to Appendices
	March 1916			
BAVINCOURT				
"	Sat. – 18th		Move continues.	
"	Sun. – 19th		Move continues. Roads now quite dry and in wonderfully good condition	
			Last 2 Battns. (13/KRR + 13/R.B.) of 111th Bde. relieved in the trenches by 12th Bde.	
LUCHEUX	Mon. – 20		~~Move con~~ Divnl. H.Q. move to LUCHEUX	
"	Tues. – 21		Move continues. 13/K.R.R. + 13/R.B. march to hutments at HALLOY. These are the last Battns. of the Divn. to move.	
"	Wed. – 22		Move completed.	
"	Thurs. – 23		NIL	
"	Fri. – 24		NIL	
"	Sat. – 25		13/R.B. to AUXI-LE-CHATEAU to be attached to 3rd Army School.	
			9/North Stafford Regt. move from BREVILLERS to OCCOCHES (evac. by 13/R.B.)	
"	Sun. – 26		NIL	
"	Mon. – 27		NIL	
"	Tues. – 28		NIL	
"	Wed. – 29		NIL	
"	Thurs. – 30		NIL	
"	Fri. – 31		NIL	

E. I. D. Gordon Major
DAA & QMG. 37th Divn.

1577 Wt. W10791/1773 500,000 1/15 D. D. & L. A.D.S.S./Forms/C. 2118.

WO 95/37/9

C O N F I D E N T I A L.

W A R D I A R Y

of

Administrative Staff 37th Divisional Headquarters

From 1st April, 1916, to 30th April, 1916.

(Volume 9).

Instructions regarding War Diaries and Intelligence Summaries are contained in F. S. Regs., Part II. and the Staff Manual respectively. Title pages will be prepared in manuscript.

April 1916

WAR DIARY
or
INTELLIGENCE SUMMARY.
(Erase heading not required.)

Administrative Staff 37th Division

Army Form C. 2118.

Place	Date	Hour	Summary of Events and Information	Remarks and references to Appendices
	April 1916			
LUCHEUX	Sat. 1st to Thurs 6th		NIL	
"	~~Fri 7th~~ Fri. 7th		NIL	
"	Sat. 8th		Following drafts arrive: 13th K.R.R. 20 men, 6th Bedfords 20, 10th L. N. Lancs. 17	
"	Sun. 9th to Wed. 12th		NIL	
"	Thurs. 13th		Leave suspended, all ranks to return not later than 15th inst	
"	Sat. 15th		Following drafts arrive:- 13/Rifle Bde 49, 11th Royal Warwicks 21. A little snow	
"	Sun. 16th		110th Bde. move into Reserve Bde area (Humbercamp, STAMAND + MUNDICOURT) + 112th Bde into SUS, LESOUICH + WARLUZEL.	
"	Mon 17th to Thurs 20th		NIL	
"	Fri. 21st		Drafts arrive:- 7th Leic. Regt. 20	
"	Sat. 22nd		110th Bde. move from Reserve Bde area to Western Bde. area (MEZEROLLES,	[illegible] L.I.G.

Instructions regarding War Diaries and Intelligence Summaries are contained in F. S. Regs., Part II. and the Staff Manual respectively. Title pages will be prepared in manuscript.

April 1916

WAR DIARY
or
INTELLIGENCE SUMMARY.
(Erase heading not required.)

Administrative Staff 37th Division

Army Form C. 2118.

Place	Date	Hour	Summary of Events and Information	Remarks and references to Appendices
	April 1916			
LUCHEUX	Sat. 22nd		BARLY + NEUVILLETTE) leaving 9/Leic. Regt. at MONDICOURT. The 111th Bde. move into the Reserve Bde. area (13th Rifle Bde. still at AUXI-LE-CHATEAU)	
"	Sun. 23		NIL	
"	Mon 24		Draft of 36 for 11/R Warwick Regt. arrives	
"	Tues-25		Leave re-opened.	
"	Wed-26		NIL	
"	Thurs-27		~~Also~~ 13th Rifle Bde. coming back from AUXI-LE-CHATEAU to rejoin 111th Bde	
"	Fri-28		Orders received to move back into the line taking over from the 4th Divn.	
"	Sat-29			
"	Sun-30		Move proceeding, 2 Battns. (10th & 13th R.F.) going into the trenches.	

C.W. Jordan Major
D.A.A. + Q.M.G. 37th Div

1577 Wt. W10791/1773 500,000 1/15 D. D. & L. A.D.S.S./Forms/C. 2118.

37 Div A & Q
Vol 10

CONFIDENTIAL.

WAR DIARY

of

ADMINISTRATIVE STAFF, 37th DIVISION.

From 1st May, 1916 to 31st May, 1916.

(Volume 10).

Instructions regarding War Diaries and Intelligence Summaries are contained in F. S. Regs., Part II. and the Staff Manual respectively. Title pages will be prepared in manuscript.

WAR DIARY
or
~~INTELLIGENCE SUMMARY.~~
(Erase heading not required.)

May, 1916

Army Form C. 2118.

Administrative Staff
37th Division

Place	Date	Hour	Summary of Events and Information	Remarks and references to Appendices
	May 1916			
LUCHEUX	Mon. 1st		Relief of 4th Divn. by 37th Divn. continues.	
"	Tues. 2nd			
BAVINCOURT	Wed. 3rd		Divnl. H.Q. move from LUCHEUX to BAVINCOURT. Relief of 4th Divn. completed.	
"	Thurs. 4th		About 2am. enemy attacked our line in 2 places, on right of 10th Royal Fus. & by the MONCHY Salient (held by 6th Bedford Regt.). Heavy bombardment by German artillery & then a small raiding party advanced & entered our trenches & retired again after a few minutes. Our total casualties:– 1 off. & 23 killed, 1 off. & ~~96~~ 102 wounded & 8 missing (believed killed). 6 of the wounded died of wounds making the total dead 1 off. & 29. Almost all the casualties were caused by shell fire, the only ones not so caused being 1 by rifle, 3 by revolver & 4 by grenade.	
"	Fri. 5th			
"	Sat. 6th		37 men for 11th R. Warwick Regt. arrive.	
"	Sun. 7th		NIL	
"	Mon. 8th		NIL	
"	Tues. 9th		Time of refilling changed from morning to afternoon. 20 men arrd. for 10th Loyal N. Lancs.	
"	Wed. 10th		NIL	

1577 Wt. W10791/1773 500,000 1/15 D. D. & L. A.D.S.S./Forms/C. 2118.

Instructions regarding War Diaries and Intelligence Summaries are contained in F. S. Regs., Part II. and the Staff Manual respectively. Title pages will be prepared in manuscript.

May 1916

WAR DIARY
or
INTELLIGENCE SUMMARY.
(Erase heading not required.)

Administrative Staff
37th Divn.

Army Form C. 2118.

Place	Date	Hour	Summary of Events and Information	Remarks and references to Appendices
	May 1916			
BAVINCOURT	Thurs 11th		NIL	
"	Fri. 12th		Following drafts arvd. :- 6th Leicester Regt. 40 (from 4th Entrenching Battn), 7th Leic. Regt. 30 10th Royal Fus. 55 men, 13th K.R.R. 20, 6th Bedford Regt. 69	
"	Sat. 13th to		} NIL	
"	Fri. 19th			
"	Sat. 20th		Ammunition Dump at SAULTY completed.	
"	Sun. 21st to		} NIL	
"	Tues. 23rd			
"	Wed. 24th		Following drafts arvd. :- 7th Leic. Regt. 53, 9th Leic. Regt. 57, 13th K.R.R. 151, ~~all from No 5 Entrenching Battn~~ 10th Royal Fus. 58, 13th Royal Fus. 77, 6th Bedford Regt. 54, 9th North Stafford Regt. 91, all from No 5 Entrenching Battn., also some small parties from 37th Infy. Base Depot. Also officers arrived from 37th Infy. Base Depot as follows:- 10th Royal Fus. 1, 13th R. Fus. 4, 11th R. Warwick Regt 6, 6th Bedford Regt. 7.	
"	Thurs 25th			
"	Fri. 26th		Following drafts arvd. :- 10th Roy. Fus. 60, 13th Roy. Fus. 60, 8th Leic. Regt. 83, all from No 10 Entrenching Bn. POPERINGHE. C.-in-C. visited Divnl. H.Q.	
~~"~~	~~Sat. 27th~~			
"	Sat. 27th to		} NIL	
	Wed. 31st			E.W. Gordon

C O N F I D E N T I A L.

W A R   D I A R Y

o f

ADMINISTRATIVE STAFF, 37th DIVISION.

from 1st June 1916 to 30th June 1916.

June

CONFIDENTIAL.

SUBJECT: War Diary.   37th Divn. 90/10a

D.A.G.,
G.H.Q.,
3rd Echelon.

Herewith War Diary of Administrative Staff 37th Division from 1st to 30th June 1916.

H. Anneau Captain for
Major General.

2/7/16.   Commanding 37th Division.

Instructions regarding War Diaries and Intelligence Summaries are contained in F. S. Regs., Part II. and the Staff Manual respectively. Title pages will be prepared in manuscript.

June 1916

WAR DIARY
or
INTELLIGENCE SUMMARY.
(Erase heading not required.)

Administrative Staff
37th Division

Army Form C. 2118.

Place	Date	Hour	Summary of Events and Information	Remarks and references to Appendices
	June 1916			
BAVINCOURT	Thurs. 1st		Brig. Gen. BAINBRIDGE, Comdg. 110th Infy. Bde., appointed to command 25th Divn.	
"	Fri 2nd		NIL	
"	Sat 3rd		Party of 10th Royal Fusiliers carried out raid at midnight 3/4 on German trenches just N. of MONCHY successfully, only having one man wounded while grenades were thrown into several German dugouts & it is believed that several Germans were killed.	
"	Sun. 4th		Raid intended to be carried out by party of 13th Royal Fus. tonight but it was abandoned on account of one of the officers being called & the other 2 being wounded.	
"	Mon. 5th		NIL	
"	Tues 6th		NIL	
"	Wed. 7th		NIL	
"	Thurs 8th		Draft of 42 for 11th R. Warwick Regt. arrived.	
"	Fri 9th		Lt. Col. W. F. HESSEY, Comdg. 9th Inniskilling Fus., appointed to command the 110th Infy. Bde.	
"	Sat. 10th		Enemy shelled Railhead (LARBRET Station) with about 100 5.9" shells. 5 or 6 wounded. Supply train off. loaded at MONDICOURT. Railhead changed to DOULLENS.	E.W.F.
"	Sun 11th		NIL	

1577 Wt. W10791/1773 500,000 1/15 D. D. & L. A.D.S.S./Forms/C. 2118.

Instructions regarding War Diaries and Intelligence Summaries are contained in F. S. Regs., Part II. and the Staff Manual respectively. Title pages will be prepared in manuscript.

WAR DIARY
or
INTELLIGENCE SUMMARY.
(Erase heading not required.)

June 1916

Army Form C. 2118.

Administrative Staff
37th Division

Place	Date	Hour	Summary of Events and Information	Remarks and references to Appendices
	June 1916			
BAYINCOURT	Mon. 12th		Nil	
"	Tues. 13th		Railhead changed back to LARBRET.	
"	Wed. 14th			
"	Thurs. 15th			
"	Fri. 16th			
"	Sat. 17th			
"	Sun. 18th			
"	Mon. 19th			
"	Tues. 20th		Major GORDON, D.A.A.+Q.M.G., apptd. to command 6/7th R. Scots Fus. (15th Divn) & Captain DUNCAN from Staff Capt. 3rd Infy. Bde. to be D.A.A.+Q.M.G.	
"	Wed. 21st		~~To Abut~~ 6 or 7 enemy aeroplanes dropped about 30 bombs on ST. POL, 3rd Army H.Q.	
"	Thurs. 22nd		Nil	
"	Fri. 23rd		~~Major Gordon pro~~ Captain Duncan arrived to take up his appointment	
	Sat 24th		Major Gordon proceeded to take up appointment	
	Sunday 25th		~~Nil~~ Aeroplane bomb dropped near ~~on~~ ammunition dump no damage was done.	
	Monday 26th		Nil.	

1577 Wt. W10791/1773 500,000 1/15 D. D. & L. A.D.S.S./Forms/C. 2118.

Army Form C. 2118.

Instructions regarding War Diaries and Intelligence Summaries are contained in F. S. Regs., Part II. and the Staff Manual respectively. Title pages will be prepared in manuscript.

WAR DIARY
or
June 1916 INTELLIGENCE SUMMARY. Administrative Staff 37th Division

(Erase heading not required.)

Place	Date	Hour	Summary of Events and Information	Remarks and references to Appendices
BAVINCOURT	Tues. 27th		Nil.	
" "	WED. 28th		Nil	
	Thursday 29th		Nil.	
	Friday 30th		Divisional Reinforcement Camp opened at HALLOY.	

1577 Wt. W10791/1773 500,000 1/15 D. D. & L. A.D.S.S./Forms/C. 2118.

SECRET

SECRET

~~CONFIDENTIAL~~.

War Diary

of

Administrative Staff

37th Division

From 1st to 31st July 1916

CONFIDENTIAL.

SECRET

Subject:- War Diaries. 37th Divn. 90/12A

D.A.G.
G.H.Q.
3rd Echelon.

Herewith War Diary for Administrative Staff 37th Division from 1st to 31st July 1916.

J. Duncan Captain DAA & QMG for
Major-General,
Commanding 37th Division.

1st August 1916.

July

37 A & Q

Vol 12

Instructions regarding War Diaries and Intelligence Summaries are contained in F. S. Regs., Part II. and the Staff Manual respectively. Title pages will be prepared in manuscript.

WAR DIARY
or
INTELLIGENCE SUMMARY.
(*Erase heading not required.*)

Army Form C. 2118.

Administrative Staff
37th Division

Place	Date	Hour	Summary of Events and Information	Remarks and references to Appendices
BAVINCOURT.	1 July.		Nil	
" "	2nd July		Nil	
" "	3rd July.		Orders received for Division to move into Corps reserve area on 4th	
" "	4th July.		Division moved into new area, Headquarters at PAS.	
			110th Bde Hq HUMBERCAMP and 3 battns. 1 battn at WARLINCOURT	
			Hqrs 111th Bde + 1 battn at MONDICOURT 2 bns HUMBERCOURT 1 bn at PAS	
			Hqrs 112th Bde GRENAS all Bns at HALLOY.	
PAS.	5th July		Division became G.H.Q. reserve from 6 AM ready to move at 3 hours notice.	
	6th July		Division taken off GHQ Reserve. Orders received for 110th Bde to join 21st Div, and 111th Bde + 112 Bde to join 34th Division. Pioneers 9 North Staffords to 34th Division. 111th Brigade and Pioneers proceeded to Bresle and Millencourt respectively by busses, the last party having left the area by 12.45 AM 7th inst.	

Instructions regarding War Diaries and Intelligence Summaries are contained in F. S. Regs., Part II. and the Staff Manual respectively. Title pages will be prepared in manuscript.

WAR DIARY
or
INTELLIGENCE SUMMARY.
(Erase heading not required.)

Army Form C. 2118.

Place	Date	Hour	Summary of Events and Information	Remarks and references to Appendices
PAS	7th July		112th Bde proceeded by busses to Breste to join 34th Division	
			110 Bde proceeded by March route to join 21st Division.	
PAS	8th July		102nd Bde and 103rd Bde arrived in busses about 1.0 pm Composition of Brigades as follows	
			102nd Bde — 20th Northumberland Fusiliers, 21st " ", 22nd " ", 23rd " "	
			103rd Bde. — 24th Northumberland Fusiliers, 25th " ", 26th " ", 27th " "	
			18th Northumberland Fusiliers (Pioneers 34th Division) arrived by busses and were billeted at PAS Huts.	
			Brigades were much below strength, estimated strengths on arrival as follows. 102nd Bde. 78 Officers 1336. O.R. 103rd Inf Bde. 89 Officers 1455. O.R 18 Northumberland Fusiliers (Pioneers) 30 off. 1019. O.R.	

1577 Wt. W10791/1773 500,000 1/15 D. D. & L. A.D.S.S./Forms/C. 2118.

Instructions regarding War Diaries and Intelligence Summaries are contained in F. S. Regs., Part II. and the Staff Manual respectively. Title pages will be prepared in manuscript.

WAR DIARY
or
INTELLIGENCE SUMMARY.
(Erase heading not required.)

Army Form C. 2118.

Administrative Staff
Hdqrs 37th Division

Place	Date	Hour	Summary of Events and Information	Remarks and references to Appendices
PAS	9th July		63rd Inf Bde arrived by March route about 3 PM and was billetted as follows. 8th Lincolns Mondicourt. 10th York & Lancs Mondicourt. 4 Middlesex HALLOY 8 Somerset L.I. HALLOY. Ammunition refilling point at GAUDIEMPRE from 6AM. Estimated strength on arrival 103 officers 2319 O.R.	
"	10th	"	18th Northumberland Fusiliers Pioneers BIENVILLERS	
"	11th		63rd Bde moved 3 battns into trenches and 1 bn to Bienvillers in relief of Bde of 46th Div	
"	12th		Casualties 10th Y & Lancs 1 O.R. wounded shell.	
	13th		Casualties 8 O.R. killed and 9 O.R. wounded.	
	14th		Orders received that 37th Div would join 4th Corps.	
	~~15th~~ "		Move commenced. 102nd and 103rd Brigade marched to new billets as follows. 102nd Bde 20th Northumberland Fus. GIVENCHY LE NOBLE 22nd Northumberland Fus. LIGNEREUIL 21st " " " ~~LIGNEREUIL~~ MANIN 23rd " " " BEAUFORT	

Instructions regarding War Diaries and Intelligence Summaries are contained in F. S. Regs., Part II. and the Staff Manual respectively. Title pages will be prepared in manuscript.

WAR DIARY
or
INTELLIGENCE SUMMARY.
(Erase heading not required.)

Army Form C. 2118.

Administrative Staff
Hdqrs 37th Division

Place	Date	Hour	Summary of Events and Information	Remarks and references to Appendices
PAS	14 July (contd.)		153rd Field Coy LIGNEREUIL. No 3 Coy Train BEAUFORT. M.G. Coy LIENCOURT.	
			49th Field ambulance HOUVIN HOUVIGNEUL. BDE. Hdqrs LIENCOURT.	
			103rd Bde. 24th & 25th Northumberland Fusiliers. HOUVIN HOUVIGNEUL	
			26th Northumberland Fusiliers } MAGNICOURT sur CANCHE. 27th Northumberland Fusiliers	
			No 4 Coy Train. SARS les BOIS.	
			50 Fd Ambulance HOUVIN HOUVIGNEUL M.G. Coy MAGNICOURT sur CANCHE.	
			154 Fd Coy R.E. " " " "	
			Bde Hdqrs " " " "	
			63rd Inf Bde, Pioneers and Artillery did not move.	
PAS	15th July		Remainder of Division move to new billets as follows.	
			Divisional Hdqrs to LIGNEREUIL. Div. Artillery to area	
			BOURET SUR CANCHE - REBREUVE ESTREE WAMIN and 1 Bde	
			at BERLENCOURT	
			63rd Bde to area HOUVIN HOUVIGNEUL - SARS LES BOIS	
			MAGNICOURT SUR CANCHE. 152 Fd Coy to REBREUVIETTE	
			48th Field Amb. REBREUVIETTE. 18 N. Fus. Pioneers to MAGNICOURT SUR CANCHE.	

1577 Wt. W10791/1773 500,000 1/15 D. D. & L. A.D.S.S./Forms/C. 2118.

Instructions regarding War Diaries and Intelligence Summaries are contained in F. S. Regs., Part II. and the Staff Manual respectively. Title pages will be prepared in manuscript.

WAR DIARY
or
INTELLIGENCE SUMMARY.
(Erase heading not required.)

Army Form C. 2118.

Administrative Staff
Hdqrs 37th Division

Place	Date	Hour	Summary of Events and Information	Remarks and references to Appendices
LIGNEUREUIL	15th July		102 and 103rd moved to new billets as follows. 102nd Bde and attached troops. Hdqrs CHELERS. remainder in area VILLERS BRULIN - BAILLEUL aux CORNAILLES - CHELERS. 103rd Bde and attached troops. Bde Hdqrs MONCHY BRETON remainder in area MONCHY BRETON - MARQUAY OSTREVILLE ORLENCOURT	
LIGNEUREUIL	16th July		102nd Bde moved to Division area with Bde Hdqrs at that place. 103rd Bde 2 bns from OSTEVILLE to MARQUAY and ORLENCOURT. 18th Northumberland Fus. Pioneers to OSTREVILLE. Div Artillery and attached to 47th Div area at GAUCHIN LE GAL. Divisional Hdqrs to BRYAS. Division came under orders of IV Corps on the completion of this move - Railhead at ST POL.	
BRYAS	17th		RAIL Head at BRUAY from this date onwards.	
" "	18		63rd Bde & attached units moved into area CAMBLIN L'ABBE - MAISNIL BOUCHE ESTREE CAUCHIE	
BRYAS	19th		103rd Brigade & attached units moved into area FREVILLERS HERMIN ESTREE	

Instructions regarding War Diaries and Intelligence Summaries are contained in F. S. Regs., Part II. and the Staff Manual respectively. Title pages will be prepared in manuscript.

WAR DIARY
or
INTELLIGENCE SUMMARY.
(Erase heading not required.)

Army Form C. 2118.

Administrative Staff
Hdqrs 37th Division

Place	Date	Hour	Summary of Events and Information	Remarks and references to Appendices
			CAUCHIE-FRESNICOURT. Bde Hdqrs at FRESNICOURT. HERMIN was found to be still occupied by a battn of 2nd Division, 26th Northumberland Fusiliers therefore billeted one night at REBREUVE	
BRYAN	20th		Div Hdqrs moved to O. 10 b. sheet 36 B. 2000 yards SOUTH of ORTON.	
ORTAN.	21st		Nil	
"	22nd		63rd Bde is placed under command of G.O.C. 47th Division from 6 AM Billets remain the same. 152nd Field Coy placed at disposal of C.R.E. 47th Division ~~and moved to~~ 153 and 154 Fd Coys placed at disposal of C.E. IV Corps and billeted at COUPIGNY and BOIS DE HAIE respectively.	
	23rd		~~Nil.~~ 33 O.R. reinforcements reported as joined 103rd Bde Machine Gun Coy. Orders received from IV Corps for 37th Div to take over section of line held by 47th Div. Relief to be completed by 10 AM 28th inst.	

1577 Wt. W10791/1773 500,000 1/15 D. D. & L. A.D.S.S./Forms/C. 2118.

Instructions regarding War Diaries and Intelligence Summaries are contained in F. S. Regs., Part II. and the Staff Manual respectively. Title pages will be prepared in manuscript.

WAR DIARY
or
INTELLIGENCE SUMMARY.
(Erase heading not required.)

Army Form C. 2118.

Administrative Staff
H.Qrs 37th Division

Place	Date	Hour	Summary of Events and Information	Remarks and references to Appendices
ORTAN	24	July	Nil	
ORTAN	25	July	63rd Infy Bde took over BERTHONVAL section of the line.	
" "	26	"	102nd and 103rd Inf Bdes concentrated at Chateau de la HAIE area and were amalgamated there for tactical purposes as 102nd/103rd Bde. Ammunition refilling point at Q.34 d.6.8 Divisional RE. dump at GAUY SERVINS. Ammunition Railhead at HOUDIN. Railhead for supplies, animals and reinforcements remains at BRUAY. Drafts for units arrived as follows.	
" "			4 Middlesex Regt 1 Officer 3 O.R.	
			8 Lincolns - 6	
			22nd Northumberland Fus. 3 -	
			23rd " " 4 175	
			26 " " 2 -	
			27 " " 1 110	
			These reinforcements being first of appreciable strength since the Bdes join this Division	

Army Form C. 2118.

Instructions regarding War Diaries and Intelligence Summaries are contained in F. S. Regs., Part II. and the Staff Manual respectively. Title pages will be prepared in manuscript.

WAR DIARY
or
INTELLIGENCE SUMMARY.
(*Erase heading not required.*)

Place	Date	Hour	Summary of Events and Information	Remarks and references to Appendices
ORTON	27 July		102/103 Inf Bde took over the CARENCY section of line. Casualties 10th York and Lancs O.R. wounded two	
			18th Northumberland Fus " " " " one	
			Reinforcements arrived as follows – Officers / O.R.	
			103rd Machine Gun Coy. – 34	
			26 Northumberland Fus. – 68	
			8 Lincoln Regt. 3 200	
			20th Northumberland Fus. – 111	
CAMBLAIN L'ABBE	28 July		Div Hdqrs moved to CAMBLAIN L'ABBE	
			Casualties 18th Northumberland Fus Wounded O.R. 1	
			124th Bde R.F.A. Killed O.R. 1 accidentally	
			Div Artillery Hdqrs situated at CAMBLAIN L'ABBE	
			" TRAIN " " " " "	
			" Engineers " " " MAISNIL BOUCHE.	
			Reinforcements arrived as follows.	
			8 Somerset Light Infantry 11 Officers.	

Instructions regarding War Diaries and Intelligence Summaries are contained in F. S. Regs., Part II. and the Staff Manual respectively. Title pages will be prepared in manuscript.

WAR DIARY
or
INTELLIGENCE SUMMARY.
(Erase heading not required.)

Army Form C. 2118.

Administrative Staff.
H.Qrs. 37th Division

Place	Date	Hour	Summary of Events and Information	Remarks and references to Appendices
			Officers — O R	
CAMBLAIN L'ABBE	28 contd.		8 Lincolns 2 —	
			10th York & Lancs 1 —	
			20th Northumberland Fus 1 —	
			21st " " " 1 —	
			22nd " " " 1 —	
			23rd " " 1 42	
			24th " " 1 103	
			26th " " — 134	
			27th " " — 65	
			4 Middlesex — 45	
" "	29 July		Casualties 25th Northumberland Fusiliers O R wounded one. 26 " " " " " " one at duty.	
"	30th July		Casualties 25th Northumberland Fusiliers O R wounded one. " 27th " " " one.	
" "	31st July		Casualties 8 Lincolns wounded O.R one. 21st Northumberland Fus wounded O.R. 3 25 Northumberland Fus. O.R wounded 1 self inflicted. 26th N.F. O.R Killed 1 bullet.	

1577 Wt. W10791/1773 500,000 1/15 D. D. & L. A.D.S.S./Forms/C. 2118.

SECRET

37 HQ Vol 13

WAR DIARY

ADMINISTATIVE STAFF

37th DIVN AUG/16

Instructions regarding War Diaries and Intelligence Summaries are contained in F. S. Regs., Part II. and the Staff Manual respectively. Title pages will be prepared in manuscript.

WAR DIARY
or
~~INTELLIGENCE SUMMARY.~~
(Erase heading not required.)

Army Form C. 2118.

Administrative Staff
Hdqrs 37th Division –

Place	Date	Hour	Summary of Events and Information	Remarks and references to Appendices
CAMBLAIN L'ABBE	1st August		Casualties 8th Somerset Light Infantry Wounded Lieut W. H. A THORNE 8 Lincolns wounded O.R. one 20th Northd Fus. Killed O R one – 18 " " wounded " one 21 " " " " " one 22 " " " " " one 26 " " " " " one –	
" " "	2nd ~~July~~ August		Casualties 8 Lincolns Wounded 1. O.R. 20th Northd Fus. " " 1. O.R 23rd " " Killed 2 O.R 25th " " wounded 1. O.R. Following drafts received. 20th Northd Fus. 30. O.R 21st " " 7 O.R. 23rd " " 23 O R.	

Instructions regarding War Diaries and Intelligence Summaries are contained in F. S. Regs., Part II. and the Staff Manual respectively. Title pages will be prepared in manuscript.

WAR DIARY
or
INTELLIGENCE SUMMARY.
(*Erase heading not required.*)

Army Form C. 2118.

Administrative Staff
Hdqrs 37th Division

Place	Date	Hour	Summary of Events and Information	Remarks and references to Appendices
CAMBLAIN L'ABBE	3rd August		Casualties 20th Northd Fus. K. O.R. 1. W O.R. 2 24 " " " " O.R. 5 26 " " " " O.R. 3.	
" "	4 Aug.		Refitting point for 63rd Bde found at E.6.b 9.7 Sheet 51 C. N.E.	
			Casualties 8 Lincolns Wounded O.R 3 10 York & Lancs. " " " 2 18 Northd Fus " " " 1 20 " " " Killed O.R. 2 Wounded officer 1. O.R 5 27 " " " wounded O.R. 1 102 Trench Mortar Batt. " " O.R. 1	
			The following Drafts arrived. 4th Middlesex Regt. 44 O.R 27th Northd Fus 58 O.R.	
CAMBLAIN L'ABBE	5th Aug.		Casualties. 8 Lincolns W O.R. 2 — 26 Northd Fus Killed O.R 1 W 1 Off 2 O.R. 22nd Northd Fus. " " 1 — 27 Northd Fus Wounded 3 O.R. 24th " " " " 2 — 154 Field Coy R.E. Wounded 1 Off 1 O.R. 25 " " " " 1	

2353 Wt. W2544/1454 700,000 5/15 D. D. & L. A.D.S.S./Forms/C. 2118.

Instructions regarding War Diaries and Intelligence Summaries are contained in F. S. Regs., Part II. and the Staff Manual respectively. Title pages will be prepared in manuscript.

WAR DIARY
or
INTELLIGENCE SUMMARY.
(Erase heading not required.)

Army Form C. 2118.

Administrative Staff - Headqrs 37th Division.

Place	Date	Hour	Summary of Events and Information	Remarks and references to Appendices
CHAMBLAIN L'ABBE	5th Aug. Contd		Following drafts arrived.	
			8 Somerset Light Infantry: 100 O.R	
" " "	6 August		Casualties.	
			8 Somersets Off K. 1. O.R W. 3.	
			18 Northd Fus W. O.R. 1.	
			20th " " W. O.R. 2	
			21st " " W. O.R. 2	
			26th " " K. O.R. 1	
			27th " " W. O.R. 1.	
CHAMBLAIN L'ABBE	7 Aug.		8 Lincolns. W. O.R. 1	
			8 Somersets: K. O.R. 1	
			10th York & Lancs. K O.R. 1. W. O.R. 1	
			24th Northd Fus. K. O.R. 1 W. O.R. 10	
			25th " " " W off 1 O.R. 12.	
			26th " " " W. O.R. 4	
			27 " " " W O.R. 1	
			102 M G Coy - W O.R. 1	

Army Form C. 2118.

WAR DIARY
or
INTELLIGENCE SUMMARY.
(Erase heading not required.)

Instructions regarding War Diaries and Intelligence Summaries are contained in F. S. Regs., Part II. and the Staff Manual respectively. Title pages will be prepared in manuscript.

Administrative Staff - Hdqrs 37th Division.

Place	Date	Hour	Summary of Events and Information	Remarks and references to Appendices
CAMBLAIN L'ABBE.	7th Aug contd		The following drafts arrived. 20th Northd Fus. 54 O.R. 21st " " 54 O.R 22nd " " 54 O.R. 23rd " " 54 O.R 24th " " 54 O.R. 25th " " 54 O R 26th " " 54 O R 27th " " 54 O. R	
CAMBLAIN L'ABBE	8th Aug.		Casualties 4th Middlesex. W. 1. O.R 10th Loyal Lancs. W. 1. O. R 22nd Northd Fus. W. 2 O.R 24th " " " K. 1. O.R. 26th " " " W. 1. off 102 MG Coy. W. O.R 1 126 Bde R.F.A. O.R. K. 1. V/37 Trench Mortar Batt. W. O.R 3. The following drafts arrived. 20th Northd Fus. 20. O.R 21st " " 20. O.R 22nd " " 50. O.R 23rd " " 40. O.R 24th " " 29 O.R 25th " " 20. O.R 26th " " 32. O.R	

Instructions regarding War Diaries and Intelligence Summaries are contained in F. S. Regs., Part II. and the Staff Manual respectively. Title pages will be prepared in manuscript.

WAR DIARY
or
INTELLIGENCE SUMMARY.
(Erase heading not required.)

Army Form C. 2118.

Administrative Staff - Hdqrs 37th Division.

Place	Date	Hour	Summary of Events and Information	Remarks and references to Appendices
CAMBLAIN L'ABBE.	9th Aug.		Casualties: 4 Middlesex Regt. W. O.R. 1. 22nd Northd Fus. W. O.R. 3 23rd " " " K. O.R. 1. W. O.R. 2. 18th " " " K. O.R. 1 W. Officer 1. O.R. 1.	
" "	10 Aug.		Casualties. 123 Bde R.F.A. W. O.R. 1 153 Field Coy R.E. W. O.R. 2 20th Northd Fus. K. O.R. 2 W. O.R. 3. 21st Northd Fus. K. O.R. 2 W. O.R. 4 26th Northd Fus. W. O.R. 1.	
" "	11th August		Order received from IX Corps for 37th Div Artillery to move to 3rd Army Area on the 17th inst. Casualties 10th Lancashires. K. O.R. 1. W. O.R. 4 — Following draft received 20th Northd Fus. W. O.R. 1. 22nd Northd Fus. W. O.R. 2. — 24th Northd Fus O.R. 29	

Instructions regarding War Diaries and Intelligence Summaries are contained in F. S. Regs., Part II. and the Staff Manual respectively. Title pages will be prepared in manuscript.

WAR DIARY
or
INTELLIGENCE SUMMARY.
(Erase heading not required.)

Army Form C. 2118.

Administrative Staff. Hdqrs 37th Division

Place	Date	Hour	Summary of Events and Information	Remarks and references to Appendices
CAMBLAIN L'ABBE	12th Aug.		Casualties 10 York & Lancs W. O.R. 1 21st North'd Fus. W. O.R. 2 22nd " " W. O.R. 2 23rd " " W. O.R. 5. 27th " " K. O.R. 1.	
" "	13 Aug.		26th Inf Bde relieved 63rd Inf Bde in Berthonval Section on night of 12/13. 63rd Bde marched to Reserve Bde area Hdqrs at CHATEAU de la HAIE. Casualties 10 York and Lancs W. O.R. 2. 18th North'd Fus. K. O.R. 1. W. officer 1. 20th " " " K. O.R. 1. W. O.R. 2 21st " " " K O.R 4 W. O.R. 7 26th " " W. O.R. 1.	
" "	14 Aug.		63rd Brigade Moved into SIEVAL area. Casualties. 10 York & Lancs. W. O.R. 1 20th North'd Fus. K Off. 1. O.R 2. W.O.R 1. 22nd " " W. O.R. 1 23rd " " K. O.R 1. W. O.R 1 103rd T.M.B. W. O.R 1.	

Instructions regarding War Diaries and Intelligence Summaries are contained in F. S. Regs., Part II. and the Staff Manual respectively. Title pages will be prepared in manuscript.

WAR DIARY
or
INTELLIGENCE SUMMARY.
(Erase heading not required.)

Army Form C. 2118.

Administrative Staff.
Hdqrs 37th Division.

Place	Date	Hour	Summary of Events and Information	Remarks and references to Appendices
BRUAY.	15th August		Divisional Hdqrs moved from CAMBLAIN L'ABBE and opened at BRUAY. Relief of 102nd/103rd Inf Bde took place during the night of 14th/15th. Bdes marched to reserve Bde area where reorganisation took place. Subsequently 102nd Bde moved to FRESNICOURT area, Hdqrs at FRESNICOURT the 103rd Bde moved to DIVION area with Hdqrs at CHATEAU de VIELFORT. Casualties 22nd North'd Fus. Killed O.R. one.	
BRUAY	16th Aug.		Nil.	
" "	17th Aug.		Divisional Artillery moved to 3rd Army area.	
" "	18 Aug.		Nil.	
" "	19 Aug.		Casualties 18 North'd Fus. attd 9th Division. Killed O.R. 1. W.O.R. 2.	

2353 Wt. W2541/1454 700,000 5/15 D. D. & L. A.D.S.S./Forms/C. 2118.

Instructions regarding War Diaries and Intelligence Summaries are contained in F. S. Regs., Part II. and the Staff Manual respectively. Title pages will be prepared in manuscript.

WAR DIARY
or
INTELLIGENCE SUMMARY.
(*Erase heading not required.*)

Army Form C. 2118.

Administrative Staff – Hdqrs. 37th Division –

Place	Date	Hour	Summary of Events and Information	Remarks and references to Appendices
BRUAY	20th Aug.		Nil.	
" "	21st "		Orders received that 102nd 103rd and 18 Northd Fus Prs are to rejoin 34th Division, and that 111th 112th and 9th North Staffords (Prs) will return to 37th Division. 63rd Bde move in to 9th Division Res. Bde area	
" "	22nd Aug.		102 103rd and 18th Northd Prs. left Division to join 34th Division. Portion of transport of each unit entrained at FOUQUEREUIL three trains in all for transport last train having left at 9. P.M.) Personnel entrained at CALONNE RICOUART four trains in all. 111th 112th Bdes and 9th North Staffs (Prs) arrived in similar trains.	
			111th Bde billeted in Division area Hdqrs at CHATEAU VIELFORT.	
			112th Bde Billeted at BRUAY Hdqrs Division CHATEAU. 9th North Staffs Billeted at HOUDAIN.	

2353 Wt. W2544/1454 700,000 5/15 D. D. & L. A.D.S.S./Forms/C. 2118.

Instructions regarding War Diaries and Intelligence Summaries are contained in F. S. Regs., Part II. and the Staff Manual respectively. Title pages will be prepared in manuscript.

WAR DIARY
or
INTELLIGENCE SUMMARY.
(Erase heading not required.)

Army Form C. 2118.

Administrative Staff – Hdqs 37th Division

Place	Date	Hour	Summary of Events and Information	Remarks and references to Appendices
BRUAY	22nd Aug Contd.		Approximate strength of units on arrival as follows:	
			111th Inf Bde. — off — O.R.	
			10th Roy Fus. — 32 — 804	
			13 " " — 34 — 798	
			13 K.R.R.C. — 31 — 873	
			13 Rifle Bde. — 16 — 888	
			111th M.G. Coy. — 10 — 152	
			112th Inf Bde. — Off — O.R.	
			11 R Warwicks Rgt. — 22 — 638	
			6 Bn Bedford Rgt. — 29 — 900	
			8 Bn East Lancs — 26 — 679	
			10th N Lancashire Rgt. — 16 — 602	
			112th M.G. Coy. — 10 — 147	
			9/N. Staff Pnrs. — 36 — 896	

2353 Wt. W2544/1454 700,000 5/15 D. D. & L. A.D.S.S./Forms/C. 2118.

Instructions regarding War Diaries and Intelligence Summaries are contained in F. S. Regs., Part II. and the Staff Manual respectively. Title pages will be prepared in manuscript.

WAR DIARY
or
INTELLIGENCE SUMMARY.
(Erase heading not required.)

Army Form C. 2118.

Administrative Staff - Hqrs 37th Division.

Place	Date	Hour	Summary of Events and Information	Remarks and references to Appendices
BRUAY	23rd Aug.		9th North Staff Pioneers move to VILLERS au BOIS and come under orders of GOC 9th Division.	
" "	24th		112th Bde move to MAZINGARBE and come under orders of GOC 16th Division.	
" "	25th		132 Field Coy R.E. moves to PHILOSOPHE and is attached 40th Division. 112th Bde move in to line held by 40th Division and are attached to that Division. Casualties MMP wounded O.R 1 (attached 40th Divn.)	
"	26th "		Casualties 11 R Warwicks attd 40th Division. Wounded O.R. one	
"	27th		Casualties 6th Bedfords attd. 40th Division Killed O.R. two Wounded O.R. four.	

2353 Wt. W2544/1454 700,000 5/15 D. D. & L. A.D.S.S./Forms/C. 2118.

Instructions regarding War Diaries and Intelligence Summaries are contained in F. S. Regs., Part II. and the Staff Manual respectively. Title pages will be prepared in manuscript.

WAR DIARY
or
INTELLIGENCE SUMMARY.
(*Erase heading not required.*)

Army Form C. 2118.

Administration Staff
Hdqrs 37th Division.

Place	Date	Hour	Summary of Events and Information	Remarks and references to Appendices
BROAY.	28th May.		111th Machine Gun Coy move to left Division area.	
			Casualties 6th Bedfords attd 40th Div. Wounded O.R. 1.	
			X 37 Trench Mortar Batt attd 9th Div (Killed O.R. 1 (Wounded O.R. 2.	
" "	29th May.		13th Royal Fusiliers and 13th KRRC moved to billets at CALONNE and are placed under orders of 63rd (RN) Division.	
			Casualties 8th L. Lancs. attd 40th Division. (Killed O.R. 1 Wounded O.R. 1.	
" "	30th May.		152 Field Coy R.E. returned and was billeted at LA CAUCHIETTE. 10th Royal Fusiliers and 13th Rifle Brigade moved to Bouvigny Huts and VERDREL under 63rd Division.	
			Casualties 13 KRRC. attd 63rd Div wounded O.R. one.	
			11th R. Warwicks attached 40th Division: Killed O.R. one	
			8 L. Lancs Regt. attd 40th Div. Killed 1 officer. W. O.R. 1.	

2353 Wt. W2544/1454 700,000 5/15 D. D. & L. A.D.S.S./Forms/C. 2118.

Instructions regarding War Diaries and Intelligence Summaries are contained in F. S. Regs., Part II, and the Staff Manual respectively. Title pages will be prepared in manuscript.

WAR DIARY
or
INTELLIGENCE SUMMARY.
(Erase heading not required.)

Army Form C. 2118.

Administrative Staff
Headqrs 37th Division

Place	Date	Hour	Summary of Events and Information	Remarks and references to Appendices
BRUAY	31st Aug.		Casualties 11 R. Warwicks att'd 40th Division. W. O. R. three.	

J Duncan Captain
DAA & QMG
37th Division

2353 Wt. W2544/1454 700,000 5/15 D. D. & L. A.D.S.S./Forms/C. 2118.

WAR DIARY Sep 1916

H.Q. 37th DIVN.

Instructions regarding War Diaries and Intelligence Summaries are contained in F. S. Regs., Part II. and the Staff Manual respectively. Title pages will be prepared in manuscript.

WAR DIARY
or
INTELLIGENCE SUMMARY.
(Erase heading not required.)

Army Form C. 2118.

Administrative Staff
Hdqrs 37th Division.

Place	Date 1916	Hour	Summary of Events and Information	Remarks and references to Appendices
BRUAY	1st September		Casualties Heavy Trench Mortar Batt. O.R. wounded one. 13 KRRC Killed O.R. 2 wounded O.R. 3 11th Royal Warwicks W. O.R. one.	
" "	2nd Sept.		112th Inf Bde rejoined 37th Division from 40th Division and were billetted in DIEVAL area. Orders for 10th York and Lancs (63rd Inf Bde) to move from ESTREE CAUCHIE to BAJUS on 3rd inst. Casualties 8 E Lancs wounded O.R. one. (accidentally)	
"	3rd Sept.		10 York and Lancs moved to BAJUS. Casualties 13 KRRC attd 63rd (RN) Division wounded O.R. two.	
" "	4th Sept.		Nil.	
" "	5th Sept.		Nil.	
" "	6th Sept.		Nil.	
" "	7th Sept.		Casualties 9th North Staffs attd 9th Division wounded O.R. one.	
" "	8 Sept.		Casualties 164 Field Coy R.E. attd 9 Division wounded O.R. one. 10th Royal Fusiliers attd 63rd (RN) Div. wounded O.R. one.	

Instructions regarding War Diaries and Intelligence Summaries are contained in F. S. Regs., Part II. and the Staff Manual respectively. Title pages will be prepared in manuscript.

WAR DIARY
or
INTELLIGENCE SUMMARY.
(*Erase heading not required.*)

Army Form C. 2118.

Administrative Staff
H.Qrs 37th Division.

Place	Date	Hour	Summary of Events and Information	Remarks and references to Appendices
BRUAY	9th Sept:		9th North Staffs (Pioneers) rejoined 37th Division from 9th Division and were billeted at DIVION. Casualties 10 R Fus. attd 63rd (R.N.) Division O.R. 4 K 4 wounded 6 Bedfords " " " Killed O.R. one. Heavy Trench Mortar Batt. attd 9th Div. wounded O.R. one.	
" "	10th Sept:		Casualties 10th R. Fusiliers attd 63rd R.N. Div wounded O.R. one	
" "	11th Sept:		Casualties 154 Field Coy. attd 9th Div. Killed O.R. one Wounded O.R. one X 37 T.M. Battery " " Wounded O.R. one.	
	12th Sept		Nil	
" "	13th Sept:		Casualties 13th Royal Fusiliers attd. 63rd (R.N.) Division. Wounded O.R. one.	
" "	14th Sept:		~~[illegible]~~ Lieut J. H. B. Morels A.O.D. appointed D.A.D.O.S. 37th Div. vice Capt. W H HARBINSON to Third Army (temporary duty).	
" "	15th Sept.		37th Division Artillery rejoined from VI Corps and were billeted at MAGNICOURT ROCOURT, and le THIEVLOVE Casualties X 37 T.M.B. attached 9th Div. Killed O.R. 2 13 KRRC at 1st Army rest camp. Drowned O.R. one.	

Instructions regarding War Diaries and Intelligence Summaries are contained in F. S. Regs., Part II. and the Staff Manual respectively. Title pages will be prepared in manuscript.

WAR DIARY
or
INTELLIGENCE SUMMARY.
(Erase heading not required.)

Army Form C. 2118.

Administrative ~~Admns~~ Staff.
HQrs 37th Division —

Place	Date	Hour	Summary of Events and Information	Remarks and references to Appendices
BRUAY.	16th Sept.		Casualties Heavy T.M. Battery attd. 37th Division Wounded O.R. two 63rd (T.M.) B attd 37th Div. Wounded O.R. one. Orders received to take over SOUCHEZ ANGRES and CALONNE Sections.	
" "	17th Sept.		Two battalions of 63rd Inf Bde took over trenches on LORRETTE Ridge, and BOIS DE NOULETTE huts from 189th Inf Bde. Two battns moved to billets at FOSSE 10. 111th Inf Bde took over CALONNE section of the line.	
" "	18 Sept.		Casualties 13 Rifle Bde wounded O.R. three	
BARLIN.	19th Sept.		37th Divisional H.Q. moved from BRUAY and opened at BARLIN. Supply Railhead + refilling point was fixed at BARLIN: the Ammunition Railhead being fixed at HOUDAIN. Brigade Grenade stores, Subsidiary Brigade Grenade Stores, and Unit Grenade Stores were arranged for. Casualties. 6th Bedfords wounded O.R one	
"	20th Sept		Casualties – 10th Royal Fusiliers wounded O.R. three 13th Royal Fusiliers Killed O.R. one (accidentally) ditto wounded O.R. one	

2353 Wt. W2544/1454 700,000 5/15 D. D. & L. A.D.S.S./Forms/C. 2118.

Instructions regarding War Diaries and Intelligence Summaries are contained in F. S. Regs., Part II. and the Staff Manual respectively. Title pages will be prepared in manuscript.

WAR DIARY
or
INTELLIGENCE SUMMARY.
(Erase heading not required.)

Army Form C. 2118.

Administrative Staff
Hd Qts. 37th Division.

Place	Date	Hour	Summary of Events and Information	Remarks and references to Appendices
BARLIN.	20th Sept.		Casualties (continued).	
			13th K.R.R.C. wounded O.R one (at duty)	
			13th Rifle Bde wounded O R one.	
"	21st Sept.		Casualties.	
			13th Royal Fusiliers wounded O.R one.	
			13th K.R.R.C. wounded O.R one (at duty)	
			8th East Lancs wounded O.R one.	
"	22nd Sept		Casualties.	
			10th Royal Fusiliers wounded O.R. four (one at duty)	
			13th Royal Fusiliers wounded O.R one	
			8th East Lancs killed O.R one.	
"	23rd Sept		Casualties. 8th Lincolns. killed O.R. two	
"	24th Sept.		Leave allotment for special cases made up to 1st October.	
			Casualties.	
			6th Bedfords. wounded O.R. one.	
			1st S.A. Regt. attached 176th Coy R.E. wounded. O.R one.	
"	25th Sept.		Casualties.	
			16th Notts & Derbys attached 255th Coy R.E. wounded O.R. one (accidentally)	

Instructions regarding War Diaries and Intelligence Summaries are contained in F. S. Regs., Part II. and the Staff Manual respectively. Title pages will be prepared in manuscript.

WAR DIARY
or
INTELLIGENCE SUMMARY.
(Erase heading not required.)

Army Form C. 2118.

Administrative Staff
Hd Qts 37th Division

Place	Date	Hour	Summary of Events and Information	Remarks and references to Appendices
BARLIN	26th Sept		Casualties. 10th York & Lancs wounded O R four 13th Royal Fusiliers killed. O R one – wounded O. R two	
"	27th Sept.		Casualties. 13th Rifle Brigade wounded O.R two (one at duty) 4th Middlesex wounded O R one (at duty) 10th York & Lancs wounded O R three	
			2/Lt R G Williams 4th Middlesex appointed O. C Div. Salvage Coy. vice Lieut R H I Rose 6th Bedfords evacuated sick, 16/9/16	
			2/Lt. H LEMARCHAND 9th Lancers (S.R) appointed A P.M and to be temp Captain while holding appointment – vice Major R G GRAHAM 5th Yorks Regt, appointed A P.M of a Corps.	
"	28th Sept.		Orders issued that all indents for the double identity discs are to be sent in by 1st October.	
			Casualties. 13th K.R.R.C. wounded O.R one 13th Rifle Bde wounded officer one 10th York & Lancs wounded O.R one 63rd M.G. Coy wounded O.R one	

Army Form C. 2118.

Instructions regarding War Diaries and Intelligence Summaries are contained in F. S. Regs., Part II. and the Staff Manual respectively. Title pages will be prepared in manuscript.

WAR DIARY
or
INTELLIGENCE SUMMARY.
(*Erase heading not required.*)

Administrative Staff
H Q 37th Division

Place	Date	Hour	Summary of Events and Information	Remarks and references to Appendices
BARLIN.	29th Sept.		Casualties: 10th York & Lancs. 2 wounded O.R	
			111th M G Coy. 1 wounded O R.	
			11th Warwicks 1 Killed OR. 3 wounded O R.	
"	30th Sept		Reinforcement of 90 O.R arrived for the 10th L N Lancs	
			Casualties. 13th K.R.R.C. wounded. O.R. one	
			10th R. Fusiliers wounded O.R one	
			10th L. N. Lancs wounded O.R one	

J Duncan Captain
DAAG & QMG
37th Division

2353 Wt. W2544/1454 700,000 5/15 D. D. & L. A.D.S.S./Forms/C. 2118.

W.D

Instructions regarding War Diaries and Intelligence Summaries are contained in F. S. Regs., Part II. and the Staff Manual respectively. Title pages will be prepared in manuscript.

87

Oct 1916

WAR DIARY

~~INTELLIGENCE SUMMARY.~~

(Erase heading not required.)

Army Form C. 2118.

Administrative Staff.
H. Q. 37th Division.

Vol 15

Place	Date 1916	Hour	Summary of Events and Information	Remarks and references to Appendices
BARLIN	Oct	1st	Winter time commenced at 1 am. Casualties. 13th K.R.R.C. wounded O.R one 11th Warwicks killed O.R. five 176th Coy R.E wounded O.R one.	
"	Oct	2nd	Reinforcements of 100 - O.R. arrived for the 4th Middlesex Casualties 8th Somerset Light Infantry wounded O.R two.	
"	Oct	3rd	Casualties. 10th L N. Lancs. wounded O.R. one (accidentally; pick axe)	
"	Oct.	4th	Casualties 13th K RRC wounded OR one (accidentally) 6th Bedfords wounded OR two - 8th E Lancs Killed OR one wounded OR two.	
"	Oct	5th	Casualties. 6th Bedfords, wounded O R two 8th E. Lancs. wounded O.R one. 10th W. Ridings att.d 176th Cy R.E. wounded O.R. one	
"	Oct	6th	Casualties. 8th Lincolns wounded O R two 10th Royal Fusiliers. Killed O.R. one — wounded O.R. one	

2353 Wt. W2544/1454 700,000 5/15 D. D. & L. A.D.S.S./Forms/C. 2118.

Instructions regarding War Diaries and Intelligence Summaries are contained in F. S. Regs., Part II. and the Staff Manual respectively. Title pages will be prepared in manuscript.

WAR DIARY
or
~~INTELLIGENCE SUMMARY.~~
(Erase heading not required.)

Army Form C. 2118.

Administrative Staff
H. Q. 37th Division

Place	Date	Hour	Summary of Events and Information	Remarks and references to Appendices
BARLIN.	Oct	7th	Casualties. 10th York & Lancs - wounded. O.R one.	
			63rd T.M Battery - wounded O.R one.	
			111th M.G. Compy. - killed Officer. one - wounded O R one.	
			13th K.R.R.C - killed. O.R. one.	
			10th L. N. Lancs . wounded officer one	
			124th Bde R.F.A - killed O.R. one.	
			49th Field Ambulance - wounded. O.R one.	
"	Oct	8th	Casualties. 4th Middlesex. - killed O.R one. - wounded O.R. two.	
			10th York & Lancs. - wounded O.R one	
			9th N Staffords. - wounded O.R. one	
			154th Field Coy R.E - wounded O.R. one	
			x/37 T.M. Battery. wounded O.R one	
"	Oct	9th	Casualties. 4th Middlesex - wounded O.R three.	
			10th York & Lancs - wounded O.R. one.	
			11th R. Warwicks - wounded O R three.	
			6th Bedfords - wounded O.R one.	
			On this day a Howitzer Battery joined the 126th Bde R.F.A	

2353 Wt. W2544/1454 700,000 5/15 D. D. & L. A.D.S.S./Forms/C. 2118.

Instructions regarding War Diaries and Intelligence Summaries are contained in F. S. Regs., Part II. and the Staff Manual respectively. Title pages will be prepared in manuscript.

WAR DIARY
or
~~INTELLIGENCE SUMMARY.~~

(Erase heading not required.)

Army Form C. 2118.

Administrative Staff
H.Q. 37th Division.

Place	Date	Hour	Summary of Events and Information	Remarks and references to Appendices
BARLIN	Oct	10th	Casualties – 4th Middlesex. killed O.R. one – wounded O.R. one. 63rd M.G. Compy wounded O.R. one. 13th R. Fusiliers wounded O.R. two 13th K.R.R.C. attached 111th T.M. Battery killed O.R. one.	
"	Oct	11th	Casualties. 4th Middlesex – wounded O.R. two. 10th York & Lancs – wounded. O.R. one 13th K.R.R.C attached 111th T.M Battery wounded O.R two. 3rd (S.R) E. Kents. attached 10th L.N Lancs, wounded – Officer – one – wounded O.R two Y/37 T.M Battery wounded – Officer – one Reinforcement of 50 O.R joined the Divisional Artillery	
"	Oct	12th	Casualties 8th Lincolns killed O.R one – 4th Middlesex killed O.R. two – wounded O.R. four. 10th York & Lancs. wounded – Officer – one – O.R. three 13th K.R.R.C attached 111th T.M Battery. wounded O.R. two. 11th R. Warwicks. killed O.R two – wounded O.R. two. 11th L.N. Lancs. killed O.R. one.	
"	Oct	13th	Reinforcement of 58 O.R. joined the 8th Somerset L.I.	

2353 Wt. W2544/1454 700,000 5/15 D. D. & L. A.D.S.S./Forms/C. 2118.

Instructions regarding War Diaries and Intelligence Summaries are contained in F. S. Regs., Part II. and the Staff Manual respectively. Title pages will be prepared in manuscript.

WAR DIARY or ~~INTELLIGENCE SUMMARY.~~

(Erase heading not required.)

Army Form C. 2118.

Administrative Staff
H. Q. 37th Division

Place	Date	Hour	Summary of Events and Information	Remarks and references to Appendices
BARLIN	Oct 13th (continued)		Casualties. 8th Lincolns wounded O.R. one.	
			8th Somerset L.I. - killed O.R. one - wounded O.R. one	
			13th Rifle Brigade - killed. O.R. two - wounded O.R. four	
			8th East Lancs wounded O.R. two.	
"	Oct 14		Reinforcements. of - 115 O.R. joined the 10th Royal Fusiliers.	
			145 O.R. joined the 13th Royal Fusiliers	
			42 O.R. joined the 11th Royal Warwicks	
			Casualties. 8th Lincolns. killed O.R. one - wounded O.R. five	
			6th Bedfords wounded O.R. One	
			Z/37 T.M. Battery wounded O.R. One	
			Administrative Arrangements issued with ref to 37th Div ORDER No 40 13/10/16	Appendix I
"	Oct 15		Casualties 8th Lincolns killed O.R. one - ~~[illegible]~~	
			8th Somerset L.I. - killed O.R. one - wounded. O.R. one	
			Lieut Colonel H. de L. Pollard - Lowsley. C.I.E. - D.S.O. - joined the Division this day on appointment as C.R.E.	
			Reinforcements of 122 Horses & Mules arrived at the Division this day from Remounts.	

2353 Wt. W2544/1454 700,000 5/15 D. D. & L. A.D.S.S./Forms/C. 2118.

Instructions regarding War Diaries and Intelligence Summaries are contained in F. S. Regs., Part II. and the Staff Manual respectively. Title pages will be prepared in manuscript.

WAR DIARY

~~or~~

~~INTELLIGENCE SUMMARY.~~

(Erase heading not required.)

Army Form C. 2118.

Administrative Staff
H Q 37th Division

Place	Date	Hour	Summary of Events and Information	Remarks and references to Appendices
BARLIN	Oct (Continued)	15th	Reinforcements of 78 O.R. joined the 8th S. Lancs	
			10 O.R " " 6th Bedfords	
			84 O.R " " 11th Warwicks.	
			133 O.R. " " 4th Middlesex	
"	Oct	16th	Casualties 176th Compy R.E. wounded O.R. one	
			Reinforcements of 76 O.R. joined the 10th L.N. Lancs	
			10 O.R " " 8th S. Lancs	
			1. Officer & 3. O.R " " 112th M.G. Company	
			65. O.R " " 11th Warwicks.	
			8. O.R " " 8th Somerset L.I.	
			3. O.R " " 63rd M.G. Company	
BARLIN	Oct	17th	111th Inf Bde relieved in CALONNE section by 4th CANADIAN Bde and billeted BARLIN - HERSIN MAISNIL LES RUITZ Area.	
			Half of 37th Div Arty relieved on night of 17/18th Oct by LAHORE Div Arty: 37th Div Arty located in PERNES - MAREST - CAMBLAIN CHATELAIN area.	
			Casualties 13 R Fus. W O.R two. 124th Bde RFA W. O.R one.	

1577 Wt. W10791/1773 500,000 1/15 D. D. & L. A.D.S.S./Forms/C. 2118.

Instructions regarding War Diaries and Intelligence Summaries are contained in F. S. Regs., Part II. and the Staff Manual respectively. Title pages will be prepared in manuscript.

WAR DIARY
or
INTELLIGENCE SUMMARY.
(Erase heading not required.)

Army Form C. 2118.

Administrative Staff
Hdqrs 37th Division

Place	Date	Hour	Summary of Events and Information	Remarks and references to Appendices
ROELLECOURT	18th Oct.		Div Hdqs closes at BARLIN at 10 AM and opens at ROELLECOURT at same hour. 63rd Inf Bde billeted VILLERS BRULIN - BETHONSART - FREVILLERS - CHELERS area H.Q. at CHELERS. 111th Inf Bde. billeted in LA THIEULOYE - MAGNICOURT - HOUVELIN area HQ at LA THIEULOYE. 112th Inf Bde billeted in AVERDOINGT - TERNAS - MAISNIL ST POL area H.Q MAISNIL ST POL	
" "	20th Oct.		112th Inf Bde billeted in BONNEVILLE - MONCHEAUX - SIBIVILLE - PIT and GRAND BOURET area. 111th Inf Bde billeted in GOUY EN TERNOIS - MAGNICOURT ~~HQ~~ SUR CANCHE area. 63rd Inf Bde MAIZIERES - SARS les BOIS area. 4th N Staffs MAIZIERES. Div Rly MAGNICOURT EN COMTE. Div Hdqs closes at ROELLECOURT and opens at LE CAUROY 10 AM. Billeting and supply arrangements attached.	Appendix II
~~Roellecourt~~	~~19th Oct~~			
LE CAUROY	21st Oct		Div Hdqs closed at LE CAUROY 9.30 AM and opened at BEAUVAL same hour. Division billeted in accordance with attached table of Billeting and Supply arrangements for 21/10/16.	Appendix III
MARIEUX	22nd		Div. HQ. closes at BEAUVAL 9.30 AM and opens at MARIEUX at same hour. Division billeted in accordance with attached table of billeting and supply arrangements for 22/10/16	Appendix IV

Instructions regarding War Diaries and Intelligence Summaries are contained in F. S. Regs., Part II. and the Staff Manual respectively. Title pages will be prepared in manuscript.

WAR DIARY
or
INTELLIGENCE SUMMARY.
(Erase heading not required.)

Administrative Staff
Army Form C. 2118.
Hdqrs 37th Division

Place	Date	Hour	Summary of Events and Information	Remarks and references to Appendices
MARIEUX	23rd Oct		R.A. group move to THIEVRES - AUTHIE area.	
" "	24th	"	Div Arty HQ SARTON	
MARIEUX	25	"	Casualties 8 Somerset L.I. wounded O.R. 2 accidentally.	
" "	26	"	Nil.	
" "	27th	"	Nil.	
" "	28	"	Nil.	
" "	29th	"	Nil.	
" "	30th		63rd Inf Bde moved to BEAUVAL area	
			111th Inf Bde " " GEZAINCOURT "	
			112th " " " " AMPLIER.	
	31st		112 Inf Bde Group less Fd Amb DOULLENS area.	

[signature]
DAA & QMG
37th Division

T2134. Wt. W708-776. 500000. 4/15. Sir J. C. & S.

Appendix I.

SECRET. 37th Division No: G42/17 A.

ADMINISTRATIVE ARRANGEMENTS.

(Reference 37th Divl. Operation Order No. 40 of 13/10/16).

I. HANDING OVER TO 2ND CANADIAN DIVISION.

1. Trench Stores.

All trench stores and material (including gum boots) are to be handed over and receipts obtained.

2. Reserves.

Reserves of S.A.A., Grenades, T. M. Ammunition and material in dumps to be handed over with statements shewing exact quantities and receipts obtained.

3. Documents.

Following documents to be handed over:-

Files of First Army R.O's.
Any First Army Circulars connected with the area or line, e.g., re lights, claims, water schemes, etc.
All plans of water supplies, trench tramways, etc.

4. Baths and Laundries.

All baths and laundries, together with plant and underclothing stored in them, will be handed over and receipts obtained. P.B. men employed in such establishments will remain in charge of them.

5. P.B. Men.

P.B. men (less those employed on baths, Y.M.C.A., or Church Army Huts, who will remain at their employment) will be assembled at Divl. Headquarters on 17th instant and handed over to 2nd Can. Division by Camp Commandant on 18th instant.

6. Town Majors.

Town Majors found by the Division will hand over their Towns and all billeting particulars with lists of village stores before leaving to representatives of incoming Division.

7. Standing tents and huts and all material connected with the construction thereof must be handed over. On no account are any of such things to be carried away.

8. A.P.M. Will arrange to hand over all Police Orders, Traffic and Straggler Posts to A.P.M. 2nd Canadian Division.

9. Canteens will be handed over to the relieving units and unsold stock disposed of by mutual agreement. The removal of such establishments or stock by either public or private transport cannot be contemplated.

P.T.O.

II. MOVING OUT.

1. Divisional Stores.

(a) Surplus kit, etc., that cannot be carried on the transport will be stored at a Divl. Store at COUPIGNY Huts, Q.17.a.1.8.

(b) The following personnel will be in charge:-

A reliable officer to be detailed by 63rd Inf. Bde.		
1 N.C.O. (A/Q.M.S.) " " " " 111th "		"
1 man detailed per Inf. Brigade		3.
1 " " each Arty.Bde. & D.A.C.		4.
1 " " by Divl. Engineers		1.
1 " " " " Pioneers		1.
1 " " " " Train		1.
1 " " " " R.A.M.C.		1.

Total: 1 officer, 1 N.C.O. and 11 men.

(c) Name of officer and N.C.O. to be submitted to Divl. Headquarters.

(d) Above personnel to assemble at Store by 10 a.m. on 14th inst. with rations for 14th and 15th October inclusive. Thereafter this personnel will be rationed by Town Major HERSIN, and will receive instructions through him. They will be liable to be detailed for local fatigues until ordered to rejoin their Division.

(e) Lists of all kit, etc., handed in must be prepared in duplicate, one copy receipted by Officer i/c Store being kept by Unit, and the other retained by Officer i/c Store. Kit should be marked with units designation.

(f) D.A.D.O.S. cannot accept any stores returned not wanted.

2. Transport.

(a) The available transport is strictly limited to:-

(i) Establishment.
(ii) That necessary for carriage of blankets (Inf. and Fd.Ambulances only).
(iii) For trench mortars.

Particulars of allotment to Infantry and R.A.M.C. will be notified later. Brigadiers and O.C., R.A.M.C. will notify Divl. Headquarters where lorries should report.

(b) Great care is necessary to prevent transport being overloaded as long marches will have to be faced. On no account are travelling kitchens to have superstructures added.

(c) C.O's will caution all ranks under their command against the following offences on the line of march:-

(i) Unauthorised persons riding on vehicles.
(ii) Hanging on to vehicles.
(iii) Putting arms and equipment on vehicles.

The military police will exercise special vigilance in these matters and will report every instance to A.P.M.

(d) O.C., Divl. Train will send baggage wagons to all units forthwith, with the exception that wagons returned to Train by Divl. Artillery to-day will not be sent back until they have been overhauled.

SALVAGE COMPANY.

(a) Headquarters will remain with Divl. Headquarters.

(b) Brigade Sections will march with their Brigades.

MEDICAL.

Field Ambulances and Rest Station will be evacuated.

VETERINARY.

Mobile Vet. Section will evacuate all animals unfit to travel.

A.D.N. Browne
Lieut-Colonel,
A.A. & Q.M.G.,
37th Division.

13th October, 1916.

SECRET. 37th Division No. 642/17A.

ADMINISTRATIVE ARRANGEMENTS.

(Reference 37th Divl. Operation Order No. 40 of 13/10/16).

In continuation of 'Administrative Arrangements' circulated to Units on 13th inst., the following will be the arrangements as regards Supplies and additional transport.

1. SUPPLIES.

Refilling Point.

16th inst.	as at present.	
17th inst.	Divl. Artillery Group.	Cross roads ½ mile W. of MAISNIL-RUITZ. J.35.d.
	63rd Brigade.Group	HERMIN
	111th Brigade Group	Cross Roads J.35.d.
	112th Brigade Group	DIEVAL.
18th inst.	Divl.Artillery Group	will be notified later
	63rd Brigade Group	same as for 17th.
	111th Brigade Group	do
	112th Brigade Group	do
19th inst.	Divl. Artillery Group	will be notified later
	63rd Brigade Group	CHELERS
	111th Brigade Group	MONCHY BRETON
	112th Brigade Group	TERNAS.

Time of Refilling on 17th, 18th, 19th insts. 2 p.m.

2. TRANSPORT.

Additional transport for the carriage of blankets etc. will be allotted to units as under. Brigades and other units mentioned will report to Divisional Headquarters by wire, the time and place the require the lorried to report. Up to and including 18th instant the lorries will be found by the Divl. Supply Column, after that date by the First Army.

One 3 ton lorry per Infantry Brigade H.Q., Infantry Battalion and Field Ambulance.

Three 3 ton lorries for Heavy and Medium Trench Mortar Batteries.

One G.S. Wagon per Field Company.

N.B. 100 bundles of 10 blankets can be loaded on a 3 ton lorry.

Captain.
D.A.Q.M.G.
37th Division.

14/10/16.

Appendix. II

BILLETING AND SUPPLY ARRANGEMENTS 20th OCT., 1916.

Unit.	Group.	Billeting Officer.	Billets	Rendezvous and time for Billeting parties.	Refilling Point and time.	Remarks.
Divl. Hd.rs. R.E., A.F. H.Q., Div.Train Sanitary Sect. Divl. Band.	Divl. Hd'rs.	Camp Commandant	LE CAUROY	LE CAUROY (Chateau) 10.30 a.m.	TERNAS 10 a.m.	
Divl. Artillery H.Q.Coy.DivlTrain. Mob.Vet.Sect.	R.A.	Staff Captain, Div.Arty.	MAGNICOURT EN COMTE - HOUVELIN - MONCHY BRETON - LA THIEULOYE and if necessary OSTREVILLE	R.A. arrangements	BOURS 10 a.m.	
63rd Inf.Bde. 152nd Fd.Co.R.E. 49th Fd. Amb. No.2 Co.D.Train	63rd Inf. Bde.	Staff Capt. 63rd Inf. Bde.	MAIZIERES - SARS LES BOIS - BERLENCOURT - HERMAVILLE - OPPY - DENIER - LIENCOURT	Bde. arrangements.	CHELERS 10 a.m.	
9th N.Staffs			MAZIERES		MONCHY BRETON 10 a.m.	
111th Inf. Bde. 154th Fd.Co.R.E. 48th Fd. Amb. No.3 Co.D.Train	111th Inf. Bde.	Staff Capt. 111th Inf. Bde.	GOUY EN TERNOIS - MAGNICOURT SUR CANCHE - HOUVIN HOUVIGNEUL - CANETTEMONT - BROUILLY - ROZIERE - REBREUVIETTE.	Bde. arrangements.	MONCHY BRETON 10 a.m.	
112th Inf. Bde. 153rd Fd.Co.R.E. 50th Fd. Amb. No.4 Co.D.Train	112th Inf. Bde.	Staff Capt. 112th Inf. Bde.	BONEVILLE - MONCHEAUX - MONTS EN TERNOIS - SIBIVILLE - SILICOURT - RONVAL - REBREUVE - LA COUTURE - PIT FOURNET - GrD. FOURET.	Bde. arrangements	TERNAS 10 a.m.	

19th October, 1916.

R.....y Capt
for Lieut-Colonel,
A.A. & Q.M.G., 37th Division.

Appendix III

BILLETING ARRANGEMENTS FOR 21st OCTOBER, 1916.

Unit	Group	Billeting Officer.	Billets.	Rendezvous and time for billeting parties.	Remarks.
Divl. Hdqrs. R.E., Div.Eng. [illegible], Div.Train Sanitary Sect. Divl. Band.	Divl. Hdqrs.	Camp Commandant	BEAUVAL	Town Major's Office, BEAUVAL 11 a.m.	
Divl. Arty. No.1 Co.D.Train Mob.Vet.Sect.	R.A.	Staff Capt. Divl. Arty.	ETREE WAMIN - REBREUVIETTE - REBREUVE - LA CAUTURE - GRD. BOURET - PIT BOURET.	R.A. arrangements	
63rd Inf. Bde. 152 Fd.Coy.R.E. 49th Fd. Amb. No.2 Co.D.Train 9th N.Staffs.	63rd Inf. Bde.	Staff Capt. 63rd Inf. Bde.	AUTHIEULE - FRESCHEVILLERS - AMPLIER - CAUMESNIL - ORVILLE.	Bde. arrangements.	
111th Inf. Bde. 154 Fd.Coy.R.E. 48th Fd. Amb. No.3 Co.D.Train.	111th Inf.Bde.	Staff Capt. 111th Inf. Bde.	GEZAINCOURT - BULEUX - BEAUVAL (two Battns. and Fd. Amb.)	Bde. arrangements	Billeting parties for troops billeting in BEAUVAL to report to Town Major 11 a.m.
112th Inf. Bde. 153 Fd.Coy.R.E. 50th Fd. Amb. No.4 Co.D.Train.	112th Inf.Bde.	Staff Capt. 112th Inf. Bde.	BRETEL - HEM - HARDINVAL - LONGUEVILLETTE - BEAUVAL (Fd.Coy.) DOULLENS (Bde.H.Q.)	Bde. arrangements	Billeting party of Fd.Coy. to report to Town Major [illegible] Billeting party of Bde.H.Q. report Town Major DOULLENS.

20th October, 1916.

J. Duncan Captain
for Lieut-Colonel,
A.A. & Q.M.G., 37th Division.

Appendix IV

BILLETING AND SUPPLY ARRANGEMENTS 22ND OCTOBER, 1916.

Unit	Group	Billeting Officer	Billets	Rendezvous and time for billeting parties.	Refilling Pt. and time.
Divl. Hd.Qrs. R.E. Div.Eng. H.Q. Div.Train. Sanitary Sect. Divl. Band.	Divl. Hd.Qrs.	Camp Commandant	MARIEUX	Town Major's Office 10 a.m.	Half mile N.W. of HULEUX on the HULEUX-DOULLENS Road. 8 a.m.
63rd Inf.Bde. 152 Fd.Coy.R.E. 49th Fd. Amb. 2 Co.,Div.Train 9th N.Staffs.	63rd Inf. Bde.	Staff Capt. 63rd Inf. Bde.	TERRAMESNIL - RAINCHEVAL - ARQUEVES (two Battns.)	Bde. arrangements	ditto.
111th Inf.Bde. 154 Fd.Coy.R.E. 48th Fd. Amb. 3 Coy.Div.Train	111th Inf. Bde.	Staff Capt. 111th Inf. Bde.	PUCHEVILLERS	Bde. arrangements	ditto.
112th Inf.Bde. 153 Fd.Coy.R.E. 50th Fd. Amb. 4 Coy.Divl.Train.	112th Inf. Bde.	Staff Capt. 112th Inf. Bde.	SARTON - MARIEUX (1 Battn).	Bde. arrangements.	ditto.

21st October, 1916.

[signature] Captain for

Lieut-Colonel,
A.A.& Q.M.G., 37th Division.

Instructions regarding War Diaries and Intelligence Summaries are contained in F. S. Regs., Part II. and the Staff Manual respectively. Title pages will be prepared in manuscript.

WAR DIARY
or
INTELLIGENCE SUMMARY.
(Erase heading not required.)

Administrative Staff
~~Hdqrs 37th Division~~ HQ ~~AQ~~ 37 D
Vol 16

Army Form C. 2118.

Place	Date	Hour	Summary of Events and Information	Remarks and references to Appendices
MARIEUX	1st Nov		63rd Inf Bde H.Q. moved to BEAUVAL.	
" "	2nd	"	Nil	
" "	3rd	"	Nil	
" "	4th	"	Nil	
" "	5th	"	Nil	
" "	6th	"	Nil	
" "	7th	"	Nil	
" "	8th	"	2 Coys 9th N. Staffs moved to ACHEUX and VARENNES for work under C.E. V Corps.	
" "	9th	"	~~Remaining~~ Coys and 9th N. Staffs less two coys moved to HEDAUVILLE for work under C.E. V Corps. Major Genl H.B. WILLIAMS C.B. D.S.O. assumed command of the division vice Major Genl SCRASE-DICKENS invalided	
" "	10th	"	Nil	
" "	11th	"	111th Inf Bde moved to PUCHEVILLERS.	
" "	12th	"	63rd Inf Bde moved to area LEALVILLERS - ACHEUX WOOD. H.Q. at LEALVILLERS. 111th Inf Bde moved to VARENNES - HEDAUVILLE H.Q at HEDAUVILLE 112th Inf Bde LOUVENCOURT - VAUCHELLES H.Q at LOUVENCOURT. Advanced Div H.Q. open at VARENNES 6 PM.	
" "	13th		V Corps attacked N of the ANCRE. II Corps S. of the ANCRE	

A5834 Wt. W4973/M687 750,000 8/16 D. D. & L. Ltd. Forms/C.2118/13.

Instructions regarding War Diaries and Intelligence Summaries are contained in F. S. Regs., Part II. and the Staff Manual respectively. Title pages will be prepared in manuscript.

WAR DIARY
or
INTELLIGENCE SUMMARY.
(Erase heading not required.)

Administrative Staff HQ 37th Division — Army Form C. 2118.

Place	Date	Hour	Summary of Events and Information	Remarks and references to Appendices
MARIEUX	13 contd.		111th Inf Bde marched to Adv 63rd (RN) Div HQ Q25.d, and was placed at disposal of GOC 63rd Div	
			112th Inf Bde moved to BERTRANCOURT. Bde placed at the disposal of 2nd Division less 2 battns (11 Warwicks and 6 Bedfords) Subsequently moved to MAILLY and placed at disposal of 2nd Div	
			63rd Inf Bde moved to Q31b and HEDAUVILLE	Appendix I
			Casualties. see appendix I	
MARIEUX	14th		63rd Inf Bde relieved a Brigade of 63rd (RN) Division in the line.	
MARIEUX	15		Adv Div Hdqrs closed at VARENNES 12 noon and opened in Dugout Q26.c.0.3 Rear Hdqrs moved to HEDAUVILLE	
			Location as follows:	
			63rd Bde HQ Q18 b	
			10 Yorks & Lancs ~~from Ruined ANCRE to R7 b 35~~ } Trenches	
			8 Lincolns	
			8 Somersets (support)	
			4th Middlesex Reserve	
			111th Inf Bde – Q18 c.0.2	
			13th Roy Fus. Front line } Trenches –	
			13th KRRC Front line	
			10th R.F. support	
			13 RB Reserve	
			112th Inf Bde with 2nd Division	
			13 KRRC suffered heavy casualties see Appendix I	

A5834 Wt. W4973/M687 750,000 8/16 D. D. & L. Ltd. Forms/C.2118/13.

Instructions regarding War Diaries and Intelligence Summaries are contained in F. S. Regs., Part II. and the Staff Manual respectively. Title pages will be prepared in manuscript.

WAR DIARY
or
INTELLIGENCE SUMMARY.
(Erase heading not required.)

Army Form C. 2118.

Administrative Staff
Hdqrs 37th Division

Place	Date	Hour	Summary of Events and Information	Remarks and references to Appendices
HEDAUVILLE	16th		SIALCOT Machine Gun Squadron attached to 37th Division Casualties see appendix I 190th Inf Bde placed at disposal of 37th Div for clearing battlefield for 1 day. Good progress in this work was made.	
" "	17th		Casualties see appendix I	
FORCEVILLE	18th		Rear HQ moved to FORCEVILLE 111th Inf Bde carried out bombing attack which was not successful Casualties see appendix I Work continued by salvage section in clearing battle field. Appendix II list of stores salved in 37th Div area to date. Pack train due to arrive railhead 11 AM did not arrive until 5 AM on 19th inst. II and V corps attached. Major H.P. BROOKE GSO 2 (Leinster Regt) wounded other casualties see Appendix I.	Appendix II
	19th		111 Inf Bde made local attack on junction MUNICH & FRANKFORT trench which failed. Casualties see appendix I Salvage section continued work of burying dead and clearing battlefield	
	20th		63rd Inf Bde was relieved by 33rd Inf Bde 11th Division the former withdrew to dugouts in the old German line. Casualties see appendix I	

Instructions regarding War Diaries and Intelligence Summaries are contained in F. S. Regs., Part II. and the Staff Manual respectively. Title pages will be prepared in manuscript.

WAR DIARY
or
INTELLIGENCE SUMMARY.
(*Erase heading not required.*)

Army Form C. 2118.

Administrative Staff
Hdqrs 37th Division

Place	Date	Hour	Summary of Events and Information	Remarks and references to Appendices
FORCEVILLE	21st		Brig Gen. BARNES C.B. D.S.O. Commdg. 111th Inf Bde appointed to command 32nd Division. 111th Inf Bde was relieved by 112th Inf Bde – Casualties see Appendix I.	
FORCEVILLE	22nd		Working party of 250 from various units employed in burying dead and clearing battlefield. Captain Sir T. R. L. THOMPSON Bt. 7th Hussars joined as GSO 2 vice Major N. P. BROOKE Leinster Regt wounded – Casualties see Appendix I.	
FORCEVILLE	23rd		37th Division attacked the TRIANGLE in R 6 C 8 2 and LEAVE AVENUE cooperating with 32nd Division. The attack was carried out by 10th L.N.Lancs, 2 officers were killed. Weather very cold and hard frost.	

A5834 Wt. W4973/M687 750,000 8/16 D. D. & L. Ltd. Forms/C.2118/13.

Army Form C. 2118.

Instructions regarding War Diaries and Intelligence Summaries are contained in F. S. Regs., Part II. and the Staff Manual respectively. Title pages will be prepared in manuscript.

WAR DIARY
or
INTELLIGENCE SUMMARY.
(Erase heading not required.)

Place	Date	Hour	Summary of Events and Information	Remarks and references to Appendices
~~MARIEUX~~ FORCEVILLE	24th		111th Inf Bde Moved from ENGLEBELMER to ACHEUX wood and LOUVENCOURT H.Q. at LOUVENCOURT.	
			8 Lincolns (63rd Inf Bde) relieved 10 LN Lancs (112th Inf Bde) in front line.	
			63rd Inf Bde less 2 Bns moved to ENGLEBELMER, 2 Bns 63rd Inf Bde moved to HAMEL and old German Line	
			10th Bn L.N. Lancs moved to ENGLEBELMER and was attached 63rd Inf Bde. Casualties see Appendix I.	
" "	25th		Rained all day. Casualties see Appendix I.	
MARIEUX	26		Rear Hqrs Q moved from FORCEVILLE to MARIEUX Chateau.	
			112th Inf Bde relieved by 97th Inf Bde (7th Division.)	
			112th Inf Bde and 2 battns 63rd Inf Bde moved to MAILLY MAILLET. 111th Inf Bde moved to PUCHEVILLERS and 63rd Inf Bde (less 2 Bns) moved to SARTON and RAINCHEVAL. Wet day.	
			Casualties see Appendix I	

A5834 Wt. W4973/M687 750,000 8/16 D. D. & L. Ltd. Forms/C.2118/13.

Army Form C. 2118.

Instructions regarding War Diaries and Intelligence Summaries are contained in F. S. Regs., Part II. and the Staff Manual respectively. Title pages will be prepared in manuscript.

WAR DIARY
or
INTELLIGENCE SUMMARY.
(Erase heading not required.)

Place	Date	Hour	Summary of Events and Information	Remarks and references to Appendices
MARIEUX	27th		112th Inf. Bde moved from MAILLY MAILLET to LOUVENCOURT and ACHEUX WOOD 2 Bns 63rd Inf. Bde moved to BERTRANCOURT 50th Field Ambulance moved from CLAIREFAYE to ACHEUX WOOD and LOUVENCOURT. Weather fine — Casualties see appendix I.	
MARIEUX	28th		Weather fine	
MARIEUX	29		One battalion 63rd Inf Bde moved from SARTON to RAINCHEVAL. Weather cold + fine. Casualties see appendix I.	
MARIEUX	30		Two battalions 63rd Inf Bde moved to ACHEUX WOOD 112th Inf Bde moved to RUBEMPRE, VAL de MAISON and LA VICOGNE Weather fine + cold. Casualties see appendix I.	

J. Duncan Capt
[illegible] 37th Division

A5834 Wt. W4973/M687 750,000 8/16 D. D. & L. Ltd. Forms/C.2118/13.

	OFFICERS			OR		
	R	W	M	R	W	M
8th Lincolns		2		13	148	
8th Somerset L.I.	4	5 (over 4)			69	10
4th Middlesex	2	3		40	45	51
10th Yorks & Lancs	1	9	-	9	87	8
63rd Machine Gun Coy	1	.	-	-	10	1
10th Royal Fusiliers	2	3		18	105	15
13th K.R.R.C.	3	6		23	149	11
13th Royal Fusiliers	1	8		32	203	14
13th Rifle Brigade	2	10		6	226	74
111th Machine Gun Coy		3		3	18	
111th T.M. Battery		1			2	
11th Royal Warwicks	1	6		30	150	41
6th Bedfords	1	7		7	120	51
8th East Lancs	16	13	4	22	108	41
10th L N Lancs	9	12		21	65	37
112th Machine Gun Co	1	2		1	8	
112th Trench Mortar Btty.					1	+
123rd Bde R.F.A.					1	
9th N Staffs	1	2		1	15	2
152 Fd Co R.E.		1		2	21	-
153 Fd Co. R.E.				[illegible]	12	-
154 Fd Co R.E.				3	20	.
48th Fd amb				1	3	.
49th Fd amb.					1	
Army Chaplains	1	1				
	4	9[illegible]	4	224	1273	354

Appendice II

37th Divn. 162/38Q.

Vth Corps "Q"

STATEMENT OF STORES SALVED ON THE BATTLEFIELD.

Vickers M.G.	3.
" TRIPODS.	9
" Spare parts, bags of	3
" S.A.A. belts ~~of~~.full	2
" S.A.A. boxes full	103
Lewis Guns	22
" " spare parts, barrels	4
" " drum carriers, full	512
" " drums loose, full	112
" " periscopes	2
Rifles	3005
Bayonets	1513
Scabbards.	41
Stokes Guns	5
" " Traversing plates	2
" " Tripods.	2
S.A.A. Boxes, full	16
" loose, bags of	15
" Bandoliers	6000 rounds.
Grenades Mills, boxes of	50
" " bags of	61
" " loose	100
Shovels	417
Picks	277
Wire Cutters pairs of	327
Waterproof sheets	429
Equipment, sets of	1006
Packs.	60
Respirators, box	29
Gloves, wire cutting, pairs of	9
Helmets, steel	307
Stretchers	7
Pistols, very light	13
Overcoats	60
Maul.	1
Water Bottles	45
Mess Tins	27
Boots, pairsof	4
Theodolite.	1

sgd. D. Duncan, Captain.
D.A.A. & Q.M.G. for
Major General.
Commanding 37th Division.

18/11/16.

Casualties *Appendix I*

13th - 24th Novr.1916.

U N I T.	OFFICERS. K.	W.	M.	R.	OTHER RANKS. K.	W.	M.	S.	R.
8th Lincolns.	-	3	-	1	13	126		66	24
8th Somersets.	4	5	1	2	12	106	2	56	69
4th Middlesex.	1	3	-	1	39	42	51	70	10
10th York & Lancs.	1	7	-	-	9	82	8	66	20
63rd M.G.Coy.	-	3	-		4	8	1	16	
63rd T.M.Battery.	1	-	-		2	9	-	3	
10th R.Fusiliers.	2	3	-	1	22	105	13	59	62
13th R.Fusiliers.	1	9	-		45	205	21	25	143
13th K.R.R.C.	2	8	-	2	21	142	11	63	238
13th Rifle Brigade.	2	10	-		96	195	73	34	276
111th M.G.Coy.	-	3	-		1	18	-	8	
111th T.M.Battery.	-	1	-		-	2	[illegible]	-	
11th R.Warwicks.	2	4	-		40	150	47	88	200
6th Bedfords.	3	10	-		7	120	41	100	16
8th East Lancs.	8	8	2	1	22	106	34	36	7
10th L.N.Lancs.	7	11	-	2	21	116	42	41	116
112th M.G.Coy.	-	1	-		2	9	-	2	
112th T.M.Battery.	-	-	-		-	1	-	-	
9th North Staffs.	-	2	-		1	15	2	30	
123rd Bde.R.F.A.	-	-	-		-	2	-	8	
124th : : : :	-	-	-		-	1	-	9	
126th : : : :	-	-	-		-	1	-	-	
37th D.A.C.	-	-	-		-	-	-	14	
152nd Coy.R.E.	-	1	-		2	19	-	6	
153rd : : :	-	-	-		-	5	-	5	
154th : : :	-	-	-		3	32	-	6	
Signals.	-	-	-		1	5	-	2	
48th Fd.Amb.	-	-	-		1	4	-	5	
49th : :	-	-	-		-	1	-	7	
50th : :	-	-	-		-	-	-	3	
Chaplains.	1	1	-						
Divl.Headquarters.	-	1	-		-	-	-	1	
T O T A L S.	35	94	3	10	364	1627	346	829	1181

K - Killed.
W - Wounded.
M - Missing.
S - Sick.
R - Reinforcement.

37

Vol 17

WAR DIARY

A. + Q.

H.Q. 34th Division

Month of December 1916.

Instructions regarding War Diaries and Intelligence Summaries are contained in F. S. Regs., Part II. and the Staff Manual respectively. Title pages will be prepared in manuscript.

WAR DIARY
or
INTELLIGENCE SUMMARY.
(Erase heading not required.)

Army Form C. 2118.

Place	Date	Hour	Summary of Events and Information	Remarks and references to Appendices
MARIEUX	Decr 1.		Weather fine with frost — 2 Battalions 63rd Inf Bde moved from ACHEUX WOOD to SARTON and RAINCHEVAL — RA headquarters moved to BERTRANCOURT — Divisional Sign changed to Golden horseshoe with points up. Casualties nil	
"	2.		Weather fine with frost — Salvage Coy returned from MESNIL. Casualties 4.	
"	3		Weather wet — 9th North Staffs moved to RAINCHEVAL	
"	4		Weather cold & fine. 4 Middlesex moved to BEAUVAL, 8th East Lancs moved to BEAUVAL. 13th R. Fus. moved to RAINCHEVAL. Divisional dump brought down from COUPIGNY.	
"	5		Weather wet —	

A5834 Wt. W4973/M687 750,000 8/16 D. D. & L. Ltd. Forms/C.2118/13.

Instructions regarding War Diaries and Intelligence Summaries are contained in F. S. Regs., Part II. and the Staff Manual respectively. Title pages will be prepared in manuscript.

WAR DIARY
or
INTELLIGENCE SUMMARY.
(Erase heading not required.)

Army Form C. 2118.

Place	Date	Hour	Summary of Events and Information	Remarks and references to Appendices
MARIEUX	6/12/16		Nil	
MARIEUX	7.12.16		Divisional Commander inspected quarters of Divisional School at BEAUQUESNE	
MARIEUX	8.12.16		Nil	
MARIEUX	9.12.16		Nil	
MARIEUX	10.12.16		Nil	
MARIEUX	11.12.16		5th Corps G 995 and G 785 ordered Division to concentrate by 13th Dec. and to march from 5th Army on 14th December. Brigades warned.	
MARIEUX	12.12.16		Orders for move issued at 12.30 p.m.	
MARIEUX	13.12.16		111th Brigade moved to DOULLENS - AUTHIEULE area } Ref. LENS SHEET 11 112th Brigade moved to BEAUVAL area. Statement of Officers & O.R. reported missing during recent operations on the ANCRE and subsequently traced sent to Army	
FROHEN-LE-GRAND ~~MARIEUX~~ 8.P.	14.12.16		112th Brigade moved to BARLY - MEZEROLLES - VILLERS L'HOPITAL area 63rd Brigade moved to NOEUX - BOFFLES - ROUGEFAY area 111th Brigade moved to WAVANS - BONNIERES - FORTEL area. Ref. LENS SHEET 11.	[signature] Lt

A5834 Wt. W4973/M687 750,000 8/16 D. D. & L. Ltd. Forms/C.2118/13.

Army Form C. 2118.

Instructions regarding War Diaries and Intelligence Summaries are contained in F. S. Regs., Part II. and the Staff Manual respectively. Title pages will be prepared in manuscript.

WAR DIARY
or
INTELLIGENCE SUMMARY.
(Erase heading not required.)

Place	Date	Hour	Summary of Events and Information	Remarks and references to Appendices
FLERS	15.12.16		63rd Brigade moved to VACQUERIE-HAUTE COTE-FILLIEVRES area. 111th Brigade moved to CROISETTE-CROIX-OEUF area 112th Brigade moved to FLERS-NUNCQ-LINZEUX area. Refilling Points at FLERS and CHAPELLE DE ST PIERRE } Ref. LENS SHEET 11	
MONCHY CAYEUX	16.12.16		63rd Brigade moved to BRYAS-MONCHY CAYEUX-VALHUON area 111th Brigade moved to TANGRY-HEUCHIN area 112th Brigade moved to BERGUENEUSE-BOYAVAL-BOURS area Refilling Point at SAINS LES PERNES. } Ref. LENS SHEET 11.	
NORRENT-FONTES	17.12.16		63rd Brigade moved to AMETTES AREA 111th Brigade moved to St HILIARE area 112th Brigade moved to ECQUEDECQUES area 154th Field Company Sent to 1st Army Bridging School, LAMBRES.	
St VENANT	18.12.16		~~Nil~~ F.R. Administrative Arrangements issued.	appendix
"	19.12.16		Bathing parades for as many men as possible.	

A5834 Wt. W4973/M687 750,000 8/16 D. D. & L. Ltd. Forms/C.2118/13.

Army Form C. 2118.

Instructions regarding War Diaries and Intelligence Summaries are contained in F. S. Regs., Part II. and the Staff Manual respectively. Title pages will be prepared in manuscript.

WAR DIARY
or
INTELLIGENCE SUMMARY.
(Erase heading not required.)

Place	Date	Hour	Summary of Events and Information	Remarks and references to Appendices
ST VENANT	20.12.16		111th & 112th Infy Bgdes. moved to VIEILLE CHAPELLE and BETHUNE ESSARS area	
LESTREM	21.12.16		111th Bgde. took over NEUVE CHAPELLE Section from 95th Infy Bgde.	
"	22.12.16		112th Bgde took over FERME DU BOIS SECTION.	
"	23.12.16		Nil	
"	24.12.16		Nil	
"	25.12.16		Nil	
"	26.12.16		Divisional School opened at ST VENANT	
"	27.12.16		The day was quiet.	
"	28.12.16		Nil	
"	29.12.16		Nil	
"	30.12.16		Nil	
"	31.12.16		Tabulated results of ~~27th~~ March of 37th Division from Fifth to First Army area, Dec. 14th to Dec. 18th 1916	Appendix III

J. [illegible] Capt. [illegible] 37 Div

SUBJECT:-Casualties. 37th Divn.No. 1/194 A

Fifth Army "A".
V Corps "A".

Appendix II

Herewith statement showing the number of Officers and Other Ranks of various Units of this Division reported Missing during the recent Operations. 195 Other Ranks have now been traced and reported to D.A.G., Base, by Units concerned.

UNIT.	Reported Missing during period 13-24th Nov.1916.		Numbers Since traced.		Numbers Still unaccounted for.	
	Officers	O.R.	Offcs.	O.R.	Offc.	O.R.
8/Somersets.	-	2	-	-	-	2
4/Middlesex.	-	51	-	44	-	7
10/ Y & Lancs.	-	8	-	6	-	2
63/M.G.Coy.	-	4	-	-	-	4
10/R.Fusiliers.	-	13	-	4	-	9
13/R.Fusiliers.	-	21	-	11	-	10
13/K.R.R.C.	-	11	-	8	-	3
13/Rif.Brigade.	-	73	-	58	-	15
11/R.Warwicks.	-	47	-	36	-	11
6/Bedfords.	-	41	-	11	-	30
8/E.Lancs.	2	34	-	7	2	27
10/L.N.Lancs.	-	42	-	10	-	32.
TOTAL.	2	347	-	195	2	152

A Duncan Capt
DAA&QMG for

Major General,
Commanding 37th Division.

13th December 1916.

Appendix I 37 Div 642/26A

SECRET.

ADMINISTRATIVE ARRANGEMENTS.

Reference 37th Divn. Order No.58 d/- 18/12/16.

A. AMMUNITION SUPPLY.

1. Ammunition railhead LESTREM.
Transport of the D.A.C. will draw direct from railhead. XI Corps Ammunition Park lorries will not be used for this purpose except for the transport of items mentioned in minute 2.

2. Trench Mortar Ammunition(Heavy,Medium and Light), Grenades, Rockets etc. will be delivered to D.A.C. by XI Corps Ammn. Park on demand.

3. The sections of the 5th and 56th D.A.C's at present supplying S.A.A. and Grenades to that portion of the front to be taken over by this Division, will continue to do so until relieved by sections of the 37th Div. Ammunition Column.

Brigade in the FERME de BOIS Section and Brigade in Reserve Area will apply to the section of the 5th D.A.C. billeted at R. 19.c.3.8. Sheet 36 A.

Brigade in the NEUVE CHAPELLE Section to section of 56th D.A.C. billeted at L.26.b.1.2. Sheet 36 A.

B. SUPPLIES.

1. Railhead BETHUNE. This will be moved about 26th instant to LA GORGUE - When the latter Railhead is used, supplies will be conveyed from LA GORGUE to LOCON on light railway. Refilling Points will be situated on the main road between LESTREM and LOCON-exact positions will be notified later.

2. Any Reserve Supplies dumped in the forward area will be taken over and a report will be rendered to Divl. H.Q. stating the quantity and condition of the supplies.

C. WATER.

In the line, is obtained from pumps and wells of which there are a considerable number.
In the FERME de BOIS Section there is a supply pumped from BREWERY CORNER (S.25.b) and piped to the right battalions H.Q.

D. R.E. MATERIAL.

37th Divl. Dump at FOSSE (R.21. Central Sheet 36 A.)
XI Corps R.E. Yard at LA GORGUE.
No. 4 R.E. Park, LILLERS.

E. TRANSPORT.

1. Companies of the Divl. Train will be billeted as follows:-

H.Q. Company		on arrival at Q. 12. c
No. 2	"	from 22nd until arrival of H.Q. Co at Q.12.c after arrival of H.Q. Co. at PARADIS.
No. 3	"	PARADIS.
No. 4	"	LES FACONS.

2. The system of transport to front line is generally as follows:- Horse transport to rear terminus of tramways thence by man-handled trucks to forward terminus, except left Battalion Sub-section of FERME de BOIS Section where transport is by carrier from TEETOTAL CORNER to FACTORY CORNER. Tramways are shown on the trench maps. Wounded can be evacuated from front line system on the tramways.
The maintenance and traffic control of the tramways will be taken over by the 9th N.Staffs(Pioneers).

F. ORDNANCE.

Ordnance Railhead, BETHUNE.
Offices of D.A.D.O.S. 7 Grand Place,
BETHUNE, until further notice.

G. HORSE STANDINGS.

A list of horse standings in 37th Divl.Area is attached.
(Appendix "A").
The following additional standings and billets are placed temporarily at the disposal of this Division by the 5th Division.
(a) Horse lines and billets for Transport of 2 Infantry Battalions at LES FACONS X.15.c.
(b) Horse lines and billets for Transport of one M.G.Co. at LESPLAUX X.14.b.7.7.
(c) Horse lines and billets for one Field Ambulance at LESPLAUX X.14.a.8.8.

H. TRENCH STORES.

Trench stores will be carefully checked on taking over and a complete list forwarded to Divl. H.Q. on A.F. W.3405 .

I. TOWN MAJORS.

Brigade Area Commanders will appoint Temporary Town Majors as far as possible for each billet area in their Brigade Area.

J. MEDICAL ARRANGEMENTS.

48th Field Ambulance	billeted at	ZELOBES will clear the Reserve Area.
49th " "	"	LESPLAUX with advanced Dressing Station at X.17.d.4.5. will clear Right Section.
50th " "	"	VIEILLE CHAPELLE with adv. Dressing Station at ST.VAAST S.32.d.6.4.and GREEN BARN S.27.d.5.2.will clear Left Section.

K. BATHS.

Baths exist at the following places:-

VIEILLE CHAPELLE	R.34.a.4.8.	400 - 600	men daily.
RICHEBOURG ST VAAST,	S.8.a.7.9	500	" "
LETOURET	X.17.c.8.6	500	" "
CROIX BARBEE		400	" "
LESTREM	R.8.b.9.7.	800	" "

L. LAUNDRY.

(a) There is a Corps Laundry at LA GORGUE L.34.c.1.1.
(b) The Corps Laundry supplies clean underclothing to Divl. Baths, in exchange for an equivalent number of dirty or unserviceable garments.
(c) The provision of coal to the Corps Laundry will be made under Division arrangements.

M. RECREATION ROOMS.

There is a Y.M.C.A. hut at VIEILLE CHAPELLE.
A Church Army hut has been promised for LETOURET.
Recreation Tent, Kings Road.
" Room, CROIX BARBEE.
Canteen at Adv.Dressing Stn. RUE de BOIS.

N. EXPEDITIONARY FORCE CANTEENS.

(a) BETHUNE
(b) LILLERS
(c) MERVILLE

O. VETERINARY.

Mobile Veterinary Section will be at LESTREM R.8.d.6.0.

P. GUM BOOT STORES.

Gum Boot stores and drying rooms exist in the forward area. Brigade Commanders in the line will arrange for these to be properly looked after by suitable men and for regular supervision by officers.

[illegible]
Lieut. Colonel.
A.A. & Q.M.G.
37th Division.

21st December, 1916.

APPENDIX "A".

MAP REFERENCE OF HORSE STANDINGS COMPLETED
IN 37TH DIVISIONAL AREA.

Location.		Accommodation.	Reserved for.
X.9.b.50/45.	Nr. Canal DE LA LAWE,) Nr. LE CASAN.)	130	
R.33.b.3/3	Nr. VIEILLE CHAPELLE.	188	
X.2.a.1/1	Nr. LE VERT LANNOT.	120	Artillery.
R.28.d.1/3.	North of E in DRAW BRIDGE.	150	-do-
R.31.d.2/5.	Nr. LA COMBE WILLOT.	150	-do-
R.19.a.9/4.	(On road running E from CHURCH (1000 yards from CHURCH	210	-do-
X.5.c.3/7.	Nr. LACOUTURE.	150	
Q.24.a.4/8.	Nr. PARADIS.	90	Train.
X.3.d.3/5	1500 yards S of VIEILLE) CHAPELLE.)	60	
X.3.d.3.4.	" " " " "	58	
X.10.c.1/4.	Nr. LE TOURET.	58	
X.4.d.5/3.	On LACOUTURE - LE TOURET RD.	56	
R.30.c.5/9.	Nr. LES 9 MAISONS.	68	
R.29.c.2.1.	Nr. LES 9 MAISONS.		Artillery.
R.28.c.2.1.	Nr. VIEILLE CHAPELLE		-do-

Appendix III

TABULATED RESULTS OF THE MARCH OF 37TH DIVISION FROM FIFTH TO FIRST ARMY AREA, Decr.14-18 1915

UNIT.	DATE. 14th			DATE. 15th			DATE. 16th			DATE. 17th			DATE. 18th		
INFANTRY.	Miles.	No. carried	No. who fell out.	Miles.	No carried	No. who fell out.	Miles.	No carried	No. who fell out.	Miles.	No. carried.	No. who fell out.	Miles.	No. carried.	No. who fell out.
63rd Brigade.															
8th Lincolns.	10	11	15	9	11	nil	14	11	10	11	11	4	10	nil	nil
8th Somerset L.I.	10	6	7	10	10	30	14	46	3	9	16	nil	7	12	nil
4th Middlesex	10	1	1	8	nil	6	13	3	14	10	6	14	7	19	2
10th Y.& L.	10	4	nil	14	4	3	13	5	4	11	6	4	10	5	nil
111th Brigade.															
10th R.Fusrs	15	nil	4	8	nil	2	13	1	nil	9	nil	nil	12	1	1
13th R.Fusrs	14	7	10	9	7	10	10	5	1	11	4	nil	11	1	nil
13th K.R.R.C.	16	10	35	10	2	10	12	7	3	10	12	1	10	13	6
13th R.Bde.	13	5	18	12	9	1	11	4	7	8	10	nil	15	7	4
112th Brigade.															
11th R.Warwicks	16	13	14	6	10	3	13	20	26	7	21	1	13	21	2
6th Bedfords.	15	nil	17	5	17	nil	13	18	20	8	20	7	7	19	6
8th E.Lancs.	16	9	28	10	3	23	11	8	32	10	18	11	10	20	2
10th L.N.Lancs.	13	6	13	7	14	5	12	14	12	9	14	5	8	20	3

P.T.O.

UNIT.	DATE. 14th			DATE. 15th			DATE. 16th			DATE. 17th			Date. 18th		
	Miles	No carried	No. who fell out.	Miles.	No carried.	No. who fell out.	Miles.	No. carried	No. who fell out.	Miles.	No. carried.	No. who fell out.	Miles.	No. carried.	No. who fell out.
Machine Gun Cos.															
63rd .G.Coy.	12	2	nil	9	3	1	13	2	nil	11	nil	nil	10	nil	nil
111th -do -	14	2	4	8	4	nil	14	nil	5	9	4	nil	10	7	nil
112th -do-	15	nil	nil	9	nil	nil	9	nil	nil	11	nil	nil	9	nil	nil
Trench Mortar Btys.															
63rd T.M.Bty.	12	1	nil	9	3	1	13	nil	2	11	nil	nil	10	nil	nil
111th T.M.Bty.	15	nil	nil	8	1	1	11	1	2	10	nil	nil	11	nil	nil
112th T.M.Bty.	15	1	nil	9	1	nil	9	1	nil	11	3	nil	9	1	nil
Field Cos.R.E.															
152nd Field Co.	15	4	2	6	4	4	14	3	1	9	4	9	10	16	nil
153rd " "	15	nil	2	15	1	1	13	8	8	10	nil	nil	8	nil	nil
154th " "	17	nil	nil	10	5	nil	13	nil	nil	Proceeded to LAMBRES					
Field Ambulances.															
48th Field Amb.	12	nil	nil	15	2	2	13	1	1	11	1	1	8	nil	1
49th " "	12	nil	nil	11	nil	nil	10	nil	nil	12	1	1	8	nil	nil
50th " "	10	nil	nil	10	nil	nil	13	7	3	8	6	5	10	nil	2

WAR DIARY HQ 37th Bde

January 1917

HQ AQ 37
Set 18

Instructions regarding War Diaries and Intelligence Summaries are contained in F. S. Regs., Part II. and the Staff Manual respectively. Title pages will be prepared in manuscript.

WAR DIARY
or
INTELLIGENCE SUMMARY.
(Erase heading not required.)

Army Form C. 2118.

Administrative Staff
H'Qrs 37th Division

Place	Date	Hour	Summary of Events and Information	Remarks and references to Appendices
LESTREM	1.1.17		G.O.C. Entertained all the children of LESTREM during the afternoon at a very lively party.	
"	2.1.17		~~Nil~~. Corps Q Conference	
"	3.1.17		Works on horse standings proceeded with.	
"	4.1.17		Nil	
"	5.1.17	}	Mild weather continues – much rain; Several roads flooded necessitating reorganisation of traffic routes	
"	6.1.17	}		
"	7.1.17		Nil	
"	8.1.17		Ceremonial Parade at MERVILLE at 2.30 p.m. Corps Commander presented medal ribbons to 130 recipients of Awards.	
"	9.1.17		~~Nil~~ Corps Q conference	
"	10.1.17		Army Commander inspects Div'l School at St VENANT	
"	11.1.17		63rd Bde Transport lines inspected: also Div'n gum boot stores	
"	12.1.17		Conference Corps H.Q.	
"	13.1.17		AA & QMG returns from leave	
"	14.1.17		Transport lines 111th & 112th Bde in same area inspected	

A5834 Wt. W4973/M687 750,000 8/16 D. D. & L. Ltd. Forms/C.2118/13.

[signature]
Lt Col
AA & QMG
37th Division

Instructions regarding War Diaries and Intelligence Summaries are contained in F. S. Regs., Part II. and the Staff Manual respectively. Title pages will be prepared in manuscript.

WAR DIARY
or
INTELLIGENCE SUMMARY.
(Erase heading not required.)

Administrative Staff H Qrs 37th Division

Army Form C. 2118.

Place	Date	Hour	Summary of Events and Information	Remarks and references to Appendices
LESTREM	15.1.17		111th Bde takes over NEUVE CHAPELLE section from 63rd who pass into reserve	
	16.1.17		Corps Q conference	
	17.1.17		Heavy snow fall arranging additional transport facilities where required	
	18.1.17		Cold weather continued with frost: question of extra fuel & [illegible] discussed	
	19.1.17		DAQMG proceeds on leave	
	20.1.17		Preparing agenda for conference of Divl administrative officers	
	21.1.17		Conference with Corps Q & Corps Park on slag question for standings & arranging for us to have extra supply.	
	22.1.17		Conference [illegible] held at LESTREM on all Q matters within the Divn	
	23.1.17		Corps Q conference	
	24.1.17		Inspection of artillery standings & arranging for them to have increased supply of slag	
	25.1.17		On receipt of outline of scheme from Corps Q as to grouping division	

[illegible] Capt. [illegible] 37th Division

A5834 Wt. W4973/M687 750,000 8/16 D. D. & L. Ltd. Forms/C.2118/13.

Instructions regarding War Diaries and Intelligence Summaries are contained in F. S. Regs., Part II. and the Staff Manual respectively. Title pages will be prepared in manuscript.

WAR DIARY
or
INTELLIGENCE SUMMARY.
(Erase heading not required.)

Army Form C. 2118.

Administrative Staff
H Qrs 37th Division

Place	Date	Hour	Summary of Events and Information	Remarks and references to Appendices
ESTREM	25.1.17	(contd)	within small area preparatory to offensive operations engaged compiling scheme & various conferences with CRE ADMS DDVS APM etc on special points concerning them	
	26.1.17 27.1.17 28.1.17		} Works on scheme	
	29.1.17		Frost having continued for 10 days arrangements were made during this time to store 3 days supply of ammunition to lessen transport during thaw	
	30.1.17		Corps Q conference	
	31.1.17		Order recd for Divn to pass into GHQ reserve 3rd prox & to be withdrawn from line forthwith	

D. Duncan Capt
DAA & QMG
37th Division

A5834 Wt. W4973/M687 750,000 8/16 D. D. & L. Ltd. Forms/C.2118/13.

Instructions regarding War Diaries and Intelligence Summaries are contained in F. S. Regs., Part II. and the Staff Manual respectively. Title pages will be prepared in manuscript.

WAR DIARY
or
INTELLIGENCE SUMMARY.
(Erase heading not required.)

Administrative Staff H.Q. 37 D
H.Q. 37th Division
Vol 19

Army Form C. 2118.

Place	Date	Hour	Summary of Events and Information	Remarks and references to Appendices
LESTREM	1.2.17		D.A.Q.M.G (Capt R. M. Airey) returned from leave. 63rd Bde relieved in line by 15th ~~Bde~~ 5th Divn: billeted in and round BETHUNE	
"	2.2.17		Divn passing 3rd into G.H.Q reserve interview with D.A.D.R.T. BETHUNE settling entraining scheme & preparing & issuing same to all concerned. 111 Bde relieved by 168 Bde 56 Divn and move into billets in and around MERVILLE	
"	3.2.17		112 Bde withdrawn into back portion of reserve division: engaged examining & readjusting new billets of all Bdes	
"	4.2.17		Artillery withdrawn from line into billets concentrating round wagon lines.	
"	5.2.17		Conference with Staff Captains discussing present administrative arrangements in new area: applying for return of all men employed away.	
"	6.2.17		Corps Q conference	
"	7.2.17		Order recd for Divn shortly to relieve 24 Div in LOOS 14 Bis and HULLUCH Sections Bdes to relieve 112. 63. 111.	
"	8.2.17		Engaged working out march table of Division to new area: visiting 24 Divn & discussing administrative arrangements in new area	
"	9.2.17		Order recd for move into new area to begin tomorrow & be complete by 13/14. Going round new area visiting Town Majors & checking accommodation etc.	
"	10.2.17		working out transport scheme for move and refilling points and supply arrangements: relieving all outstanding working parties etc.	
"	11.2.17		Preparing & issuing administrative instructions for new area: 112 Bde take over LOOS Section: rearranging billets owing to overcrowding in ~~billets~~ BETHUNE	
	12.2.17		111 Bde take over HULLUCH Section H.Q. at PHILOSOPHE.	

A5834 Wt. W4973/M687 750,000 8/16 D. D. & L. Ltd. Forms/C.2118/13.

WAR DIARY
or
INTELLIGENCE SUMMARY.
(Erase heading not required.)

Instructions regarding War Diaries and Intelligence Summaries are contained in F. S. Regs., Part II. and the Staff Manual respectively. Title pages will be prepared in manuscript.

Administrative Staff
HQ 37th Division

Army Form C. 2118.

Place	Date	Hour	Summary of Events and Information	Remarks and references to Appendices
NOEUX-LES-MINES	13-2-17		D.H.Q. moved from LESTREM to NOEUX LES MINES : 63 Bde took over 14 Bis section H.Q at MAZINGARBE	
"	14-2-17		Dealing with difficulties in providing water for troops in trenches and for baths owing to pipe lines & boilers burst. 9th N. Staffs (Pioneers) complete relief of LOOS defences.	
"	15-2-17		Taking over Laundry at NOEUX LES MINES from 6th Divn	
"	16-2-17		Going into system of ammunition supply and surveying tram lines etc.	
"	17-2-17		D.A.A. & Q.M.G (Capt. D. Duncan M.C.) proceeded on leave.	
"	18-2-17		Corps Q conference	
"	19-2-17		Restriction of lorry traffic owing to thaw	
"	20/21-2-17		Organising divisional Coy of P.U. men under Major ESS	
"	22-2-17		Inspection of transport by O.C. Train & A.D.V.S.	
"	23-2-17		Calling for returns of officers & O.R. not received ribands with view to medal riband parade	
	24-2-17		Further inspection of transport Orders recd that Divn wld be withdrawn from line & move to St HILAIRE area : period 1-6 prox : preparatory to march to VI Corps 3 Army area.	
"	25-2-17		Reconnaissance of St HILAIRE area from billeting point of view : engaged preparing scheme to form basis of march table	
"	26-2-17		Visit to various Town Majors concerned and completing march table for move from 1-6 march	
	27-2-17		Preparing & issuing administrative instructions re leaving present area & occupying St HILAIRE area	
"	28-2-17		Settling with 6th Divn as to taking over : preparing detailed billeting scheme for each village to be occupied on march & issuing to all concerned.	

D. Duncan Capt.
DAA & QMG 37 Division

A5834 Wt. W4973/M687 750,000 8/16 D. D. & L. Ltd. Forms/C.2118/13.

WAR DIARY MAR 1917

HEADQUARTERS 37 DIVN Vol 20

ADMINISTATIVE BRANCH

Instructions regarding War Diaries and Intelligence Summaries are contained in F. S. Regs., Part II. and the Staff Manual respectively. Title pages will be prepared in manuscript.

WAR DIARY
or
INTELLIGENCE SUMMARY.
(Erase heading not required.)

Army Form C. 2118.

Headquarters
37th Division
Administrative Branch

Place	Date	Hour	Summary of Events and Information	Remarks and references to Appendices
NOEUX LES MINES	1917 March 1		Relief of Divn commenced 6th Divn taking over part of part of LOOS Section from 112 Bde and part of HULLUCH section from 111 Bde: arranging final details re billets in staging areas on way to ST HILAIRE area	
	2		Relief continued: all 112th Bde being withdrawn from LOOS section: visit to VI Corps to which Divn was to march from ST HILAIRE area: going over ROELLECOURT area visiting TOWN MAJORS etc verifying particulars of accomodation & arranging for Field Coys & Pioneers to come straight through to complete bunking etc: Divisional School moves to FOUFFLIN RICAMETZ in ROELLECOURT area	
	3		DAA & QMG (Capt Duncan MC) returned from leave: conference with 6th Divn Q Staff re handing over. Relief continued in HULLUCH section & begun in 14 Bis section: visiting troops in new billets	
NORRENT FONTES	4		DHQ moved to NORRENT FONTES: railhead to LILLERS: difficulty with Arty billets in BERQUETTE area: visiting FIRST ARMY & settling same & subsequently seeing S.C. on spot & explaining position to 66th Divn: relief continued	
	5		G.O.C. proceeds on leave Divn commanded by C.R.A. Brig Genl POTTS: relief completed except for arty: visiting Bdes in new area 63 RELY 111 FONTES 112 LAIRES: DADOS moves to ROELLECOURT area	
	6		Visit to VI Corps & pointing out inadequacy of ST MICHEL area in ROELLECOURT area for Div Arty & they arranged to ask THIRD army for tents	
	7		Order recd for transfer of Divn from FIRST to THIRD ARMY in VI Corps area move to be complete by 10th working out march table accordingly one staging area for each Bde group & Arty: visiting staging areas and checking accomodation tables. Working out transport and supply arrangements for move: 9 N Staffs reach MONCHEAUX	
	8		112th Bde move from LAIRES to VALHUON area: DADOS reporting non receipt of tents for Arty area ST MICHEL in ROELLECOURT visiting VI Corps to expedite delivery: Corps stated their laundry at FREVENT was temporarily out of order but would soon be running: baths in ROELLECOURT area very defective.	
ROELLECOURT	9		DHQ moved to ROELLECOURT: Arty to ANVIN area: 112 Bde to REBREUVIETTE area: 63 to VALHUON area: 111 to PERNES area: visiting various units on march & Bde H.Q & clearing up billeting difficulties: calling at VI Corps & they stated III Army had promised 100 tents for Arty by tomorrow morning.	
	10		Move to ROELLECOURT area completed: Div Arty to ST MICHEL area: 63 to HOUVIN HOUVIGNEUL: 111 to BUNEVILLE tents for Arty recd: visiting units on the march.	

A5834 Wt. W4973/M687 750,000 8/16 D. D. & L. Ltd. Forms/C.2118/13.

Instructions regarding War Diaries and Intelligence Summaries are contained in F. S. Regs., Part II. and the Staff Manual respectively. Title pages will be prepared in manuscript.

WAR DIARY
or
INTELLIGENCE SUMMARY.
(Erase heading not required.)

Army Form C. 2118.

Place	Date 1917	Hour	Summary of Events and Information	Remarks and references to Appendices
ROELLECOURT	March 11		Preparing & issuing administrative instructions for ROELLECOURT area: conference at DHQ of S.C's & representatives of administrative services etc: discussing arrangements for present area & outlining scheme of anticipated offensive operations just E. of Arras.	
	12		Perusing VI Corps administrative instructions for offensive operations: visit to Corps discussing certain points and arranging to put forward suggestions & requirements for special articles.	
	13		Issuing scheme as to pack transport water crates etc: visit to Corps laundry at FREVENT investigating delay in starting work & arranging to provide extra personnel	
	14		Visit to 3. 12. 15th Divs in forward area: discussing dump sites water & transport arrangements; also site for D.H.Q.	
	15		G.O.C. Div^n returns from leave: order recd for Div Art^y less SAA portion of DAC to move to VII Corps area tomorrow: issuing administrative instructions in relation thereto.	
	16		Relieving Town Majors throughout ROELLECOURT area: visit to ARRAS & forward area for reconnaissance generally: Art^y march to GROUCHES area & come under VII Corps.	
	17		Conference of all parties interested at 63 Bde H.Q on pack transport: settling on types of various articles required: discussing trump lines & Lewis gun slings	
	18		Visiting baths in area: also laundry at FREVENT not yet working: further visit to ARRAS: Brig Gen CHALLONER assumes command 63 Infy Bde vice Brig Genl HILL to ENGLAND	
	19		Making slight readjustment of Bde areas consequent on increased accomodation through tending: arranging to draw all supplies by horse transport Corps requiring all lorries from Supply Col except those for Art^y DADOS & Postal.	
	20		Order recd for Div^n to be held in readiness to move at short notice: issuing instructions as to dumping withdrawing of personnel etc: visit to staging area round LIGNEREUIL making out accomodation table of same: medical conference 63 Bde H.Q: Corps Q conference	
	21		Preparing & issuing scheme for medal ribbon parade at HOUVIN on 23rd by Army Commander: Corps allot Div^n 6 lorries daily in addition to ordnance & postal: taking dump offr 2/Lt WILLIAMS 4/Middx to forward area & showing him site at AGNEZ LES DUISANS for main div^l dump & E. of ARRAS for iron ration dumps	

A5834 Wt. W4973/M687 750,000 8/16 D. D. & L. Ltd. Forms/C.2118/13.

Instructions regarding War Diaries and Intelligence Summaries are contained in F. S. Regs., Part II. and the Staff Manual respectively. Title pages will be prepared in manuscript.

WAR DIARY
or
INTELLIGENCE SUMMARY.
(Erase heading not required.)

Headquarters 37th Division Administrative Branch

Army Form C. 2118.

Place	Date	Hour	Summary of Events and Information	Remarks and references to Appendices
	1917			
BELLECOURT	March 22		Choosing site at HOUVIN for ceremonial parade tomorrow: arranging details with 63rd Bde & 152 Field Coy: instructing DADOS as to ribands required: visit to 3.12.& 15 Divns settling details as to dumps etc: visit to VI Corps on question of iron rations & oats to be dumped & as to supplies for Cavalry attd.	
	23		Army Commander presented medal ribands at HOUVIN: superintending the dumping of one day's iron rations for fighting troops at forward dump E. of Arras & similar no at AGNEZ dump: artillery railhead moves to BOUQUEMAISON	
	24		Owing to shortage of blank for firing 23 grenades arranging with Corps to draw 2000 direct from SAVY railhead: inspecting Corps laundry FREVENT & obtg figs present posn: obtaining from Bdes specimens L.G. strips & arranging with DADOS as to pattern for divn	
	25		C/E on DADOS' accident when firing rifle grenade with shortened rifle: visiting & inspecting refilling points: notification Artillery railhead changes WARLINCOURT tomorrow: British Army in France adopts summer time midnight of day to conform to French arrangements.	
	26		Discussing with AAG Third Army mixed scheme for reporting estimated casualties during heavy fighting: visit from Corps Salvage Offr arranging dumps etc: instructing divnl Burial Offr (2nd Bromage 13 RB) as to his duties & his proceeding to ARRAS: visit to Bde Corps & 3 12 & 15 Divns arranging outstanding details.	
	27		Visit to AGNEZ DUISANS with Camp Commandant settling with him as to accomodation for D.H.Q: inspecting site of advanced DHQ in ARRAS which CRE was building: arranging for RE to carry out ... at VILLERS: inspecting Russian steam baths ... by all units.	
	28		Corps Q conference: arranging to dump E. of Arras further iron & oats rations: applying for small supply gum boots: detailing party to draw remounts from BOULOGNE returning by road.	
	29		G.O.C. inspects pack saddlery at Bde HQ: visit to ARRAS looking for sites for Bde HQ when divn moves through: inspecting CCS etc: visiting Divnl Burial Offr: issuing instructions as to Corps depot school & what personnel was to go there with divl & gas schools	
	30		Visit to Corps discussing staging area accommodation and how to fit in just W. of Arras: striking St Michel camp & arranging to send tents to our forward area: issuing instructions about dumps: preparing administrative instructions of a general nature for the active operations	
	31		Preparing scheme showing supply posn at various stages of operations: visit to D.D.S.&T. discussing same: conference with S.Cs explaining. Visit to AGNEZ WAGNONLIEU & WARLUS choosing sites for camps when Divn closing up W. of ARRAS.	

A5834 Wt. W4973/M687 750,000 8/16 D. D. & L. Ltd. Forms/C.2118/13.

S. ... Capt
DAA & QMG
37 Div

Vol 21

War Diary

Apl 1917

Administrative Staff

37th Divn

Instructions regarding War Diaries and Intelligence Summaries are contained in F. S. Regs., Part II. and the Staff Manual respectively. Title pages will be prepared in manuscript.

WAR DIARY
or
INTELLIGENCE SUMMARY.
(Erase heading not required.)

Hdqrs 37th Division
Administrative Staff

Army Form C. 2118.

Place	Date	Hour	Summary of Events and Information	Remarks and references to Appendices
ROELLECOURT	1917 April 1		Railhead moves tomorrow to AGNEZ-DUISANS: Supply Col. allotted to Divn & ordered to move tomorrow to VILLERS-SIR-SIMON: arranging administrative conference School HOUVIGNEUL 5 p.m. tomorrow and preparing agenda for same: engaged revising administrative instructions A. & Q.	
	2		Visit to Corps discussing areas to be occupied W X & Y nights especially with reference to tent accommodation required on Y night: subsequently visiting areas especially forward ones: completing & issuing administrative instructions A & Q: conference with S.C.'s etc. at school HOUVIN.	
	3		Engaged working out march & accommodation tables for forward march of Division: visit to WARLUS deciding on site for camps on Y night & for transport seeing T.M. as to billets for senior officers: applying for return of all [illegible] employed away; visiting Corps Depot Camp FREVENT where Div School was now established & explaining system as to reinforcements etc:	
	4		Preparing transport & supply scheme for forward move: issuing instructions to Bdes as to collecting tents which were to be taken into forward area for camps on Y night: visit to D.D.O.S. Third Army as to certain outstanding articles [illegible]: also to 17 Divn who were to take over ROELLECOURT HQ tomorrow	
AGNEZ-LES-DUISANS	5		D.H.Q. moved from ROELLECOURT to AGNEZ-LES-DUISANS: 63 Bde to MANIN area 111 to IZEL LE HAMEAU 112 to HABARCQ: seeing various units on march: visit to Corps as to grenades etc. not yet in at dumps: visit to Third Army as to wagons of DAC not yet returned: Z day being postponed 24 hours going round Bdes notifying them accordingly everything being postponed 24 hours	
	6		Arranging various details to improve DHQ camp: visit to FREVENT depot camp settling outstanding points with O.C. Div School: inspecting refilling points: conference with O.C. Corps mounted troops on transport & supply questions: visit to Bde H.Qs arranging as to supplying Bde equipment dumps from Div Dump at AGNEZ.	
	7		Visiting alternative spots for transport E. & W. of Arras & arranging sites with Div. Transport Offr: all Bdes move forward 63 round LATTRE St QUENTIN 111 DUISANS 112 HABARCQ: filling Bde equipment dumps: visit to forward Div Dump at BLANGY E. of ARRAS: visit to BACHIMONT ordering detachment B echelon DAC to return & arranging details: arranging for tents for tomorrows camps.	
	8		Bdes move forward to camping grounds 63 DUISANS 111 LOUEZ 112 WARLUS: visiting Bdes & settling final details: Zero time fixed for 5.30 a.m. tomorrow: part of DHQ move up to advanced H.Q at Horseshoe Cave just E. of Arras: clearing AGNEZ dump & moving remainder of staff to forward dumps: arranging for dumping blankets packs etc. at camping grounds.	
	9 10 11 12		Active operations just E. of Arras. Divn move through town and after passing through 3. 12. & 15 Divs advance & capture their objective MONCHY LE PREUX: relieved by 12 Divn & withdrawn to ARRAS	

A5834 Wt. W4973/M687 750,000 8/16 D. D. & L. Ltd. Forms/C.2118/13.

Instructions regarding War Diaries and Intelligence Summaries are contained in F. S. Regs., Part II. and the Staff Manual respectively. Title pages will be prepared in manuscript.

APRIL 1917

WAR DIARY
or
INTELLIGENCE SUMMARY.
(Erase heading not required.)

Army Form C. 2118.

Hdqrs 37th Division
Administrative Staff

Place	Date	Hour	Summary of Events and Information	Remarks and references to Appendices
AGNEZ-LES-DUISANS	13		Advanced DHQ returns from Horse Shoe cave: 112 Bde move by M.T. to HABARCQ: 111 Bde to AGNEZ: 2 Bns 63rd to DUISANS: making out march table to accompany G order for move tomorrow: preparing statement of estimated casualties (Appendix A): returning blankets packs etc: arranging to draw 11 limbered G.S. wagons for Lewis guns from AUXI LE CHATEAU	Appendix A
LIGNEREUIL	14		D.H.Q. moves to LIGNEREUIL: 112 Bde moves to AMBRINES area: 111 to IZEL LES HAMEAU area: 63 Bde to AGNEZ: seeing Bdes on march; arranging transport and supply questions: Divn today comes under XVIII Corps: visit to Corps H.Q: arranging for clean clothes from VI Corps laundry FREVENT	
	15		Preparing statement of officer casualties (Appendix B): 63 Bde move to MANIN area: arranging with Corps for extra accomodation & re arranging area: visit to Corps Depot & arranging for reinforcements to come up tomorrow: preparing administrative instructions as to refitting etc: visit to Bde H.Qs: applying for C.Os & 2nd i/c to replace casualties.	Appendix B
	16		Railhead moves to TINCQUES: arranging to draw from tomorrow by horse transport: 152 Field Coy move to St POL: visiting & inspecting refilling points: preparing statement of other rank casualties (Appendix C): conference at DHQ on recent operations: arrangements about baths.	Appendix C
	17		Supplies drawn by horse transport from railhead lorries under S.M.T.O: preparing notes on refitting: asking Bdes to supply information & suggestions re special articles used in recent operations: visit to D.O.S. Third Army & Heavy & Medium workshops as to making portable anti aircraft Lewis gun mountings: ordering up all reinforcements from Corps Depots.	
	18		Orders recd for Divn to come under orders of 17th Corps: working out march table for Bdes move: going round billeting area with Staff Capt: visit to 17th Corps: ordering up remaining reinforcements from Corps Depot & as there were no M.T. available arranging to stage them at BEAUFORT: issuing supply & transport arrangements for move.	
	19		63 Bde move to GOUVES & MONTENESCOURT 'B' echelon in latter place: 111 Bde to AGNEZ: 112 to HABARCQ area: orders recd to relieve 4th Div N. of Scarpe Bde at a time: arranging for lorries to bus 63rd up to ARRAS: visit to 4th Divn and 17th Corps as to administrative arrangements on relief: sending up Lt Williams to take over Div dump: visit to BEAUFORT superintending arrangements for reinforcements.	
	20		Preparing & issuing administrative arrangements: arranging for Corps Park to supply ammn gum boots etc: to St Nicholas dump: superintending debussing of 63 Bde at ARRAS who take over line from 4th Divn: 111 Bde march up to support trenches: arranging for camp for 112 Bde near St NICHOLAS as Divl Res: sending Lt ROBINSON forward to take over forward Divl dump: collecting reinforcements at BEAUFORT to join Bdes at transport lines.	
ETRUN	21		D.H.Q move to ETRUN: helping 112 Bde on march to new camp near St Nicholas: inspecting & arranging transport lines of Bdes: advanced DHQ move to dug outs near Railway embankment G 14 A 0 8: signal car practically destroyed by shell: arranging for flares etc: demanded by Bdes.	
	22		Railhead moves to ARRAS: 111th Bde move to front line on left of 63rd Bde: completing equipment of Bdes etc:	
	23		Division attacks N. of Scarpe: heavy loss in C.Os: asking Army for officers to replace: preparing estimated casualties: also casualty list No 5 ~~(see appendix)~~	
ARRAS	24 25 26		Active operations continue: visits from time to time to advanced H.Q dumps transport lines etc: estimated casualty returns Appendix D: casualty lists 6.7. & 8.: getting up all reinforcements from Depot: Rear H.Q move to ARRAS	Appendix D

A5834 Wt. W4973/M687 750,000 8/16 Forms/C. 2118/13.

Instructions regarding War Diaries and Intelligence Summaries are contained in F. S. Regs., Part II. and the Staff Manual respectively. Title pages will be prepared in manuscript.

WAR DIARY
or
INTELLIGENCE SUMMARY.
(*Erase heading not required.*)

Army Form C. 2118.

H.Q. 37th Division
Administrative Staff

Place	Date	Hour	Summary of Events and Information	Remarks and references to Appendices
ARRAS	27		Active operations continue	
	28		37th Divn attack & gain their objective GREENLAND HILL: casualty list No 9: further estimated casualty wire: orders rec'd for 9th Div to relieve 37th: arranging for busses to take back 63rd & 112th Bdes to LIGNEREUIL area: working out march table for G.S. order: in the course of night 28/29 63rd & 112th are relieved from line & concentrate round transport lines St NICHOLAS.	
	29		Divn ~~come~~ under XVIII Corps noon 30th: working out details of embussing arrangements for 63 & 112 Bdes: supply & further transport arrangements for move: superintending embussing & debussing 130 lorries & buses: issuing administrative arrangements for move: 111th Bde night 29/30 move from line to transport lines St Nicholas.	
LIGNEREUIL	30		Advanced H.Q and rear H.Q. (ARRAS) move to LIGNEREUIL: embussing 111 Bde Pioneers & all details 130 M.T. vehicles double journey: spell of brilliantly fine weather starts: 63rd Bde MANIN area 111 IZEL LES HAMEAU 112 AMBRINES.	

D Duncan Capt
DAAG 37th Division

A5834 Wt. W4973/ . 750,000 8/16 Forms/C2118/13.

List No. I
14/4/17

37th DIVISION.

	Officer Casualties. Name.	Nature.	Date.	Remark
63rd Inf. Brigade.			Aprl.	
8th Lincolns.	Major F.W.Greatwood.	Wounded.	9th.	
	Lieut.F.W.Allbones.	"	9th.	
	2/Lt.F.W.Smith.	"	9th	
	2/Lt.R.J.Godfrey.	"	9th	
	2/Lt.D.C.Hodgson.	"	9th	
	2/Lt.F.J.Hansell.	"	9th	
	2/Lt.G.Tolhurst.	"	10th	
	2/Lt.S.G.Knight.	"	10th	
	2/Lt.B.Jevons.	"	10th	
8th Somerset L.I.	2/Lt.C.H.Thornton.	Missing.	9th	
	2/Lt.J.H.B.Gegg.	Wounded.	11th	
	2/Lt.H.C.Frost.	"	11th	
4th Middlesex.	Maj.A/Lt-Col. W.I.Webb-Bowen.	"	9th	
	Capt.C.G.Moran.	"	10th	
	2/Lt.A/Capt. D.Cutbush.	Killed.	10th	
	2/Lt.A.C.Terrell.	Wounded.	10th	
	2/Lt.J.C.Lyal.	Wounded.	10th	At Duty.
	2/Lt.A.D.Trowell.	"	10th	
	2/Lt.W.E.Stockley.	"	10th	
	Lt.A/Capt. S.A.Willis.	"	11th	At Duty.
	2/Lt.H.M.Williams.	"	11th	
	2/Lt.J.H.Hodgson.	"	11th	
10th York & Lancs.	Capt.E.G.J.Fairnie,	Wounded	11th	
63rd M.G.Company.	2/Lt.E.Hemsoll.	Wounded.	9th	
111th Inf. Brigade.				
10th Royal Fusiliers.	2/Lt.L.H.J.Herridge.	Wounded.	9th	
	2/Lt.H.L.Betts.	"	9th	
	2/Lt.C.M.Jenkin.	"	9th	
	Maj.A/Lt-Col. C.E.Rice.	"	10th	
	Capt.C.F.A.Warner.	"	10th	
	Lt.A/Capt.G.R.St John.	"	10th	
	2/Lt.P.G.Twyman.	"	10th	
	2/Lt.H.S.Redding.	"	10th	
	2/Lt.M.R.Fuller.	Killed.	11th	
	Lt.A/Capt.F.W.S. Shutes .	Wounded.	11th	
	2/Lt.C.R.H.Heywood,	"	11th	
	2/Lt.C.W.Mollison,	"	11th	9th London Rgt.attd.
13th Royal Fusiliers.	2/Lt.H.V.Day.	Killed.	9th	
	Capt.J.E.Walker.	Wounded.	9th	
	Lieut.F.M.M.Troup.	Killed.	10th	
	Lieut.P.C.F.Gibson.	Killed.	10th	
	2/Lt.W.Davies.	Killed.	10th	
	2/Lt.A/Capt.D.S. Harding,M.C.	Wounded & missing believed killed.	10th	
	2/Lt.T.S.Yandle.	Wounded & missing believed killed.	10th	
	2/Lt.C.D.Thompson.	Wounded.	10th	

Contd.

	Officer Casualties. Name.	Nature.	Date.	Remarks.
111th Inf. Brigade.			Apl.	
13th Royal Fusiliers.	2/Lt.Pearson W.D.	Wounded.	10th	
	2/Lt.T.J.C.Munford.	"	10th	
	2/Lt.R.S.Harrison.	"	10th	
	2/Lt.C.F.Bishop.	"	10th	
	2/Lt.S.W.A.Tubb.	"	10th	
13th Kings Royal Rifles.	Capt.E.W.Webster.	Killed.	9th	
	2/Lt.H.Cairns.	Wounded.	9th	
	2/Lt.J.D.C.Beaver.	"	10th	
	2/Lt.H.B.English.	"	10th	
	2/Lt.A.H.Dawe.	Killed.	11th	
	Capt.& Adjt. F.Fisher,M.C.	Wounded.	11th	
	Lt.H.E.Milliken.	"	11th	
	2/Lt.T.W.Penhale.	"	11th	
	2/Lt.J.N.Evans-Jackson.	"	11th	
	2/Lt.F.S.Pemberton.M.C.	"	11th	At Duty.
	Lt.A/Capt. J.W.N.Dorrington.	"	12th	At Duty.
	2/Lt.F.Atkinson.	"	12th	At Duty.
13th Rifle Brigade.	Capt. J.W.Bowyer.	Killed.	10th	
	2/Lt.W.E.Hobday.	Wounded.	11th	
	2/Lt.W.J.Carlile.	"	11th	
	2/Lt.P.J.Spooner.	"	11th	
	2/Lt.J.C.Reepmaker.	"	11th	
	2/Lt.N.N.Wardlaw.	"	11th	
111th M.G.Company.	Lt.C.A.Robinson.	Killed.	9th	
	2/Lt.F.R.Arnold.	Wounded.	9th	
	2/Lt.F.E.Click.	"	9th	
112th Inf. Brigade.				
11th R.Warwicks.	Capt.E.L.Routh,M.C.	Wounded.	10th.	
	Lieut.A.G.Jenkins.	Wounded.	10th	
	2/Lt.H.E.Surplice.	"	10th	
	2/Lt.E.E.Brett.	"	10th	
	2/Lt.P.R.Brown.	"	10th	
	2/Lt.R.W.T.Thorowgood.	"	11th	
	Lieut.F.H.Layman.	"	11th	
	2/Lt.J.W.Alabaster.	"	11th	
	2/Lt.R.C.Leeson.	"	11th	
8th E.Lancs.	Capt. R.C.Beattie.	Wounded	10th	
	2/Lt.A.H.Parks.	"	10th	
	2/Lt.L.Prada.	"	10th	
	Lieut.C.D.Haywood.	"	10th	
	2/Lieut.C.M.Heard.	" & Missing.	10th	
	2/Lt.C.L.Taylor.	Wounded.	10th	At Duty.
	Capt. F.Edmondson.	Missing.	11th	
	Capt.E.M.Wright.	Missing.	11th	
	Lieut.M.Forman.	Died of Wounds.	11th	2/Lt.in Army List.
	2/Lt.M.G.Loudon.	Wounded	11th	
	2/Lt.G.P.Raeburn.	Died of Wounds.	11th	
	2/Lt.H.S.Webb.	Wounded.	11th	

Contd/

	Officer Casualties. Name.	Nature.	Date.	Remarks.
112th Inf. Brigade.			Aprl.	
10th L.N.Lancs.	2/Lt.D.C.Logan.	Wounded.	9th	
	Capt.H.St.H.Peskett.	"	10th	
	2/Lt.R.Cliffe.	"	10th	(In Army List 'Cliff')
	2/Lt.R.E.Quesnil.	"	10th	(Not in Army List)
	Lt.K.C.Watson.	Killed.	11th	
	2/Lt.J.Goodman.	Killed.	11th	
	2/Lt.G.Parker.	Killed.	11th	
	2/Lt.E.Ibbotson.M.C.	Killed.	11th	
	2/Lt.W.B.Waye.	Wounded.	11th	
	2/Lieut.W.W.Deacon.	Wounded.	11th	5th Kings Own Lancs. attd.
	2/Lt.J.P.Sheridan.	Wounded.	11th	1st Bn.L.N.L. in Army List.
	2/Lt.H.Bracewell.	"	11th	6th Bn.Lancs. Fusrs.attd.
	2/Lieut.W.E.Crossley.	"	11th	Not in Army List.
6th Bedford Rgt.	2/Lt.H.C.Iredale.	Wounded.	9th	In index in Army List only.
	Lieut.G.H.Shaw.	Killed.	10th	In Army List as 2/Lieut.
	2/Lt.J.D.Forman.	Wounded.	10th	
	2/Lt.F.W.Hedges.	"	10th	
	2/Lt.H.A.L.Pattison.	"	10th	
	2/Lt.S.H.Davidson.	"	10th	
	2/Lt.F.G.Thompson.	Killed.	11th	
112th Machine G.Co.	Lieut. R.C.Wace.	Wounded.	10th	
	2/Lt. J.S.Penman.	"	11th	
	2/Lt.W.V.Baker.	"	11th	At Duty.
Divisional Troops.				
152nd Field Coy.RE.	Capt.A/Maj.W.F. Hanna.M.C.	Wounded.	11th	
9th N.Staffs.	2/Lt.R.H.F.Coleman.	Wounded.	10th	At Duty.
Northampton Yeo.	Lieut. A.F.Chaplin.	Killed.	10th	
	Capt. J.G.Lowther. M.C.	Wounded.	11th.	11th Hussars attd.
R.A.M.C.	Capt. G.R.Plaister.	Killed.	11th	attd.10th York & Lancs.
	Capt. R.A.W.Procter.	Wounded.	10th.	attd. 13th Royal Fusrs.

Appendix A

SECRET

ESTIMATED CASUALTIES UP TO

12 Noon 13th April, 1917.

	Offrs.	O.R.
63rd Inf. Bde. H.Q.		
8th Lincolns.	4	150
8th Somersets.	2	100
4th Middlesex.	6	200
10th York & Lancs.	3	200
111th Inf. Bde.H.Q.		
10th R. Fusrs.	12	250
13th " "	14	350
13th K.R.R.C.	11	200
13th Rif. Bde.	7	300
112th Inf. Bde.H.Q.		
11th R.Warwicks.	7	150
8th E.Lancs.	10	150
10th L.N.Lancs.	15	200
6th Bedfords.	5	150
9th N. Staffs.		
Machine Gun Corps.	8	100
	104	2500

APPENDIX B

OFFICER CASUALTIES. LIST No 1.

63rd Inf.Bde.	Killed.	Missing.	Wounded.	Remarks.
8th Lincolns.			9	
8th Somersets		1.	2	
4th Middlesex Regt.	1		9	2 at Duty.
10th Yorks & Lancs.			1	
63rd M.G.Coy.			1	
TOTAL BRIGADE.	1	1.	22.	
111th Inf.Bde.				
10th Royal Fusiliers.	1		11	
13th Royal Fusiliers.	4	2 ø	7	ø Wounded believed kille
13th Kings Royal Rifle Corps	2		10	3 at Duty
13th Rifle Brigade.	1		5	
111th Machine Gun Coy.	1		2	
TOTAL BRIGADE.	9	2	35	
112th Inf.Bde.				
11th Royal Warwicks.			9	
8th East Lancs.	2ø	3x	7	1 at Duty ø Died of wounds. x wounded & missing (1)
10th Loyal North Lancs.	4		9	
6th Bedfords.	2		5	
112th Machine Gun Coy			3	1 at Duty.
TOTAL BRIGADE.	8	3	33	
Divisional Troops.				
152nd Field Coy.R.E.			1	
9th North Staffs (Pioneers)			1	at Duty.
R.A.M.C.	1		1	
Northampton Yeomanry.	1		1	
	2		4	
T O T A L.	20	6	94 x	x includes 8 at duty.

120

Remarks Column addenda to list No 1

37th DIVISION.

	Officer Casualties.	Remarks.
63rd Inf.Bde.		
8th Lincolns.	Lieut.F.W.Allbone.	2/Lt Lincoln Regt.
	2/Lt F.W.SMITH	5th Battn
	2/Lt.F.JHansell	11thBn Training Reserve.
	2/Lt.G.Tolhurst.	5th Battn.
	2/Lt.S.G.Knight.	4th "
	2/Lt.B.JEVONS	Lincolnshire Regt.
8th Somerset.L.I.	2/Lt.C.H.Thornton.	West Somerset Yeomanry.
	2/Lt J.H.BGegg	Attd Somerset.L.I.
	2/Lt.H.C.Frost.	-do-
4th Middlesex.	Capt.C.G.Morgan.	Attd Middlesex Regt.
	2Lt a/Capt D.Cutbush.	5th Battalion.
	2/Lt.A.C.Terrell	5th "
	2/Lt.W.E.Stockley	6th "
111th Inf.Bde.		
10th Royal Fusiliers.	2/Lt.H.L.Betts.	Attd Royal Fusiliers
	2/Lt.C.M.Jenkin.	City of London Rough Riders.
	Maj.A/Lt-Col.C.E.Rice.	Scottish Horse.
	Capt.C.F.A.Warner.	Lt.Royal Fusiliers.
13th Royal Fusiliers.	2/Lt.H.S.Redding.	Army List incorrect RODDING.
	Capt.J.E.Walker.	Attd Royal Fusiliers
	Lieut.F.M.M.Troup	Royal Fusiliers
	Lieut.P.C.F.Gibson.	31st Bn Training Res
	2/Lt.W.Davies.	Attd Royal Fusiliers
	2/Lt C.D.Thompson	5th Battalion.
	2/Lt Pearson.W.D.	Not in Army List
	2/Lt T.J.C.Munford	Attd Royal Fusiliers
	2/Lt S.W.A.Tubb	Not in Army List.
13th Kings Royal Rifles	2/Lt.J.D.C.Beaver	Attd.K.R.R.C.
	Lt.A/Capt.J.W.N.Dorrington	2/Lt 6th Bn.
13th Rifle Brigade.	2/Lt W.E.Hobday.	Special list.
	2/Lt W.J.Carlile.	Rifle Brigade.
	2/Lt P.J.Spooner	Army List incorrect B.J.
112th Inf.Bde.		
11th Royal Warwicks.	2/Lt.P.R.Brown.	Attd Warwickshire Rgt
	Lt.F.H.Layman	-do-
	2/Lt R.C.Leeson.	-do-
8th E.Lancs.	2/Lt L.Prada.	Not in Army List
	Lt.C.D.Haywood.	Attd.E.Lancs Regt
	2/Lt C.N.Heard	-do-
	2/Lt.C.L.Taylor	3rd R.
	Capt.F.Edmondson	Attd E.Lancs Regt.
	Capt.E.M.Wright.	2/Lt 5th Bttn.

	Officer Casualties.	Remarks.
8th E.Lancs.	2/Lt.M.G.Loudon.	3rd Battalion.
	2/Lt.H.S.Webb.	4/East Surrey Regt. Attd
10th L.N.Lancs.		
	2/Lt.D.C.Logan.	5th Bn.
	2/Lt.R.Cliffe.	4th R.E.Lancs Regt.
	2/LT. J.GOODMAN	5th Bn. R.Lanc Regt
	2/Lt.G.Parker	4th Bn.
	2/Lt.W.B.Waye	4th Bn.
6th Bedford Rgt.		
	Lieut.N.H.Shaw (g)	5th Battalion.
	2/Lt.H.A.L.Pattison.	Attd Bdfordshire Regt
	2/Lt.F.G.Thompson.	7th Battalion.

SUBJECT: Casualties. 37th Divn. No.190/149A.

Third Army "A".
VIth Corps "A"
XVIII Corps "A".

It is regretted that the additional information in accompanying list was not included in LIST No.1 sent to you yesterday.

S Duncan Captn
for AA&QMG

Major General.

16/4/17.
GR.

Commanding 37th Division.

APPENDIX D

ESTIMATED CASUALTIES. 25/4/17 up to Noon.

	Officers.	O.Ranks.
8th Lincolns.	10	300
8th Somerset L.I.	14	300
4th Middlesex.	10	250
10th York & Lancs.	18	300
63rd M.G. Coy.	4	50
10th R. Fusiliers.	9	200
13th -do-	2	50
13th K.R.R.C.	5	150
13th Rifle Brigade.	6	300
111th M.G. Co.	1	25
11th R. Warwicks.	8	250
8th E. Lancs.	8	250
10th L.N. Lancs.	6	200
6th Bedfords.	6	200
112th M.G. Coy.	-	12
	10~~5~~7	2837

APPENDIX C.

List No.1.

37th D I V I S I O N.

	Date	Killed.		Wounded		Missing		T O T A L			
		Ofrs.	O.R.	Ofrs.	O.R.	Ofrs.	O.R.	Ofrs.	O.R.	Ofrs.	O.R.
63rd Inf. Bde											
8th Lincolns	9.4.17		4	6	22			6	26)		
	10.4.17		12	3	69		8	3	89)		
	11.4.17		8		53		12		73)	9	210
	12.4.17		3		18		1		22)		
8th Somerset L.I.	9.4.17		3		10	1		1	13)		
	10.4.17		14		39		3		56)	3	103
	11.4.17		9	2	22		3	2	34)		
4th Middlesex	9.4.17		2	1	17			1	19)		
	10.417	1	6	5 1 @ duty	88		12	6	114)	10	223
	11.4.17		6	3 1 @ duty	72		12	3	90)		
10th York &L	9.4.17		8		34				42)		
	10.4.17				47				47)	1	165
	11.4.17			1	45			1	45)		
	12.4.17				27		4		31)		
63rd M.G.Coy.	9.4.17			1	9			1	8)		
	10.4.17				6				6)	1	16
	11.4.17		1		1				2)		
T O T A L		1	78	22	578	1	61			24	717
111th Inf. Bde											
10th R.Fuslrs.	9.4.17		6	3	46			3	52)		
	10.4.17		20	5	51		48	5	119)	12	238
	11.4.17	1	19	3	23		25	4	67)		
13th R.Fuslrs	9.4.17	1	10	1	62 1 at duty		15	8	77)		
	10.4.17	3	21	6	104	2 Wd. Believed killed	12	11	137)	13	281
	11.4.17		11		51		5		67)		
13th K.R.R.C.	9.4.17	1	5	1	18		2	2	25)		
	10.417		7	2	73		13	2	93)		
	11.4.17	1	14	5 1 at duty	70		7	6	91)	12	212
	12.4.17			2 at duty	1		2	2	3)		
13th R.Bde.	9.4.17		2		19				21)		
	10.4.17	1	2		28			1	30)	6	180
	11.4.17		13	5	87		29	5	129)		
111th M.G.Coy.	9.4.17	1	1	2	3			3	4)		
	10.4.17				3				3)	3	15
	11.4.17		2		6				8)		
T O T A L		9	133	35	635	2	158			46	926

List No.1. Contd.

	Date	Killed. Ofrs.	Killed. O.R.	Wounded. Ofrs.	Wounded. O.R.	Missing. Ofrs.	Missing. O.R.	TOTAL Ofrs.	TOTAL O.R.	Ofrs.	O.R.
112th Inf.Bde.											
11th R.Warwicks.	9.4.17		1		12				13)		
	10.4.17		14	5	35		4	5	53)		
	11.4.17		5	4	86		10	4	101)	9	183
	12.4.17.				15		1		16)		
8th E.Lancs.	9.4.17.		3		8		1		12)		
	10.4.17.		9	5 1 @ duty.	37	1 Wnd.	1	6	47)	12	162
	11.4.17.	2	5	2	81	2	17	6	103)		
10th L.N.Lancs.	9.4.17.		5	1	16		2	1	23)		
	10.4.17.			3				3	)		
	11.4.17.	4	26	5	180 2 @ duty.		34	9	240)	13	263
6th Bedfords.	9.4.17.		12	1	20			1	32)		
	10.4.17.	1	3	4	17		3	5	23)	7	183
	11.4.17.	1	17		83		9	1	109)		
	12.4.17.				19				19)		
112th M.G.Co.	9.4.17.				6		1		7)		
	10.4.17.			1	9			1	9)		
	11.4.17.		7	2 1 @ duty	16			2	23)	3	39
112th T.M.Bty.	9.4.17.		2		2				4)		
	10.4.17.		1				2 Believed Wnd.		3)		7
TOTAL		8	110	33	642	3	85			44	837
Divl.Troops.											
152 Fld.Co.RE.	11.4.17.			1	2			1	2)		
153 " " "	10.4.17.				2				2)		
	11.4.17.				3				3)	1	10
154 " " "	11.4.17.				3				3)		
37th Signal Co.	11.4.17.				4				4)		
Wireless Depot Co.attd. 37th Sig.Co.	11.4.17.				2				2)		6
9th N.Staffs.	10.4.17.		2	1@ duty.	7			1	9)		
	11.4.17.				2				2)	1	12
	14.4.17.				1				1)		
R.A.M.C. ~~48th Fd. Amb.~~	10.4.17.			1				1	)		
	11.4.17.	1						1	)		
48th Fd. Amb.	12.4.17.				1				1)	2	17
49th " "	11.4.17.				3				3)		
	12.4.17.				7				7)		
	13.4.17.		2		4				6)		
Northampton Yeo.	10.4.17.	1						1	)	2	
	11.4.17.			1				1	)		
TOTAL.		2	4	4	41					6	45

16/4/17

[signature] Major General,
Commanding 37th Division.

List No 2.

37th D I V I S I O N.

	Date.	Killed. Off	Killed. O.Rks	Wounded. Offr	Wounded. O.R.	Missing. Offr	Missing. O.Rks	Name of Officers
63rd Inf Bde								
8th Lincolns	16-4-17	-	1	-	1	-	-	
10th Y & Lancs	13-4-17	-	-	1	-	-	-	2nd Lt CAJ Nicholson, Middx Rgt attached.
111th Inf Bde								
10th R.Fusrs	16-4-17.	-	-	-	1	-	-	
13th R.Fusrs.	16-4-17.	-	-	-	1.	-	-	
13th K.R.R.C.)	9-4-17.	-	-	-	1	-	2.	
)	11-4-17.	-	-	-	6	-	1.	
13th R.Bde	9-4-17.	-	-	-	-	-	1.	
112th Inf Bde.								
8th N.Lancs.)	11-4-17.	-	-	1	-	-	-	
)	16-4-17.	-	-	-	1	-	-	2nd Lt R.J. Phennah diagnosed shell shock wounded No 6 Staty Hp Certificate OC unit atthd
6th Bedfords.	16-4-17.	-	1	-	-	-	-	
9th N.Staffs.	16-4-17.	-	-	-	1	-	-	
TOTAL.		-	2.	2.	12.	-	4.	

A M E N D M E N T T O L I S T No 1.

DELETE THE FOLLOWING.

		KILLED. O.Ranks.	WOUNDED. O.Ranks.	MISSING. O.Ranks.
111th Inf Bde.) 13th K.R.R.C.)	9-4-17	1.	-	-
" "	10-4-17	-	-	3.

AMENDMENT TO LIST No 1 REPORTED BY 37th DIVISION WIRE No A/909 D/17-4-1917.

D E L E T E.

	MISSING. Officers.	REMARKS.
63rd Infantry Brigade. 8th Somerset L.I.	1.	2/20 C.H. THORNTON Traced to Base Hospital [illegible] 14.

18th April 1917.
[illegible]

Major General.
Commanding 37th Division.

List No: 3.

37th DIVISION.

	Date	Killed. Ofrs.	Killed. O.R.	Wounded Ofrs.	Wounded O.R.	Missing Ofrs.	Missing O.R.	Name of Officer.
111th Inf. Bde.								
13th Rifle Bde.	11.4.17		3 ✗					
Divl. Troops.								
9th N.Staffs (Pioneers)	18.4.17			1 (at duty)	7 (3 at duty)			2/Lieut. A.B.L. GODSON att. N. Staffs Regt.
		-	3	1	7	-	-	

Further amendment to LIST No: 1.

Delete

111th Inf. Bde. 13th Rifle Bde	11.4.17						3 ✗	✗ Same men inaccurate first report.

19.4.17.

Major-General.
Commanding 37th Division.

List No. 4

37th DIVISION.

111th Inf. Bde.	Date.	Killed. Offrs.	O.R.	Wounded. Offrs.	O.R.	Missing Offrs.	O.R.
13th Rifle Bde.	11/4/17.				1		
Divl. Troops.							
9th N. Staffs.	19/4/17.				2		
		-	-	-	3	-	-

Major General.
Commanding 37th Division.

21/4/17.
GR.

37th DIVISION.

Total estimated Casualties(o.r. to nearest 50 excluding M.G.Cos.) of Infantry Battalions and Machine Gun Companies from 22nd - 30th April, 1917.

63rd Inf. Bde.	Offrs.	O.R.	Offrs.	O.R.
8th Lincolns.	12	300		
8th Somerset L.I.	18	300		
4th Middlesex.	10	300		
10th York & Lancs.	15	300		
63rd M.G.Coy.	5	40	60	1240
111th Inf. Bde.				
10th R. Fuers.	9	300		
13th -do-	3	200		
13th K.R.R.C.	5	150		
13th Rifle. Bde.	7	300		
111th M.G. Co.	1	30	25	980
112th Inf. Bde.				
11th Warwicks.	11	200		
8th E.Lancs.	7	200		
10th L.N.Lancs.	8	200		
6th Bedfords.	11	250		
112th M.G.Co.	-	15	37	865
		TOTAL.	122	3085

Affaudirott

37th DIVISION.

Statement of accurate Casualties for period 21st - 30th April 1917. (Lists 5 - 12.)

	Officers.							Other Ranks.									
	Killed	Wounded	Missing	Believed K.	W.	P.	Total	Killed	Wounded	Missing	Believed K.	W.	P.	Total	Total C'lties	Total Bde C'lties	Total Divl. C'slties.
63rd Inf.Bde																	
8th Lincolns	2	13 z	2	1	1	-	17	25	149	119	27	92	-	293	310		
8th Somerset L.I.	4	15 x	-	-	-	-	19	16	191	99	22	68	9	306	325		
4th Middlesex	2	7 x	1			1	10	20	168	98	36	48	14	286	296		
10th York & L's	4	17 x	1	1	-	-	22	29	226	128	55	55	18	383	405		
63rd M.G. Coy	1	2	1	1	-	-	4	7	28	-	-	-	-	35	39	1375.	

z 1 at duty 2 W & M. x 1 at duty.

	Killed	Wounded	Missing	Believed K.	W.	P.	Total	Killed	Wounded	Missing	Believed K.	W.	P.	Total	Total C'lties	Total Bde C'lties	Total Divl. C'slties.
111th Inf.Bde																	
10th R. Fusilrs	3	8 x	-	-	-	-	11	43	194	17	17	-	-	254	265		
13th "	2	4 y	2	2	-	-	8	41	194	94	16	18	60	329	337		
13th K.R.R.C.	4	5 z	-	-	-	-	9	35	134 y	7	3	1	3	176	185		
13th Rifle Bde	2	8	-	-	-	-	10	28	211	19	12	7	-	258	268		
111th M.G. Coy	-	1	-	-	-	-	1	6	25 x	-	-	-	-	31	32	1087.	

x 1 at duty. y 1 previously at duty z(1 attd T.M. Bty (1 prvsly at duty — y 1 at duty. x includes 2 K.S.L.I. attached 111 T.M. Bty

	Killed	Wounded	Missing	Believed K.	W.	P.	Total	Killed	Wounded	Missing	Believed K.	W.	P.	Total	Total C'lties	Total Bde C'lties	Total Divl. C'slties.
112th Inf.Bde																	
11th R.Warwick	2	7 x	1	-	1	-	10	36	187	59	-	-	-	282	292		
8th East Lancs	-	7 y	-	-	-	-	7	33	127	27	-	-	-	187	194		
10th L.N.Lancs	1	6 z	1	-	-	-	8	19	113	52	-	-	-	184	192		
6th Bedfords	3	10 %	-	-	-	-	13	48	176	57	5	-	-	281	294		
112th M.G. Coy	-	-	-	-	-	-	-	5	21	2	2	-	-	28	28	1000.	

x 1 at duty y 1 at duty 1 W & M. z 1 W & M. % 1 W & M. 1 previously at duty.

	Killed	Wounded	Missing	Believed K.	W.	P.	Total	Killed	Wounded	Missing	Believed K.	W.	P.	Total	Total C'lties	Total Bde C'lties	Total Divl. C'slties.
Divl Troops																	
37th Div.Arty	2 x	-	-	-	-	-	2	1	1	-	-	-	-	2	4		
37th Divl Engrs	1	5	-	-	-	-	6	6	25 x	-	-	-	-	33	39		
37th Signal Coy	-	-	-	-	-	-	-	1	10	-	-	-	-	11	11		

x Died of wounds. — x 3 at duty.

(Continued).

37th Division.

Statement of accurate Casualties for period 21st - 30th April 1917 (Lists 5 - 12)

	Officers.							Other ranks									
	Killed	Wounded	Missing	Believed K.	W.	P.	Total.	Killed	Wounded	Missing	Believed K.	W.	P.	Total	Total C'ltles	Total Divl Troops C'ltles	Total Divl C'ltles.
Brought Forward	33	115	9	5	2	1	157	401	2180	778	195	289	104	3359	3516	3462	
Divl Troops (Contd)																	
9th N. Staffs.	1	5 X	-	-	-	-	6	7	60 X	-	-	-	-	67	73		
R.A.M.C.	1 X	2 Y.	-	-	-	-	3	3	15 Y.	-	-	-	-	18	21		
Chaplains	1	1	-	-	-	-	2	-	-	-	-	-	-	-	2		
ASC & MMP	-	-	-	-	-	-	-	1	2	-	-	-	-	3	3	153	3615
Totals.	36	123	9	5	2	1	168	412	2257	778	195	289	104	3447	3615	3615.	

X Died of Wounds.

X 2 at duty
Y 1 at duty

X 8 at duty
Y. 1 at duty.

Instructions regarding War Diaries and Intelligence Summaries are contained in F. S. Regs., Part II. and the Staff Manual respectively. Title pages will be prepared in manuscript.

WAR DIARY
or
INTELLIGENCE SUMMARY.
(Erase heading not required.)

Army Form C. 2118.

Administrative Staff
H.Q. 37 Division

Vol 22

Place	Date	Hour	Summary of Events and Information	Remarks and references to Appendices
	1917			
LIGNEREUIL	May 1		Visit to Corps obtaining authority to bring up all reinforcements from Depot: visit there & arranging for them to come by march route: visit to Bdes: casualty list No 10: railhead moves to TINQUES exchanging parks with 4th Div: orders for withdrawing winter clothing.	
	2		Administrative conference of Q Staff with DADOS: visit to refilling points: brilliant weather continues very dusty: visit to THIRD ARMY on question of officers	
	3		Preparing & issuing refilling and A & Q notes: going round each battn checking rolls of officers with adjutants and clearing up doubtful points: Casualty list No 11: arranging for Canteen & Laundry lorries to be at DHQ.	
	4		Visit to Div Depot deciding on questions of policy for reinforcements: officers to be sent up at once other ranks after 24 hours clear at Depot: visit to Bdes going into question of lost Vickers & Lewis guns & equipment generally.	
	5		Arranging move of 154 Field Coy to St POL: re-arranging area in consequence of Corps school taking over GIVENCHY LE NOBLE: making out lists of captured material: preparing administrative map of area & going round area obtaining necessary materials.	
	6		Visit to Corps on question of officers leaving rolls by battns showing position of all officers on strength: engaged on honours & awards: leave to PARIS for various officers.	
	7		Casualty list No 12: making out statement of accurate casualties (Appendix A): arranging for inspection 1st Line transport by O.C. train & ADVS: visit to railhead: visit to Div Artny	Appendix A
	8		Arranging for Lt GUNSON to be trained ammn railhead as Divl ammn offr: preparing scheme for divisional ammn dumps etc: gully: engaged Honours & awards	
	9		Transport show at DHQ	
	10		Visit to Corps & 3 Inf Bdes: further transport inspections: fine weather continues: arranging for Col. 700 gall motor lorry tanks to supply additional water	
	11		ADVS leaves divn on promotion to DDVS XI Corps: engaged on Honours & Rewards courts martial & promotions	
	12		Engaged on question of officers including cross posting C.O's: visit to XVIII Corps Laundry PAS.	
	13		Officers chargers competition & jumping show D.H.Q.	
	14		Riding round area: engaged on ammunition scheme: casualty list No 13: revising pending F.G.C.M proceedings	
	15		Warning recd that on 18th Divn will come under VI Corps & relieve 56 Divn in line relief to be completed by 21st: visit to Arras to 56 Divn discussing relief: visit to VI Corps.	
	16		Visit to 56 Divn at Arras inspecting dumps etc: arranging bus for various administrative officers to exchange views with their opposite Nos of 56 Divn: asking for extra tents from Corps for DAC.	
	17		Lecture by Corps Comdr at DHQ on battle of ARRAS: preparing march table for "G" orders: supply and transport arrangements for move including fresh refilling points	
	18		Railhead moves tomorrow to ARRAS: 63rd group march to SIMENCOURT: 111 to BERNEVILLE 112 to GOUVES & MONTENESCOURT: visit to area & on to ARRAS & ACHICOURT: arranging about tentage with 56 Divn	

A5834 Wt. W4973 750,000 8/16 J.J.K. & Co. Ltd. Forms/C.2118/13.

Instructions regarding War Diaries and Intelligence Summaries are contained in F. S. Regs., Part II. and the Staff Manual respectively. Title pages will be prepared in manuscript.

WAR DIARY
or
INTELLIGENCE SUMMARY.
(*Erase heading not required.*)

Administrative Staff
HQ. 37 Division

Army Form C. 2118.

Place	Date	Hour	Summary of Events and Information	Remarks and references to Appendices
WARLUS	19		112th Bde move up to support trenches.	
"	20.		112th Bde move up to take over front line from 56th Division. 111th Bde group moves up to support line. 63rd Bde billeted in DAINVILLE and ACHICOURT.	
ARRAS	21		Relieve 56th Div. HdQrs who go back to occupy our recent HdQrs at WARLUS. 2 Bns 63rd Bde move into ARRAS.	
"	22.		Leave to England for various officers and men is opened. Capt Sheringham (A.D.C.) leaves for England to attend Staff course at Clare College, Cambridge.	
"	23.		Forward area visited to find out if any bodies still remain unburied after recent fighting. a few still remain. Burial party is working daily until the work is completed.	
"	24		NIL.	
"	25		Transport lines of 3 Brigades moved back just WEST of ACHICOURT. Improvement of fixing and carrying entrenching tool submitted to Div. HdQrs for approval.	
"	26.		Visit D.D.R at AVESNES on the question of making up horse deficiencies as soon as possible.	
"	27.		NIL	
"	28.		112th Bde on being relieved by 111th Bde less 2 MG sections move back to ACHICOURT billets. AA+QMG and D.A.QMG visit HdQrs concerning relief of Division with 61st Division.	
	29.		NIL	
	30.		NIL	
	31		112th Bde move to DUISANS. 63rd Bde move from TILLOY to ARRAS. 52 L.D. horses are received for the Division from AUBIGNY. Very good stamp of horses.	
	1		63rd Bde group move to BEAUFORT - MANIN area.	
LIGNEREUIL	2		111th Bde move to AMBRINES area. Div. HdQrs move to LIGNEREUIL.	
	3		NIL	

D. Heneage? Capt.
DAAG 37 Division

A5834 Wt. W4973/M687 750,000 8/16 D. D. & L. Ltd. Forms/C.2118/13.

Vol 23

H.Q. Administrative Staff

37th Divn

June 1917

Instructions regarding War Diaries and Intelligence Summaries are contained in F. S. Regs., Part II. and the Staff Manual respectively. Title pages will be prepared in manuscript.

WAR DIARY
or
INTELLIGENCE SUMMARY.
(Erase heading not required.)

Administrative Staff
H.Q. 37 Divn

Army Form C. 2118.

Place	Date JUNE	Hour	Summary of Events and Information	Remarks and references to Appendices
ARRAS.	1		63rd Bde Group move to BEAUFORT – MANIN area	
LIGNEREUIL	2		111th Bde move to AMBRINES area. Divl Hdqrs moves to LIGNEREUIL	
	3		NIL	

A5834 Wt. W4973/M687 750,000 8/16 D. D. & L. Ltd. Forms/C.2118/13.

Army Form C. 2118.

Instructions regarding War Diaries and Intelligence Summaries are contained in F. S. Regs., Part II. and the Staff Manual respectively. Title pages will be prepared in manuscript.

WAR DIARY
or
INTELLIGENCE SUMMARY.
(Erase heading not required.)

Place	Date	Hour	Summary of Events and Information	Remarks and references to Appendices
IGNEREUIL	JUNE 4		9th N. Staffs ~~[illegible]~~ moved from BRYAS to PREDEFIN. 152 & 154 Field Coys. moved from ~~GAUCHIN - VERLOIGNT~~ to ECQUIRRE, 153 Field Coy from IZEL-LEZ-HAMEAU to GAUCHIN-VERLOIGNT. Administrative Orders for BOMY area published.	
	5		63rd Infy. Bgde. bussed to BEAUVOIS-CROIX area. 152 Field Coy moved to HEZECQUES, 153 to ECQUIRRE & 154 to VINCLY.	
	6		63rd Infy. Bgde. bussed to TANGRY-ANVIN area. 111th Infy Bgde. bussed from AMBRINES area to PERNES - BOYAVAL area.	
	7		111th Infy Bgde moved to BOMY area; 63rd Bgde to FRUGES area.	
	5?		112th Bgde. from IZEL-LEZ-HAMEAU area to VALHUON area. Following reinforcements arrive - 4th Mdx. 2 offs. 3 O.R., 10th Y&L 2 offs. 68 O.R., 10th R.F. 2 offs. 87 O.R., 13th R.F. 1 off. 59 O.R., 8th E Lancs. 1 off. 7 O.R., 10th L.N.L. 4 O.R.	
BOMY	8		112th Bgde. move to DELETTE-COYECQUES AREA. Following reinforcements arrive:- 4th Mdx. 10 O.R., 10th Y&L 79 O.R. 10th R.F. 44 O.R., 13th R.F. 15 O.R.	
	9		Following reinforcements arrive - 13th K.R.R. 1 off. 76 O.R. 13th R.B. 12 O.R. 11th Warwicks 94 O.R. 6th Beds. 2 offs. 12 O.R.	
	10		Divisional Employment Coy. under Major Christie join Division ~~[illegible]~~ relieves as many Class A men as possible. Lithento [illegible] extra-regimentally employed. Divisional Band takes part in La Fête Dieu procession.	
	11		Town Majors appointed for villages in the Area.	

A5834 Wt. W4973/M687 750,000 8/16 D. D. & L. Ltd. Forms/C.2118/13.

Instructions regarding War Diaries and Intelligence Summaries are contained in F. S. Regs., Part II. and the Staff Manual respectively. Title pages will be prepared in manuscript.

WAR DIARY
or
INTELLIGENCE SUMMARY.
(Erase heading not required.)

Army Form C. 2118.

Place	Date JUNE	Hour	Summary of Events and Information	Remarks and references to Appendices
BOMY	12th–14th		NIL	
	14th		A A & Q M G, C R E & G.S.O. 3 proceed on 10 days leave.	
	15th		D.A.Q.M.G returns from leave. 75 O R reinforcements arrive LILLERS.	
	16th		D.A.D.O.S proceeds on leave.	
	17th		112th Bde hold sports at CAPELLE-sur-la-LYS. Leave to England is suspended.	
	18th–19th		NIL	
	20th		Field companies commence to move. 9th N Staffs move to ROMBLY	
	21st		Presentation of medals in FRuges Square to Division by army commander. 9th N Staffs move to STEENBECQUE.	
	22nd		63rd Bde move to LIGNY by AIRE area. 9th N Staffs to VERTERUE and 3 Field Coys to CAUDESCURE.	
STEENBECQUE	23rd		Div^l H.Qrs move to STEENBECQUE. 63rd Bde move to STEENBECQUE area. 111th Bde to ISBERGUES area. 112th Bde to BOESEGHEM area. 9th N Staffs 3 Field Coys to LOCRE.	
LOCRE	24th		Brigades move to CAESTRE area. Div^l H.Qrs to LOCRE.	
	25th		Brigades move to LOCRE area. A.A. & Q.M.G & C.R.E. return from leave.	
	26th		G.O.C inspects men of Bdes who fell out during march on 24th inst.	
	27th		G.O.C continues inspection of men who fell out. BOMY cleared of all kit left behind when division moved. D.A.D.O.S returns from leave.	
	28th		Div^l front is considerably cut down. 2 Bns 63rd & 111th Bdes move up to line.	
	29th		Conference with area commandants to determine area for 63rd & 112th Bdes. ADVS returns from leave.	
DRANOUTRE	30th		Div^l H.Qrs move to DRANOUTRE & take over H.Qrs from 36th Division.) Railhead at HAEGERDOONE. Ammunition railhead at LINDENHOEK.	

R [illegible] for D A A [illegible]

A5834 Wt. W4973/M687 750,000 8/16 D. D. & L. Ltd. Forms/C.2118/13.

Nat Dairy

Administration Staff

[illegible]

NC-24

Administrative Staff
37th Div.

Army Form C. 2118.

Instructions regarding War Diaries and Intelligence Summaries are contained in F. S. Regs., Part II. and the Staff Manual respectively. Title pages will be prepared in manuscript.

WAR DIARY
or
INTELLIGENCE SUMMARY.
(Erase heading not required.)

Place	Date JULY.	Hour	Summary of Events and Information	Remarks and references to Appendices
DRANOUTRE	1st July		Visit by A.A.G. 2nd army. 9th North Staffs move to KEMMEL HILL. Railhead at BRULOOZE from tomorrow 2nd inst. From 4th inst horsed transport will draw direct from railhead.	
"	2nd		Visit by A.Q.M.G. ~~+ D.A.G.~~ & G IV Corps. Corps dump to start at LINDENHOEK. 63rd Bde less M G coy relieved and move to Nos 2 + 3 areas. Dumps (ammunition) handed over to 19th Div which are in our old area.	
"	3rd		63rd M.G. Coy on being relieved in front line, move to KEMMEL.	
"	4th		Visit to KEMMEL by the King during morning. Passes through DRANOUTRE and LOCRE to BAILLEUL in afternoon.	
"	5th		D.A.A.G. proceeds to England on 10 days leave.	
"	6th		36th Arty HdQrs on relief by 14th Arty HdQrs leave ULSTER CAMP. Visit by A & Q.M.G. 2nd army. Mobile Veterinary Section moves to DRANOUTRE from LOCRE. Notification received that Capt R M AIREY MC. D.A.Q.M.G. on relief will proceed to ENGLAND.	
"	7th		Lecture by Divl Gas officer on attachment to Box respirator.	
"	8th		Capt Landon MC. arrives to take over duties of D.A.Q.M.G.	
"	9th		Capt Airey MC. proceeds to England.	
"	10th		A A & Q M G visits area with Corps Q to decide what huts can be moved forward.	
"	11th 12th 13th		~~102~~ 111th Inf Bde goes back to DRANOUTRE. 63rd Bde go into the line and 112th Bde go in support.	
"	14th		Nil	
"	15th		DAAG returns from leave	
"	16th			
"	17th			
"	18th		Lecture and demonstration by Capt Dunwater on the Yukon pack. 63rd Inf Bde is relieved by 111th Bde in the line.	

J H Billiat Capt
for D.A.A.G. 37th Div.

Instructions regarding War Diaries and Intelligence Summaries are contained in F. S. Regs., Part II. and the Staff Manual respectively. Title pages will be prepared in manuscript.

WAR DIARY
or
INTELLIGENCE SUMMARY.
(Erase heading not required.)

Army Form C. 2118.

Place	Date JULY	Hour	Summary of Events and Information	Remarks and references to Appendices
DRANOUTRE	19th		247th M.G. Coy (Divl M G Coy) arrived with transport. Lt Col Jackson takes over command from Major Leach.	
	20th		1st Portuguese Railway Bn arrived in Divl Area on 18th inst and are rationed by Division	
	21-22		Nil	
	23rd		Capt Dunwaters lectures and demonstrates the Yukon pack to Trench mortar battery.	
	24th		Army Commander visits Divl ~~HdQrs~~.	
	25th		63rd Bde moves up into line and 112th Bde into support. L Special Coy RE is billeted in KEMMEL CHATEAU for special work in line. 153 Fd Coy and Company of 9th N Staffs ordered to move out of water catchment area. G.O.C. inspects agricultural [illegible] proceeding to FLETRE.	
	26th		111th Bde moves up into line. 112th Bde in support (KEMMEL). 63rd Bde at DRANOUTRE.	
	27th		Capt Shering has appointed staff captain 14th Bde.	
	28th		Authority for issue of rum to Bdes has to be obtained from Corps on all occasions.	
	29th		63rd Bde move into line and 111th Bde into support. All M G coys in the line with exception of 8 guns of 247th M G Coy.	
	30th		Nil	
	31st		Operations in which 63rd 111th and 1 Bn 112th are involved. Casualties so far estimated to roughly 11 officers and 350 OR.	

A5834 Wt. W4973/M687 750,000 8/16 D. D. & L. Ltd. Forms/C.2118/13.

War Diary

HQ Administrative Staff

37th Divn

Vol 25

17

Instructions regarding War Diaries and Intelligence Summaries are contained in F. S. Regs., Part II. and the Staff Manual respectively. Title pages will be prepared in manuscript.

WAR DIARY
or
INTELLIGENCE SUMMARY.
(Erase heading not required.)

Administrative Staff
37th Division

Army Form C. 2118.

Place	Date August	Hour	Summary of Events and Information	Remarks and references to Appendices
DRANOUTRE	1st		Supply train arrives very late. Supplies are drawn from railhead at 1.15 pm. An issue of rum is made to all troops not in billets or huts.	
	2nd		Issue of rum to all troops not in billets or huts. Visit by DDAG 9th Corps concerning employed men. 63rd Bde move to DRANOUTRE and 112th to KEMMEL. Supply train arrives railhead at 11 a.m.	
	3rd		10th York & Lancs come to DRANOUTRE and are relieved by 8th E LANCS.	
	4th		Issue of rum to whole division. 500 pairs of gum boots issued to Divl Arty.	
	5th		Warning order as to relieving 19 Div in next sector N. & being relieved by Australians making preliminary arrangements accordingly	
	6th		March table for Q operation order: visit to Corps & 19 Div: round new area: move of 112 Bde from KEMMEL area to Support Bde area 19 Div & coming under orders GOC 19	
	7th		Arranging for Claims Offr to act as Disbursing Offr 10–11 am. daily BAILLEUL station: Supply & transport arrangements for move; 111th Bde relieved in line & withdraw to KEMMEL area: 112 Bde take over front line in new sector: visit to 19 Div & round new area	
SCHERPENBERG CAMP near LOCRE	8th		63 Bde move to Support Bde area: HQ FAIRY HOUSE: DHQ move from ULSTER Camp DRANOUTRE to SCHERPENBERG Camp 1 mile N. of LOCRE: 111 Bde move to Reserve Bde area HQ LOCRE: Location list.	
	9th		Rearranging DHQ camp & making provision for Div artª to come in: suggesting 112 Bde who had brigaded transport SIEGE FARM should spread it out: arranging additional artª accomⁿ as 19 were leaving a bde & ½ DAC: applying for 111 Bde school remain in old area.	
	10th		DAQMG Capt Landon proceeds on leave: Div artª join Div & take over command of artª covering front: 19 Div leave Bde artª & 1 Sect DAC	
	11		Arranging daily supply 800 clean socks Bdes in line: supply arrangements for Bdes in line re rum and soda tablets: supply table for change of railhead to Brulooze 12th	
	12		Going round areas inspecting camps & transport lines: preparing scheme for improving DONCASTER Huts LOCRE	
	13		Arrangements for funeral Brig Genl Maclachlan GOC 112th Bde killed by sniper 11th: projected reliefs in line.	

A5834 Wt. W4973/M687 750,000 8/16 D. D. & L. Ltd. Forms/C.2118/13.

Instructions regarding War Diaries and Intelligence Summaries are contained in F. S. Regs., Part II. and the Staff Manual respectively. Title pages will be prepared in manuscript.

WAR DIARY
or
INTELLIGENCE SUMMARY.
(Erase heading not required.)

Administrative Staff
37th Division

Army Form C. 2118.

Place	Date	Hour	Summary of Events and Information	Remarks and references to Appendices
SCHERPEN-BERG CAMP M. LOCRE	Aug 14th		Orders for 63 Bde to relieve 112 in line 15/16: arranging issue 1400 pr new gum boots 63rd: issuing administrative instructions re relief	
	15th		Divn to extend line northwards 111 Bde to take over 19/20 from Bde of ~~[illegible]~~ 39 Divn: visit to them talking matters over: arranging site for Pioneers & Fld Coys 30th Divn in our area to work under C.E. Corps; Bde 30th Divn to take over LOCRE area 20th arranging for them to view to-day	
	16th		Arranging for move of 111 Bde to new line 19/20 & reconnoitring site for their new transport lines: G.O.C. receives former car back in exchange for present one	
	17th		Arranging supply of water for D.H.Q. by motor trailer from Loc: projected extension of Divnl line N cancelled for the present	
	18th		Going round area with heads of administrative services considering hutting & standing proposals for winter	
	19th		Orders issued for 112 to relieve 63 in line 21/22: scheme for making DONCASTER HUTS sanitary approved. Major CHRISTIE OC Divl Employment Coy to superintend.	
	20th		D.A.Q.M.G. returns from leave: leave allotment altered to CALAIS & consequently halved: working out fresh schemes: making suggestions for increasing the trench tramway system	
	21st		Owing to increase of night attacks by German aeroplanes issuing special instructions as to precautions re lights etc.	
	22nd		Special instructions for preventative measures against dysentery & issuing circular thereon & arranging for lectures in each unit: scheme for DONCASTER HUTS approved & arranging to move battn 111 to CORUNNA Camp: during night 112 relieve 63 in line latter moving to support area	
	23rd		Arrangements for handing over LA POLKA ammn siding to 30th Divn: for 10 M to visit B/123 guns in action: completing scheme for horse standings at BRULOOZE and 4 Batty wagon lines in vicinity.	
	24th		Owing to increasing number of dysentery cases special visits to units testing water tracing reinforcements as to introduction from Base depots.	
	25th		Making arrangements for accommodation in area M Special Coy RE & Tunnel Company: sandbag walls 18" high round tents in permanent camp to be built.	
	26th		111 Bde move to support area & 63 to reserve: transport lines are exchanged: Divn are defeated in officers cricket match v Corps H.Q.	

A5834 Wt. W4973/M687 750,000 8/16 D. D. & L. Ltd. Forms/C.2118/13.

Instructions regarding War Diaries and Intelligence Summaries are contained in F. S. Regs., Part II. and the Staff Manual respectively. Title pages will be prepared in manuscript.

WAR DIARY
or
INTELLIGENCE SUMMARY.
(Erase heading not required.)

37th Division Army Form C. 2118.

Place	Date	Hour	Summary of Events and Information	Remarks and references to Appendices
CHERPEN-BERG CAMP [illegible] LOCRE	Aug 27		Successful raids by Warwicks in night; issue of new appts to troops & art'y in line; owing to new huts for Div Art'y HQ being ready arranging for offices on S. side of hill to move round; orders for taking over extra bit of line northwards received.	
	28		111th Bde relieve 112th in front line latter withdrawing to support area; sailings have been suspended owing to stormy weather; visit to 39 Div discussing administrative arrangements on taking over portion of their area; bussing 63 Inf Bde to new area.	
	29		63 Bde take over line northwards up to Canal having the 2 front line battns & T.M. Batty; issuing administrative instructions & arranging for supply [illegible] from boats [illegible] food containers; arranging site for 63 Bde Transport by Cheapside close to Pioneer HQ & obtaining [illegible] tents	
	30		Leave still stopped owing to stormy weather; 19 Div ordered to complete work on RIDGE defences visit from them as to finding room for one Bde in KEMMEL-VIERSTRAAT area; visit to new area & arranging salvage work there; GOC inspects train coys.	
	31		Visit to DAC lines with CRE as to sites for winter standings; subsequent visit to Corps discussing the whole question of winter accommodation; visit from DDMS Sanitation on question of outbreak of dysentery; arranging visit from naval detachment.	

D. Duncan [illegible]
DA&QMG
37 Division

War Diary Sep. 1917

Vol 26 HQ Administrative Staff

37th Division

17

Instructions regarding War Diaries and Intelligence Summaries are contained in F. S. Regs., Part II. and the Staff Manual respectively. Title pages will be prepared in manuscript.

WAR DIARY
or
INTELLIGENCE SUMMARY.
(Erase heading not required.)

Army Form C. 2118.

Adqrs Administrative Staff 37th Division

Place	Date	Hour	Summary of Events and Information	Remarks and references to Appendices
SCHERPEN-BERG CAMP Nr. LOCRE	Sept 1		Orders rec'd to take over further sector N from 39 Div: to hand over present right sector to 30 Div: visit to 39 Div obt'd particulars as to what wld be handed over etc: visit from 30 Div giving them information about the sector they were taking over	
	2		Supply train very late arranging to take one day's preserved rations off Supply Col: new system of one day's fresh on Train in lieu of one day's preserved on Col: surveying site for Reserve batt'n Left Bde BOIS CARRE & obt'g tents & shelters from Corps: getting certain roads 2 way for traffic leading to new area to facilitate ration transport	
	3		111 Bde are relieved night 2/3 by Bde of 30 Div & withdraw to Support area: similarly 112 take over new right section from Bde of 39 Div: visiting neighbourhood VIERSTRAAT with 19 Div'n choosing sites for Pioneers & 2 Field Coys that Div'n: meeting naval party & conducting them to guides	
	4		Supervising return of naval party: conference with Corps Staff off'rs concerned CRE etc on whole question of winter accomodation hutting standings etc: visit to new sector arranging salvage scheme etc: owing to re arrangement Div area arranging accomodation for displaced units.	
	5		Conference with Corps as to accomodation for various extra outside units going round area and submitting scheme & sites: visit from 19 Div who in about 10 days were to relieve us & giving them information about area	
	6		19 Div adv'd HQ taken over from ours at SCHERPENBERG: going round area with 19 D.A.S.C explaining accomodation: Selecting sites for additional units in accordance with list sent by Corps & submitting suggestions: preparing & issuing administrative instructions re forthcoming relief of 63 by 111 Bde: all leave by BOULOGNE etc: supervising arrival another party sailor guests.	
	7		Supervising departure sailors: further engaged on accomodation scheme and as to moving our own DAC: visit to Corps on general accomodation in area: visit to 112 Bde arranging salvage & amm'n dumps forward area.	
	8		Relief of 63 in right section by 111 completed night 7/8: 63 withdraw to Support area: visit to 19 Div ST JANS CAPPEL obt'g information as to reserve div'l area: 30 Div ask for one batt'n IRISH HOUSE to be moved out: engaged working out table of moves for forthcoming withdrawal to reserve area: visit to Corps & 19 Div discussing same.	
	9		Further engaged on working out tables for relief of div'n by 19th & it was found 2 extra camps wld be reqd: visit to Corps explaining & obt'g tents: reconnoitring sites & arranging pitching of camps: preparing & issuing administrative instructions for move	

Instructions regarding War Diaries and Intelligence Summaries are contained in F. S. Regs., Part II. and the Staff Manual respectively. Title pages will be prepared in manuscript.

WAR DIARY
or
INTELLIGENCE SUMMARY.
(*Erase heading not required.*)

Army Form C. 2118.

Hdqrs Administrative Staff 37th Division

Place	Date	Hour	Summary of Events and Information	Remarks and references to Appendices
CHERPENBERG CAMP Nr LOCRE	10th		63 Bde march to Mt KOKEREELE area: supervising traffic arrangements: visit from Q 19 Divn as to transport lines; arranging moves of train coys etc.: issuing supply table & postal arrangements: visit to 30 Div as to relief.	
	11		Start of relief of 111 by Bdes of 30th Div and 112 by Bdes of 19 Divn: preparing matters for handing over to 19 Divn with maps: selecting sites for additional Batteries coming into area.	
St JANS CAPPEL	12		DHQ move to St JANS CAPPEL leaving Field Coys RE PIONEERS & Divnl M.G. Coy behind: completion of move by 112 to MONT VIDAIGNE area: 111 Bde reach FAIRY HOUSE area early morning their further withdrawal to LOCRE DRANOUTRE area cancelled: handing over to 19 Divn.	
	13		Visit to 19th Divn & 111 Bde making arrangements for latter's move into line: visit to 63 Bde area train coys & refilling points: arrangements for Horse Show 18th subsequently postponed to 25th	
	14		arranging to move Q office tomorrow to CHATEAU 1/2 mile off so as to be with G: arranging supply training stores for 63 & 112: visit to 63 Bde area	
	15		111 Bde go into line under orders 19 Divn night 14/15: 325 reinforcements for 9 N Staffs equivalent no of men now with unit to be returned making necessary arrangements: round 112 Bde area with G.O.C.	
	16		9 N Staffs reinforcements moved to Corps reinforcement camp under Army orders exchange not to be effected at present: visit to Field Coy transport with G.O.C.: arrangements for ammn & RE stores for re-equipping Bdes when they move forward	
	17		Preparing administrative instructions relative to forthcoming offensive operations: preparing papers etc for G.C.M. trial of 2/Lt King 13 R.B. Sec 19: visit from Corps discussing offensive question: visit to 19 Divn as to accommodation for our 2 Bdes in forward area.	
	18		Start of relief of 111th Bde by 19th Divn: sending ammn off to YORK HOUSE and arranging for equipment ammn flares etc. & RE Stores for 63 & 112 to be sent there & drawn tomorrow by units: visit to 19 Divn & LOCRE DRANOUTRE area ascertaining there was room for 111 Bde	
	19		111 Bde complete relief night 19/20 & withdrawn to LOCRE DRANOUTRE area: visit to 19 Divn & to area to be occupied by 63 & 112: not later than 4 a.m. 20th: issuing instructions as to [illegible]	
	20		63 Bde night 19/20 move to FAIRY HOUSE area & 112 to area betw CHEAPSIDE and IRISH HOUSE: transport with units; orders issued for 10 L N Lancs to move to BOIS CARRE & come under 19 Divn 4 M.G. Coys moving up to Irish House to take their place and 13 R F taking place of 4 M.G. Coys at CLEM CAMP transport of all 3 units remaining on existing lines	
	21		orders for Div artly to withdraw from 30 Div area to No 11 Sub area night 21/22: visit with CRE round hutted camps now in course of erection under his supervision: visit to Bdes: orders for 63 & 112 Bdes to move back to original areas forthwith informing Sub area Comdt accordingly: 13 RF move back to LOCREHOF FARM.	

2353 Wt. W2544/1454 700,000 5/15 D. D. & L. A.D.S.S./Forms/C. 2118.

Army Form C. 2118.

WAR DIARY
or
INTELLIGENCE SUMMARY.
(Erase heading not required.)

Instructions regarding War Diaries and Intelligence Summaries are contained in F. S. Regs., Part II. and the Staff Manual respectively. Title pages will be prepared in manuscript.

Administrative Staff 37th Division

Place	Date	Hour	Summary of Events and Information	Remarks and references to Appendices
St JANS CAPPEL	Sept 22nd		Orders for 3 Infy Bdes to move 2 hours notice: arranging bussing programme accordingly: visit to 39 Div Offrs all information & map of their area: eventually orders recd for 112 Bde to move up by bus & take over from Bde of 39 Div and subsequently to come under orders 19 Div on latter extending their front N: supervising embussing in Mont VIDAIGNE area & debussing near RVS area: Div Arty withdrawn to Croix de POPERINGHE area less DAC.	
	23		111 Inf Bde are bussed up to assist 19 Div: DAC withdrawn to CROIX de POPERINGHE area: visit to 19 Div: arranging for withdrawal of 267 Inf Coy: visit to Div Arty area & asking Corps for further tents: visit to Corps settling certain general outstanding points: GOC throws Chateau grounds open to villagers 4-6:	
	24		Engaged on Honours & Rewards: visit to 112 Bde & 19 Div: visiting hutted camp sites & arranging for Ranch & 111 Bde to find necessary working parties	
	25		Divl Horse Show which lasts all day: 247 Inf Coy march from KLEINE VIERSTRAAT to MONT KOKEREELE area	
	26		Visit to Bde Schools: Superintending arrival remounts BAILLEUL station: visit to 39 Div Offrs information as to their present area in case we were ordered to relieve them: arrangements as to bussing 111 Inf Coy from line to LOCRE: also as to withdrawal 112 Bde from line under 19 Div to FAIRY House area	
	27		Orders to relieve 39 Div: 63 & 111 to move into line: arranging embussing programme and superintending embussing & debussing: 112 Bde complete withdrawal to FAIRY HOUSE area: preparing & issuing administrative instructions & list of new locations: visit to 39 Div & from them recd & giving particulars of respective areas	
ZEVECOTEN	28		D.H.Q move from St JANS CAPPEL to ZEVECOTEN: 112 Bde move to camps in neighbourhood of VIERSTRAAT — HQ & transport stand fast: visit from & to Corps on subject of accomodation in area many of 39 Div sites into which units had moved being outside new IX Corps area: visit round area choosing fresh sites & ascertaining that all 39 Div Arty wagon lines were outside	
	29		Moving 63 & 111 transport lines to new sites within area along Cheapside: selecting sites for 39 DAC & wagon lines within area & issuing orders for move tomorrow: applying to Corps for more tentage: readjusting certain 112 camps to conform to area boundary	
	30		Arranging accomodation for various units moving into area as Corps troops & clearing out certain X Corps troops	

Dept 37 Division
DAAG 37

WO 95/27

War Diary
A.Q. Administrative Staff
34th Divn
Oct 1917

16

Instructions regarding War Diaries and Intelligence Summaries are contained in F. S. Regs., Part II. and the Staff Manual respectively. Title pages will be prepared in manuscript.

WAR DIARY
or
INTELLIGENCE SUMMARY.
(Erase heading not required.)

Administrative Staff
H.Q. 37th Division

Army Form C. 2118.

Place	Date	Hour	Summary of Events and Information	Remarks and references to Appendices
DE ZON Camp near LA CLYTTE	Oct. 1		DHQ move from ZEVECOTEN to DE ZON Camp: survey of tramways in area & as to extensions: equipping Div bomb store in view of operations: visit round area completing arrangements of accommodation: visit to railhead & refilling points.	
	2		Issuing instructions as to drawing RE material: also as to additional supplies in view of operations: arranging for extra grenades etc: called for by 111 Bde & Varley bombs by 63 Bde: preparing & issuing administrative instructions: arranging for Div Bomb: Salvage & Burial Offrs to be accommodated in VOORMEZEELE.	
	3		Arranging for 112 Bde to move their H.Q. forward to near CONFUSION CORNER: meeting at Corps H.Q. of T.T. Board: subsequently conference as to Divnl boundary: arranging additional supplies of amm: etc: called for by Bdes taking part in operations	
	4		Visit to 19 Div as to accommodation should 112 take over from both Bdes in line: arranging accommodation for 353 A.T. Coy RE & Q Special Coy RE: visit to 112 Bde as to their equipment for relieving in line: subsequently visit to VOORMEZEELE as to casualties: estimated casualty since 28 and 660.	
	5		Orders for 112 to take over line from 63 & 111 the latter each leaving their strongest battn in reserve under orders 112: preparing & issuing administrative instructions: arranging programme for embussing 3 battns 63 at Bus House & 3 of 111 SHRAPNEL CORNER & supervising same: arranging with 19 Div for use of LITTLE KEMMEL & FERMOY: inspecting camps to be occupied tonight by troops from line & arranging accommodation	
	6		Orders for 37 Div Arty to take over tonight & tomorrow night from our Arty 39 & 52 A.F.A., DAC &c: arranging with S.C. as to accommodation & with Train as to H.Q. Coy: Orders for 63 M.G. Coy & T.M. Batts & 111 M.G. Coy to be relieved by 112 M.G. Coy & T.M. Batts & arranging busses accordingly: preparing statement of ration strengths for Army Comdr: interview visit to Corps Reinforcement Camp & Bde Schools offrs [illegible]: visit to 112 Bde in line.	
	7		Orders for 13 R. Bde to relieve 10 4th in line arranging to bus both parties: X Corps having asked 28 [illegible] to move from this area arranging accommodation DEVIZES Camps: Corps [illegible] provisionally settling Divnl boundaries: arranging additional accommodation for DAC	
	8		13 KRRC relieve 10 RF in line arranging busses accordingly: owing to inclement weather obtd sanction for issue of rum to whole Div: visit to Corps on hutting and tracks: on receipt of [illegible] from Corps visit to 19 Div re agreeing boundary	
	9		Orders for 63 to relieve 112 in line night 10/11: preparing & issuing administrative instructions: arrangements for 2 days rations for 63: going round camps making necessary adjustments: compiling and circulating bus programme: visit to train camps & ato's wagon lines	
	10		63 are bused up in afternoon and 112 back during night 10/11: superintending whole transaction: sending to CALAIS for gum boots for 63 Bde: arranging to clear camps for 112.	
	11		Visit to Army A R P with S.C. Div Arty & ADLR II fixing on site for new A.R.P: [illegible] programme for M.G. & T.M. relief and supervising arrangements: obtd extra tents for M.G. camps.	

2353 Wt. W2514/1454 700,000 5/15 D. D. & L. A.D.S.S./Forms/C. 2118.

Instructions regarding War Diaries and Intelligence Summaries are contained in F. S. Regs., Part II. and the Staff Manual respectively. Title pages will be prepared in manuscript.

WAR DIARY
or
INTELLIGENCE SUMMARY.
(*Erase heading not required.*)

Administrative Staff H.Q. 37th Division

Army Form C. 2118.

Place	Date	Hour	Summary of Events and Information	Remarks and references to Appendices
DE ZON Camp near LA CLYTTE	Oct. 12		Warning that 39 Div would relieve us 14/15: visit from their A & Q officers giving them information about area location list [illegible] etc: working administrative map for them: preparing papers for G.C.M. Lt COLLINS Rawe [?] GOC 112 president 13th	
	13		Orders issued for relief 14/15 troops in line to be bussed back. Bdes to move to former areas: preparing and issuing administrative instructions & fresh supply table: preparing embussing programme: 112 Bde less HQ move	
	14		Mont VIDAIGNE area: orders for move to be postponed 24 hours. 112 Bde HQ move near Mont NOIR: compiling [illegible] of Div area for 39 Div: visit to St JANS CAPPEL Settling accomodation there: visit to 39 Div & Corps: issuing amendments to adm. instructions & fresh supply table:	
	15		Orders from Army to move 1000 working party II Anzac Corps arrangements with 112 accordingly. Bussing programme for 16/17 [illegible]: arranging site for Pioneers near St JANS CAPPEL: superintending move 1000 men from 112 Bde to N. of YPRES by bus & visiting camps: helping 2 battns 111 embus from line: supervising	
St JANS CAPPEL	16		embussing 63 from line to Mt KOKEREELE area through night ~~16/17~~ 15/16. DHQ move from DE ZON to St JANS CAPPEL: visit to Corps Reinforcement Camp: writing corps on subject suggesting improvements: visit to Bdes & Corps.	
	17		A.A. & Q.M.G. proceeds on leave: visit to Battns 112 Bde detached N. of YPRES settling accomodation	
	18		Supply [illegible] ordnance [illegible]: visit from Corps ADVS arranging staff clipping [illegible] as to [illegible] of equipment & vehicles: [illegible] to units: arranging to [illegible] transport on [illegible] 111 Bde: visit to Div [illegible] Corps Reinforcement Camp Corps & Bdes.	
	19		Preparing programme whole units transport competition by Bdes in first instance but whole unit to compete in Divnl show in a fortnight: visit to 19 Div as to extra men to help in our hutting work: Gen Francis arrives to take command 111 Bde	
	20		GOC proceeds on leave: Genl Compton GOC 111 Bde proceeds to England 6 months tour of duty at home: orders for 63 Bde to move tomorrow MERRIS area: visit to area arranging accomodation etc: orders for [illegible] to send company for work LOCRE & arranging daily details of M.T.: orders for 2 bns 111 Bde to relieve the 2 bns 112 Bde 22nd working on [illegible] NE of YPRES arranging M.T. accordingly	
	21		63 Bde move Merris area: visit to 111 Bde arranging details for 2 battns move & inspecting transport lines: visit to Divl wing Corps reinforcement camp: instns re relief to working parties N. of YPRES.	
	22		Visit to 63 Bde & round battns & through area [illegible]; preparing & issuing instns re use of clipping establishment	
	23		KRABBENHOF FARM: supervising move 2 bns 111 in relief of 2 bns 112 working party N. E. YPRES. Applying for move back 112 Bde refused; visit to clipping establishment & making arrangements with DADVS: with Battn offr to take over METEREN baths on STRAZEELE road: 400 reinforcements for [illegible] equivalent no to be sent to other units.	
	24		Visit to Corps reinforcement Camp 37 Div wing: visit to Bde Schools & 111 Bde: arrangements for continuing manufacture VARLEY bombs	
	25		Obtd Corps auth'y for move of another Bde to MERRIS area provided we kept a full Bde in LOCRE: orders issued accordingly for 111 less 2 bns NE YPRES move MERRIS area 112 to LOCRE: issuing administrative instns.	

Instructions regarding War Diaries and Intelligence Summaries are contained in F. S. Regs., Part II. and the Staff Manual respectively. Title pages will be prepared in manuscript.

WAR DIARY
or
INTELLIGENCE SUMMARY.
(Erase heading not required.)

Administrative Staff H.Q. 37th Division

Army Form C. 2118.

Place	Date	Hour	Summary of Events and Information	Remarks and references to Appendices
ST JANS CAPPEL	Oct. 26		111 Bde less 2 bns march to STRAZEELE and 112 less 6 Bedfords to LOCRE: visiting them on arrival: obtd Corps auth for use of DONCASTER HUTS	
	27		6 Beds march to DONCASTER HUTS LOCRE and 9 N. Staffs leave their camp for billets in the KORTE-REELE area vacated by 6 Beds: orders for 2 bns 63 to relieve 2 bns 111 N.E. of YPRES on 29th: making the arrangements	
	28		9 N Staffs find another coy for work on forward roads under CE IX Corps: A.A. & Q.M.G. returns from leave: Addl leave extended from Nov 1 to 14 days: Col DILL GSO I leaves for GHQ.	
	29		2 composite bns 63 brought up N.E. YPRES 1260 all ranks in relief 111 Bde who return to STRAZEELE: supervising arrangements & fixing accomodation: visit from Corps re hastening hutting work: visit to Bdes: D.A.A.G. proceeds on leave; Major MAKIN joins as G.S.O. II.	
	30		G.O.C. returns from leave: preparing scheme for YUKON pack competition: visit to Corps Dunwaters 2nd Army Sniping School arranging for him to act as judge.	
	31		Visit round area fixing on site for transport competition: visit to Corps re winter accomodation & posting of additional offrs.	

J. Duncan Capt.
DAAG 37th Division

1917

Instructions regarding War Diaries and Intelligence Summaries are contained in F. S. Regs., Part II. and the Staff Manual respectively. Title pages will be prepared in manuscript.

AAQ

WAR DIARY
or
INTELLIGENCE SUMMARY.
(Erase heading not required.)

Administrative Staff
H.Q. 37th Division
Vol 28

Army Form C. 2118.

Place	Date	Hour	Summary of Events and Information	Remarks and references to Appendices
ST JANS CAPPEL	Nov 1		Engaged making arrangements for transport and YUKON pack competitions : visit to Div wing of Corps Reinforcement Camp	
	2		Going round hutted camps with CRE : visit to Corps and round Bdes : Corps having asked for observations on their administrative arrangements during recent offensive operations – engaged compiling same	
	3		Attd G.O.C. on his inspection of artillery wagon lines : choosing site for YUKON pack competition : visit to Field Coys Pnrs & Fld Ambces	
	4		Attd 112 Bde memorial service : leave allotment increased by 3 per diem to 37 working out fresh divisional sub-allotment	
	5		Orders recd that Div would relieve 19 Div in line by 10th : visit to Corps & subsequently to 19 Div discussing relief & obtg information re area	
	6		Arrangements for relief of 2 bns 63 Bde NE of YPRES bringing them back to MERRIS area : visit round new area : working out march table : YUKON pack competition	
	7		Preparing & issuing administrative instructions & new supply table : arranging billeting [illegible] for move : visit to 19 Div & Bdes as to moves etc : Divl transport competition.	
	8		112 Bde move from LOCRE area to BOIS (support) area : 111 Bde move from STRAZEELE area to KEMMEL area HQ FAIRY HOUSE : visit round new area including calls at Corps & 19 Div	
	9		112 Bde take over line 9/10 : arranging gum boots for them : 63 Bde march from MERRIS area to LOCRE area : DAAG returns from leave	
SCHERPENBERG nr LA CLYTTE	10		DHQ moves from ST JANS CAPPEL to SCHERPENBERG : Field Coys & Pnrs move to new area : 63 Bde march from LOCRE to BOIS area HQ KEMMEL CHATEAU : visit to Bde in line inspecting tunnels & accommodation generally	
	11		Making fresh location list : visit round wagon & transport lines generally : preparing scheme for tunnel supervision & maintenance in SPOIL BANK & LARCH WOOD	
	12		Leave allotment increased to 42 daily working out fresh sub allotment : arranging for autos to take over made wagon lines : visit to Bdes on accommodation generally	
	13		Going round the area inspecting camps & transport lines generally, paying special attention to Salvage.	
	14		Visited Bde in the line.	
	15.		Nil.	
	16.		Visited Hutted Camps with reference to accommodation of Cinema.	
	17.		111 Inf Bde relieved 112 Inf Bde in the line. 63rd Inf Bde moved to Reserve area.	

Instructions regarding War Diaries and Intelligence Summaries are contained in F. S. Regs., Part II. and the Staff Manual respectively. Title pages will be prepared in manuscript.

WAR DIARY
or
INTELLIGENCE SUMMARY.
(Erase heading not required.)

Administrative Staff, HQ. 37th Division

Army Form C. 2118.

Place	Date	Hour	Summary of Events and Information	Remarks and references to Appendices
SCHERPENBERG Nr LA CLYTTE	Nov 18		Major-Gen WILLIAMS to temporary command IX Corps. Brig-Gen T. POTTS to temporary command 37th Div.	
	19		Visited the Support area re accommodation in hutted camps.	
	20, 21		Nil.	
	22		Ascertaining from Commandants the accommodation question in Tunnels.	
	23		Going round the area inspecting standings in transport lines.	
	24		Nil.	
	25		The 63rd Inf Bde relieved the 111th Inf. Bde. in the line. The 111th Bde moved on relief to into the Support Area. The 112th Inf Bde moved into reserve HQ at LA CLYTTE	
	26		Visited Area Commandants.	
	27		Went round the area generally, visiting camps & horse lines, and informing Salvage Officer of where salvage material lay.	
	28		Nil.	
	29		Orders received for the relief of 63rd Inf Bde.	
	30		Visited the forward area inspecting the tramways etc.	

[illegible] Capt
DAAG 37th Division

2353 Wt. W2544/1454 700,000 5/15 D. D. & L. A.D.S.S./Forms/C. 2118.

19

Administrative Staff
H.Q. 37th Division

Army Form C. 2118.

37

Instructions regarding War Diaries and Intelligence Summaries are contained in F. S. Regs., Part II. and the Staff Manual respectively. Title pages will be prepared in manuscript.

WAR DIARY
or
INTELLIGENCE SUMMARY.
(Erase heading not required.)

Vol 29

Place	Date	Hour	Summary of Events and Information	Remarks and references to Appendices
HERPENBERG	1st Dec		Visited 37th Div Roads Company at BEDFORD HOUSE reference accommodation, Ordnance	
LA CLYTTE			stores and equipment, and work being done by this unit.	
"	2nd.		Went round the camps with Area Commandants to see about additional accommodation.	
	3rd		Nil.	
	4th		Going round the forward area inspecting ammunition dumps.	
	5th		112th Infantry Brigade relieved the 63rd Infantry Brigade in the line. The 111th Infantry Brigade moved into support area.	
	6th		} Nil.	
	7th		}	
	8th		Present at the entraining of working parties on the Light Railway System.	
	9th		Inspected the work being done on the forward roads by Divisional Roads Company.	
	10th		Nil.	
	11th		Visited the three Brigade Headquarters.	
	12th		Visited the Brigade in the line, inspecting soup kitchen and canteens	

T2134. Wt. W708–776. 500000. 4/15. Sir J. C. & S.

Instructions regarding War Diaries and Intelligence Summaries are contained in F. S. Regs., Part II. and the Staff Manual respectively. Title pages will be prepared in manuscript.

WAR DIARY
or
INTELLIGENCE SUMMARY.
(Erase heading not required.)

Administrative Staff H.Q. 37th Division

Army Form C. 2118.

Place	Date	Hour	Summary of Events and Information	Remarks and references to Appendices
			near there.	
	13th		111th Infantry Brigade relieved the 112th Infantry Brigade in the line. Present at the entraining on Light Railway System of relieving parties and of the working parties.	
	14th		Visited Headquarters of Battalions in the line, inspection quarters with reference to Ordnance Stores, Gas proofing etc.	
	15th		Conference at IX Corps Headquarters on Recreation, Amusements etc for the Winter.	
	16th 17th		} Nil	
	18th		Going round the area visiting horse standings.	
	19th		Visited the Brigade in the Line.	
	20th		Visiting the forward area inspecting the dumps & arranging for a site for a new Salvage Dump.	
	21st		63rd Infantry Brigade relieved the 111th Infantry Brigade in the line by Trench Tramway.	

T2134. Wt. W708—776. 500000. 4/15. Sir J. C. & L.

Instructions regarding War Diaries and Intelligence Summaries are contained in F. S. Regs., Part II. and the Staff Manual respectively. Title pages will be prepared in manuscript.

WAR DIARY
or
INTELLIGENCE SUMMARY.
(Erase heading not required.)

Administrative Staff
H.Q. 37th Division

Army Form C. 2118.

Place	Date	Hour	Summary of Events and Information	Remarks and references to Appendices
	22nd		Conference of Div Staff, representatives of Brigades re Recreation, Amusements etc for Winter.	
	23rd		Drawing up a scale on which to issue furniture to various kinds of hutted camps.	
	24th		Visited the Brigade in the Line. Preparing accommodation return for the Divisional Area.	
	25th		Went to BEDFORD HOUSE to see what arrangements had been made for the Christmas Dinner of the men of the Divisional Roads Company.	
	26th		Inspecting Baths & gum boot drying rooms.	
	27th		Visited the Brigade in the line & the Brigade in Support with reference to equipment.	
	28th		Nil.	
	29th		112th Infantry Brigade relieved the 63rd Infantry Brigade in the line. The 111th Infantry Brigade moved to the Reserve Area.	
	30th		Visited the various entraining points on the Light Railway of the detraining points. Visited the Brigade in the Line.	

T2134. Wt. W708–776. 500000. 4/15. Sir J. C. & S.

Army Form C. 2118.

37th Division

Instructions regarding War Diaries and Intelligence Summaries are contained in F. S. Regs., Part II. and the Staff Manual respectively. Title pages will be prepared in manuscript.

WAR DIARY
or
INTELLIGENCE SUMMARY.
(Erase heading not required.)

Place	Date	Hour	Summary of Events and Information	Remarks and references to Appendices
	31st.		Reconnoitring the Reserve Area at BLARINGHEM.	

[illegible] Capt.
[illegible] 37 Div.

72

Instructions regarding War Diaries and Intelligence Summaries are contained in F. S. Regs., Part II. and the Staff Manual respectively. Title pages will be prepared in manuscript.

WAR DIARY
or
INTELLIGENCE SUMMARY.
(Erase heading not required.)

Administrative Staff 37th Division

Army Form C. 2118.

Vol 30

Place	Date	Hour	Summary of Events and Information	Remarks and references to Appendices
	Jan[y]			
CHERPENBERG & LA LUYTTE	1st		Leave of DAQMG Capt LANDON extended by medical certs and board ordered	
	2nd		Visit to Corps on various outstanding administrative questions	
	3rd		Arrangements for Art[y] relief CRA 37 remaining in command	
	4th		Train arrangements for forthcoming Corps relief: concentrating on salvage work	
	5th		Visit to BLARINGHEM area working out accommodation: one Bde has to be left behind for work on Corps line and 2 Field Coys	
	6th		111 Bde relieve 112 in line: latter move to Support: 63rd move from support to Reserve area	
	7th		administrative arrangements in connection with raid to be carried out on 9th by 13 KRRC	
	8th		Arranging accommodation for 63 Bde when left behind for work on Corps line	
	9th		Work on train supply etc arrangements for move of Div to BLARINGHEM area 10th 11th & 12th mounted personnel staging at STRAZEELE	
	10th & 11th		Engaged entraining troops etc & supervising move of Div to Reserve area less 63 Bde who remain behind for work on Corps defence line: handing over to 4 Aust Div & giving them information about area.	
BLARINGHEM	12		DHQ move to BLARINGHEM	
	13		DAQMG Capt Landon given one month's sick leave & 6 months duty at home struck off.	
	14 to 19		Generally getting Reserve area into shape: obtg 4 TARRANT Huts as Recreation Rooms: working out scheme with CRE for improvement of billets	

T2134. Wt. W708-776. 500000. 4/15. Sir J. C. & S.

Instructions regarding War Diaries and Intelligence Summaries are contained in F. S. Regs., Part II. and the Staff Manual respectively. Title pages will be prepared in manuscript.

WAR DIARY
or
INTELLIGENCE SUMMARY.
(Erase heading not required.)

Administrative Staff
H.Q. 37th Division

Army Form C. 2118.

Place	Date	Hour	Summary of Events and Information	Remarks and references to Appendices
	Jan			
BLARINGHEM	18		Scheme for Re-organisation of battns of Infantry into Bdes of 3 battns each issued by G.S. battns affected 10th Yorks & Lancs of 63: 10th L.N. Lancs 11/Warwicks & 8/E Lancs of 112 Bde	
	19		Arrangements for 112 to relieve 63 in forward area on 21st	
	20-23		General routine work	
	24		AG's instructions recd as to disposal of personnel of disbanded battns: Div receives 1/Essex from 29 Div complete plus transport. QMG's instructions for disposal of transport & stores	
	25		Preparing detailed instructions re re-organisation: applying for certain Offrs & W.O's to be retained within Div	
	26		Arrangements for move on 27th to forward area of Pnrs & 152 Field Coy battn in relief of 153	
	27		Capt ALLEN (R of O) arrives as DAQMG	
	28		Fresh instructions from QMG re retaining 3 surplus infantry battns in each Div: 37 Div [illegible] over to 29th	
	29		GSO 1 Lt Col Walker sick with mumps leave extended	
	30		AA & QMG proceeds on leave	
	31		Instructions for sending away draft from 8/E Lancs	

A Duncan Capt
DAAG
37 Div

T2134. Wt. W708-776. 500000. 4/15. Sir J. C. & S.

16

HQ 37 DW
Administrative Staff

Vol 31

Instructions regarding War Diaries and Intelligence Summaries are contained in F. S. Regs., Part II. and the Staff Manual respectively. Title pages will be prepared in manuscript.

WAR DIARY
or
INTELLIGENCE SUMMARY.
(Erase heading not required.)

Army Form C. 2118.

Place	Date	Hour	Summary of Events and Information	Remarks and references to Appendices
	Feb			
BLARINGHEM	1st		Div comes under 22 Corps (formerly 2nd ANZAC) leaving IX Corps	
	2nd		Visit to 112 Bde in forward area as to sending away 8/E Lancs draft	
	3rd		Arrangements for relief 112 Bde forward area by 111 Bde trains supply etc	
	4th		Seeing off 8th Lancs from ARQUES : supervising entraining & detraining 111 & 112 : arrangements for meeting 1/Essex who arrive by train to join the Div transport coming by road	
	5th		Orders for sending away drafts from 10/4 Lancs & 11/Warwicks – 10 LN Lancs to go to surplus as a battn	
	6th & 7th		Engaged supervising despatch of above drafts checking rolls etc reporting off's posted : also arranging for reception of drafts for 10th & 13th R.F.	
	8th–10th		Engaged on reorganization work including receipt of drafts from w/Lancs 6/Beds 1/Essex. 13 R Fus join 112 Bde from 111 Bde : 112 becoming 13 RF 6 Beds 1/Essex.	
	11th		8th Lancs chosen as transport to be sent to 29 Div asking for instructions to despatch	
	12 & 13		Orders recd for Div to relieve 20th Div 15th 16th & 17th in MENIN road Sector : a/c of staff returns from leave	
	14th		Working lorry & train arrangements for move : visit to 20th Div & 22nd Corps	
	15/16		Supervising move including entraining & detraining : looking round accommodation new area	
WESTOUTRE	17		D.H.Q. move to WESTOUTRE	

Instructions regarding War Diaries and Intelligence Summaries are contained in F. S. Regs., Part II. and the Staff Manual respectively. Title pages will be prepared in manuscript.

WAR DIARY
or
INTELLIGENCE SUMMARY.
(Erase heading not required.)

Army Form C. 2118.

Place	Date	Hour	Summary of Events and Information	Remarks and references to Appendices
	Feby			
WESTOUTRE	18		Visiting accommodation in area with GOC with a view to move all infantry forward	
	19		Going carefully round area visiting transport lines and conditions CHATEAU SEGARD near CAFE BELGE where DHQ were to move 24th: baths at VIJVERHOEK Off. club DICKEBUSCH etc	
	20		General accommodation conference at BEDFORD HOUSE on reorganisation of front into 3 Bde fronts: one battn line one support one reserve hutted camp: visit from AA&QMG 49 Div who take over left Corps Sector 21–24th.	
	21		Necessary reliefs on Div front being held equally by the two Bdes: 111 Bde take over Northern sub-section on left HQ Halfway house: 112 centre: 63 right: re-organising transport lines so as to give each Bde standing for forward echelon: giving each Bde details camp round DICKEBUSCH	
	22		DAAG proceeds on leave to U.K: preparing & issuing instructions re tunnels schedule of accommodation: Corps lecture on economy in food	
	23		Round forward area visiting tunnels etc: reserve rations ammunition dumps: visit to Bdes & subsequently to Corps: arranging move DHQ to CHATEAU SEGARD 25th	
	24		Surveying salvage arrangements & preparing scheme	
CHATEAU SEGARD	25		DHQ move to CHATEAU SEGARD between CAFE BELGE & KRUISSTRAATHOEK.	
	26		Round tunnels on general tour of inspection: re-grouping transport lines: preliminary instructions re Kings Birthday Gazette.	

T2134. Wt. W708–776. 500000. 4/15. Sir J. C. & S.

Instructions regarding War Diaries and Intelligence Summaries are contained in F. S. Regs., Part II. and the Staff Manual respectively. Title pages will be prepared in manuscript.

WAR DIARY
or
INTELLIGENCE SUMMARY.
(Erase heading not required.)

Army Form C. 2118.

Place	Date	Hour	Summary of Events and Information	Remarks and references to Appendices
CHATEAU SEGARD	27		Owing to expected German attack arranging dump extra rations forward for Infy & Arty: preparing & issuing admin instructions for Precautionary period: forming forward transport Echelon near Derby Ammn Dump	
	28		Regrouping of areas: 63 bringing details to SCOTTISH WOOD CAMP: 111 to bring Bde School up to details camp MICMAC batten camp: engaged on Honours & Rewards Kings Birthday Gazette	

R. [illegible] Gorell
a/DAA&QMG
37 Div
1/3/18

T2134. Wt. W708–776. 500000. 4/15. Sir J. C. & S.

16 SECRET

Administrative Staff
H.Q. 37th Div

Vol 32

WAR DIARY
or
INTELLIGENCE SUMMARY.
(Erase heading not required.)

Instructions regarding War Diaries and Intelligence Summaries are contained in F. S. Regs., Part II. and the Staff Manual respectively. Title pages will be prepared in manuscript.

Army Form C. 2118.

Place	Date	Hour	Summary of Events and Information	Remarks and references to Appendices
	MARCH			
CHATEAU SEGARD	1		Engaged on re-organisation of M.G. Coys into Divnl MG Battn : allotment of Divnl rewards & mentions for K.B. Gazette : preparing & issuing salvage scheme for Div area	
	2		Preparing administrative notes & appendices for Defence Scheme :	
	3		Visit to 3 Infy Bde H.Q. discussing scheme for improving tunnels generally	
	4		Engaged on recommendations for K.B. despatch	
	5		Major Bowly appd GSO1 : visit round area inspecting new hutting etc.	
	6		Making careful inspection & reconnaissance of all tunnels in forward area with a view to improvements including Canada St Sussex St HEDGE St TOR TOP JACKDAW	
	7		Engaged on recommendations for Kings Birthday Despatch	
	8		DAAG returns from leave : estimated casualty returns owing to GERMAN attacks & our counter attacks 5 & 200	
	9		Round area & visiting Bdes & further tunnel inspection : visiting prohibited area E of ZILLEBEKE & arranging for removal of inhabitants	
	10		DAQMG proceeds on leave : visit to 111 Bde transport lines near YPRES with DADVS	
	11		Visit round battery wagon lines & rear transport lines principally to inspect bomb proof protection	
	12		General Divs conference Halfway house on proposed readjustment forward Div area : subsequent administrative conference : 111th Bde move HQ to Warrington Rd by ZILLEBEKE Lake.	
	13		Conf Corps HQ as to storing ammunition water rations etc forwards	

T2134. Wt. W708–776. 500000. 4/15. Sir J. C. & S.

Instructions regarding War Diaries and Intelligence Summaries are contained in F. S. Regs., Part II. and the Staff Manual respectively. Title pages will be prepared in manuscript.

WAR DIARY
or
INTELLIGENCE SUMMARY.
(Erase heading not required.)

Army Form C. 2118.

Place	Date	Hour	Summary of Events and Information	Remarks and references to Appendices
	MARCH			
CHATEAU SEGARD	14		Visit to Div Wing with GOC	
	15		Working out ammn water ration storage scheme for forward area	
	16		Engaged on immediate rewards for recent fighting: visit to Bdes & round intermediate area	
	17		Memorial Service 13/KRRC: visit to Area Comdts re maps of camps & standings reqd by Corps: preparing points of policy for Salvage Offr	
	18		Conf with OC Train & DADVS as to propd reduction of horses: circular to all units re reduction rations	
	19		Working out with DADOS scheme for propd reduction of certain mob. store table stores & equipment: visit to 63 Bde and round DICKEBUSCH	
	20		Visit round back areas preparing scheme for moving up surplus infantry batts: engaged on immediate Honours & Rewards: preparing return ammn water rations etc. stored forward	
	21		Corps Comdr inspects 10 RF & presents ribands won in recent fighting: back areas shelled moving 111 reserve batt from Ferme to Malplaquet: DADVS leaves DICKEBUSCH for WESTOUTRE: 1/Essex transport move from DICKEBUSCH for CROYDON Lines near ZEVECOTEN.	
	22		Conference Corps HQ general administrative questions:	
	23		Engaged working on maps of area showing hutted camps & horse standings: all leave stopped	
	24		Arrangements for holding line on 2 Bde front: 112 to come out.	

T2134. Wt. W708-776. 500000. 4/15. Sir J. C. & S.

Army Form C. 2118.

Instructions regarding War Diaries and Intelligence Summaries are contained in F. S. Regs., Part II. and the Staff Manual respectively. Title pages will be prepared in manuscript.

WAR DIARY
or
INTELLIGENCE SUMMARY.
(Erase heading not required.)

Place	Date	Hour	Summary of Events and Information	Remarks and references to Appendices
CHATEAU SEGARD	March 25		Preparing & issuing advance instrns re 111 giving up part of line to 49: 63 taking over additional from 1/Aust & 111 taking over line held by 112 & latter withdrawing to Reserve	
	26		Above reliefs completed night 25/26: completing map 1/10000 giving sites & names & merits for use suitable of all camps & horse standings in Divl area: visit to Westoutre supervising handing over of kitchens & LGS wagon from surplus transport to 5th Aust M.G. Battn	
	27		Visit to ABEELE re surplus kit dump: supervising arrangements at Station re returning leave parties all leave having been stopped & all offrs recalled: all students returned from Courses: preparing scheme for billeting an extra Div but artly in Westoutre HALLEBAST & DICKEBUSCH area & for Bde group in KRUISSTRAATHOEK: conferring with area comdts	
	28		Further re-arrangements of transport lines consequent on Corps troops leaving HALLEBAST area: Orders for Divn to move to 3rd Army by strategical trains: consequential administrative arrangements.	
TOUTENCOURT	29		Divn moved by rail from CAESTRE and HOPOUTRE to MONDICOURT and BOUQUEMAISON: supervising entraining & detraining and arranging billets lorries supplies etc. Div 3rd Army Res. administered by VII Corps.	
PAS	30		Orders for Div to move N. to IV Corps and relieve 62 Div: whole Div moves accordingly supervising same: visit to Corps & 62 Div	
	31		Toured area: conference with DA & QMG IV Corps: 112 Bde take over left sector line night 31st/1st: preparing & issuing administrative instrns	

[illegible signature]
Major
DAAG 37 Divn.

A5834 Wt. W4973/M687 750,000 8/16 D. D. & L. Ltd. Forms/C.2118/13.

IV.Corps.

WAR DIARY

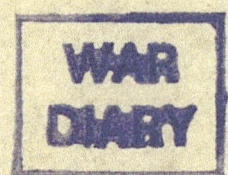

ADMINISTRATIVE STAFF

37th DIVISION

APRIL

1918

E19

Instructions regarding War Diaries and Intelligence Summaries are contained in F. S. Regs., Part II. and the Staff Manual respectively. Title pages will be prepared in manuscript.

WAR DIARY
or
INTELLIGENCE SUMMARY.
(*Erase heading not required.*)

Army Form C. 2118.

Administrative Staff. 37th Division

V8 33

Place	Date	Hour	Summary of Events and Information	Remarks and references to Appendices
	April			
SOUASTRE	1		112th Bde complete taking over left sub-sector : 63 take over right subsector night 1/2 : 111 Bde move into support with HQ FONQUEVILLERS Church : preparing & issuing additional admin instns : conference Corps HQ settling Divl boundaries 37 allotted COUIN (DHQ) COIGNEUX BAYENCOURT SAILLY AU BOIS : arranging to clear this area of outside troops & move all Div within : visit to rear Bde HQrs 62nd & 42nd Divs : DHQ moves PAS to SOUASTRE except rear echelon : Major HUNTER 1/Queens takes over appt DAQMG.	
	2		Supervising move of transport & rear Bde HQ to Div area : conference with all units 41-47-62 Div arrys 10 & 13 Mob squadrons & arst Inf Bde 93 APA Bde : visit to 3 Inf Bde HQ with APM.	
COUIN	3		Art. GOC's conference DHQ : arranging supply ammn etc : DHQ move from SOUASTRE to COUIN & rear echelon join up from PAS : visit 3 Army HQ for ammn : leave parties being returned BELLE EGLISE sending Disbursing Offr there to supervise & visit there making arrangements	
	4		Conference Corps HQ re traffic etc : visit with DADMS as to medical arrangements for proposed attacks : round area fixing additional watering places for horses :	
	5		63 Bde & 4 Aust attack : 112 Bde are attacked : getting up extra ammn : supervising withdrawal of prisoners : obtg information as to casualties from M.D.S : arranging & withdrawing 112 & MG transport owing to shelling of BAYENCOURT-COIGNEUX : estimated casualty wire	
	6		Visit to Corps HQ on subject of baths : visit to R.P : arranging rest station at COUIN : further estimated casualty wire.	

T2134. Wt. W708–776. 500000. 4/15. Sir J. C. & S.

Instructions regarding War Diaries and Intelligence Summaries are contained in F. S. Regs., Part II. and the Staff Manual respectively. Title pages will be prepared in manuscript.

WAR DIARY
or
INTELLIGENCE SUMMARY.
(Erase heading not required.)

Administrative Staff 37th Division

Army Form C. 2118.

Place	Date	Hour	Summary of Events and Information	Remarks and references to Appendices
	April			
COUIN	7		Bath started at FONQUEVILLERS: tour of back area up horse watering points: owing to outbreak trench foot arranging for each Bde to open near their HQ a preventive estmt: conference with S.C's CRE & ADMS & going round with former inspecting: visit Corps HQ.	
	8		C/124 Batty arrive at AUTHIEULE arranging accomodation: Medium TM Batts arrive from 2nd Army by lorry with Div Artly advance parties: arranging accomodation in COUIN: visit to C/124: round Bde HQ finally on admin questions: conf with CRE Corps troops on roads to be kept up E. of DGT line: arranging for formation of all Bde details into composite battn.	
	9		Visit to Bdes & round artly wagon lines: 37 D.A. HQ arrive & batts & DAC into SARTON area: visit to Corps: Supply arrangements & allocation of lorries in case of a move	
	10		Getting up ammn for reserve line & strong points: 63rd relieve 112th in line 9/10th: 1/Essex withdrawn round BAYENCOURT: 111th take over part of Aust front: batts of 37 D.A. march into area: visit to Corps	
	11		Full Q conference DHQ attended by all SCs including artly artly & representatives admin services etc discussing precautionary measures system of supply & ammn in mobile warfare MT position etc: riding round area with G.O.C.: visit to Composite Battn: arranging receipt of various reinforcements.	
	12		Artly Corps Q conference: readjustment of line side slipping a bit S. with all Bdes & 4 Aust in line: orders for all units of Div to move E. of St LEDGER reconnoitring sites for 3 Train Coys & DAC HQ & 2 Sects & MVS & altering Div Troops R.P.: visit to other R.P.	
	13		Conference at COIGNEUX with S.C's etc re Composite Battn: 14th M.G. Squadron arrive as a mounted unit	

Instructions regarding War Diaries and Intelligence Summaries are contained in F. S. Regs., Part II. and the Staff Manual respectively. Title pages will be prepared in manuscript.

WAR DIARY
or
INTELLIGENCE SUMMARY.
(Erase heading not required.)

Administrative Staff
37th Division

Army Form C. 2118.

Place	Date	Hour	Summary of Events and Information	Remarks and references to Appendices
	April			
COUIN	13th (contd)		arranging a location in wood near CHATEAU COUIN & issuing tents & shelters: conference with AA & QMG 42 Div as to possible accommodation in COUIN for their MG Battn	
	14th		Preparing & issuing admin instructions as appendix to Div Defence Scheme including table of action to be taken on precautionary measures being ordered: going round purple line visiting ammn dumps: visit to 42 Div at Pas as to handing over & to MONDICOURT railhead: visit from DA & QMG IV Corps	
	15th		Orders for 42 Div to relieve 37 Div in line 15/16 & 16/17: 57 Div in Army Reserve also to close up into area: visits to 42.57.62 Divs & Corps re adjustment of billeting accommodation: preparing & issuing admin instructions: attd G conference	
AUTHIE	16th		63rd Bde moved from line to HENU: attd conference of AA & QMGs with DA & QMG Corps on billeting proposals: DHQ forward echelon moves to AUTHIE rear to PAS: 63rd Bde moves across to AUTHIE WOOD: visit to Bdes & PAS as to accommodation: issuing amended admin instructions.	
	17th		111th Bde withdrawn from line during night & after resting proceed to LOUVENCOURT: 112th Bde withdrawn to St LEGER & BOIS de WARNIMONT: visit to NZ Div at BUS & to Bdes: visit from DA & QMG Corps: attd G conference	
	18th		Preparing & issuing admin instructions as to action on G orders of battle positions: M.G. Battn withdrawn from line to AUTHIE WOOD: arranging to move them to BOIS de WARNIMONT: getting up ammn to Bde HQ for fighting purposes: moving part of rear echelon from PAS to AUTHIE: providing HQ for 63 Bde in AUTHIE	
	19th		Engaged on command & staff recommendations SS 627;	

T2134. Wt. W708-776. 500000. 4/15. Sir J. C. & S.

Instructions regarding War Diaries and Intelligence Summaries are contained in F. S. Regs., Part II. and the Staff Manual respectively. Title pages will be prepared in manuscript.

WAR DIARY
or
INTELLIGENCE SUMMARY.
(Erase heading not required.)

Army Form C. 2118.

Place	Date	Hour	Summary of Events and Information	Remarks and references to Appendices
AUTHIE	20/4/18		Visited 62nd Div HENU, making arrangements for relief of 24th inst. Reconnoitred accomodation in PAS, where it is proposed to accomodate Composite Battalion and Reinforcements.	
" "	21/4/18		Lieut R.E. TAYLOR 4th Middx Regt attached Div HQ as "A" learner appointed Staff Captain 189 Brigade, proceeded to TOUTENCOURT to assume duties.	
	22/4/18		Preparing administrative instructions for relief. ADMS held conference of Regtl M.Os. AA & QMG & DAQMG attended	
	23/4/18		63rd Infantry Brigade relieved Brigade of 62nd Div in trenches. Engaged in reconnoitring alternative waggon lines for Div train in neighbourhood of MARIEUX and SARTON also Refilling point on the AUTHIE-MARIEUX Road	
HENU	24/4/18		Div HQ. moved to HENU relieving 62nd Div. 111th Inf Bde moved to line from LOUVENCOURT, in relief of Brigade of 62nd Div. 112th Inf Bde moved to reserve line from BOIS de WARNIMONT in relief of	

T2134. Wt. W708 - 776. 500000. 4/15. Sir J. C. & S.

Instructions regarding War Diaries and Intelligence Summaries are contained in F. S. Regs., Part II. and the Staff Manual respectively. Title pages will be prepared in manuscript.

WAR DIARY
or
INTELLIGENCE SUMMARY.
(Erase heading not required.)

Administrative Staff
37th Division

Army Form C. 2118.

Place	Date	Hour	Summary of Events and Information	Remarks and references to Appendices
			Brigade of 62nd Div. Bt Lieut Col A S M BROWNE appointed AQMG IX Corps	
HENU	25		Bt Lt Col ASM Browne proceeded to assume duties at IX Corps. Major H M A HUNTER DAQMG 37th Div appointed AA & QMG 37th Div. assumed duties. Captain J. CARRUTHERS appointed DAQMG. Div Composite Battalion reformed at PAS under command of Major P. G WHITE 4th Middx Regt approximate strength 62 off 650 OR composed of reinforcements and personnel kept back in accordance with SS135.	
" "	26		Visited composite Bn at PAS, accomodation unsatisfactory too scattered and place unsuitable for purpose.	
" "	27		Reconnoitred P of W Camp at ORVILLE, allotted by corps to Div for Composite Bn. ordered advanced party to proceed from PAS and take over camp from Labour Coy at present in occupation. Visit to Corps.	
	28		Composite Bn moved to ORVILLE. Div Wing strength 4 officers 154 OR	

Instructions regarding War Diaries and Intelligence Summaries are contained in F. S. Regs., Part II. and the Staff Manual respectively. Title pages will be prepared in manuscript.

WAR DIARY
or
INTELLIGENCE SUMMARY.
(Erase heading not required.)

Army Form C. 2118.

Administrative Staff
37th Division

Place	Date	Hour	Summary of Events and Information	Remarks and references to Appendices
			arrived from XXII Corps at ABBEELE. accomodated in PAS for the night. Engaged in preparation of administrative instructions in connection with defence scheme.	
HENU.	29th		Div Wing moved to ORVILLE, Maj D C R HAY in command also assumed command of Composite Bn and Reinfts on arrival. visit from AA&QMG 82nd Div, visit to corps with reference to moving hundred huts from forward area to ORVILLE	
HENU.	30th		Visited three Infantry Brigade rear HQ at SOUASTRE. and visited transport lines. Reclassification of cold shoers as shoeing smiths completed by board, of which Lt Col G.H. Humphrey commdg 37th Div Train is President.	

J Duncan Major
DAAG 37th Division

T2134. Wt. W708-776. 500000. 4/15. Sir J. C. & S.

11

Instructions regarding War Diaries and Intelligence Summaries are contained in F. S. Regs., Part II. and the Staff Manual respectively. Title pages will be prepared in manuscript.

WAR DIARY
or
INTELLIGENCE SUMMARY.
(Erase heading not required.)

Army Form C. 2118.

Administrative Staff
HQ 37th Division

Vol 34

Place	Date	Hour	Summary of Events and Information	Remarks and references to Appendices
HENU.	1/5/18		Address to Composite Battalion officers by Divisional Commander. Visit to WARLINCOURT to see arrival of reinforcements and Div Reinforcement officer.	
			112th Inf Bde relieve 63rd Infantry Brigade in front line. 63rd moving to reserve trenches with 1 battalion in billets in SOUASTRE.	
HENU.	2/5/18		Lecture to Div [illegible] at ORVILLE by AA&QMG, system of supplies.	
"	3/5/18		Engaged in reconnoitring site for DAC to move from COUIN to HENU. Captain J.A.T. Langdon [?] & Learner [?] attached Div HQ since Feb 18 rejoined unit. Visit from Corps Horsemaster.	
"	4/5/18		Rear H.Q. 112th Inf Brigade move from SOUASTRE to HENU on account of shelling at the former place. DAC move to HENU from COUIN. Prince C. [?] visited Div HQ about 4.30 PM.	

T2134. Wt. W708–776. 500000. 4/15. Sir J. C. & S.

Instructions regarding War Diaries and Intelligence Summaries are contained in F. S. Regs., Part II. and the Staff Manual respectively. Title pages will be prepared in manuscript.

WAR DIARY
or
INTELLIGENCE SUMMARY.
(Erase heading not required.)

Administrative Staff H.Q. 37th Division

Army Form C. 2118.

Place	Date	Hour	Summary of Events and Information	Remarks and references to Appendices
HENU.	5/5/18		Engaged in arranging accommodation for labour company in FONQUEVILLERS, sent up to work on forward roads under C.R.E. 37th Div.	
"	6/5/18		Five American Officers including 1 Staff Officer, and 7 O.R. arrive for attachment to Brigades in the line.	
			Visit to Corps, arranging accommodation in connection with forward main dressing station for 50th Fd Amb at P.A.F. A few shells in the vicinity of Div H.Q. 1 man killed M.G.C. and 2 wounded.	
HENU.	7/5/18		Visit to Div Wing at ORVILLE also to Reinforcement Railhead MARIEUX. 63rd B. de H.Q. moved to FONQUEVILLERS from SAULTRE.	
HENU	8/5/18		Orders received from IV Corps that 1/1st Hertfordshire Regt would be transferred from 39th to 37th Division forthwith. On arrival 1/1st Herts to absorb 6th Bedford Regt the total of Battalions in	

T2134. Wt. W708–776. 500000. 4/15. Sir J. C. & S.

Instructions regarding War Diaries and Intelligence Summaries are contained in F. S. Regs., Part II. and the Staff Manual respectively. Title pages will be prepared in manuscript.

WAR DIARY or INTELLIGENCE SUMMARY.

(Erase heading not required.)

Administrative Staff HQ 37th Division

Army Form C. 2118.

Place	Date	Hour	Summary of Events and Information	Remarks and references to Appendices
			amalgamated not to exceed 40 officers and 900 O.R. Remainder to form nucleus of training battn for American army, on establishment laid down, the balance i.e. surplus being sent to Base. McInf Bde carried out a minor operation and captured 2 officers and 28 O.R.	
HENU	9/5/18		1/1st HERTS arrived CANDAS and were conveyed by bus to Div Composite Bn at ORVILLE. Strength 22 off 449 OR	
	10/5/18		Div Commander visited Composite Bn and saw Lt Col R WILKINSON DSO Commanding 1/1st HERTS.	
	11/5/18		1/1st HERTS moved from ORVILLE to Old British trenches E of FONQUEVILLERS and came under orders of 112th Infantry Brigade. Heavy Bombardment of FONQUEVILLERS during the night with gas shell. 49 officers and 1014 OR of this division casualties as result.	
	12/5/18		Visit to [illegible] arranging details of relief with 62nd Division.	

T2134. Wt. W708–776. 500000. 4/15. Sir J. C. & S.

Instructions regarding War Diaries and Intelligence Summaries are contained in F. S. Regs., Part II. and the Staff Manual respectively. Title pages will be prepared in manuscript.

WAR DIARY
or
INTELLIGENCE SUMMARY.
(Erase heading not required.)

Administrative Staff H.Q. 37th Divn

Army Form C. 2118.

Place	Date	Hour	Summary of Events and Information	Remarks and references to Appendices
HENU	13/3/18		Visit to Corps discussing position of left Division [illegible] suggested alteration of Div Boundary. Reconnoitring accommodation at AUTHIE and visit to Fd Coys and Pnrs who were accommodated in Red line and Chateau de la HAIE & [illegible]	
HENU.	14/3/18		Engaged in supervising unloading of surplus kit dump [?] by rail from ST OMER at WARLINCOURT. Two trucks sorted and dispatched direct to owners. Orders received for Captain W. B. Belcher GSO 3 to proceed and take up duties of Brigade Major 19 Bde 63rd Div.	
HENU	15/3/18		Engaged in reconnoitring wagon lines for SAA section of DAC near AUTHIE. meeting of remounts, and preparation of administrative instructions for relief by 62nd Div on 16/17th. Hostile aeroplane dropped bombs in village about 11 PM setting two lorries of 42nd Div M/T Coy on fire and causing about 12 casualties	

T2134. Wt. W708–776. 500000. 4/15. Sir J. C. & S.

Instructions regarding War Diaries and Intelligence Summaries are contained in F. S. Regs., Part II. and the Staff Manual respectively. Title pages will be prepared in manuscript.

WAR DIARY
or
INTELLIGENCE SUMMARY.
(Erase heading not required.)

Administrative Staff HQ 37th Divn

Army Form C. 2118.

Place	Date	Hour	Summary of Events and Information	Remarks and references to Appendices
HENU	16/5/18		Visit from AAG Third Army discussing strengths, estimated casualties, and reinforcements for 10th Royal Fusiliers and Machine Gun Battn. 63rd Inf Bde relieved in the line by a Brigade of 62nd Div, and withdrawn to St Leger les Authie.	
AUTHIE.	17/5/18		62nd Div relieve 37th Div. Div H.Q. moving to AUTHIE. 111th Inf Brigade to AUTHIE and 112th Inf Brigade to LOUVENCOURT. Visit from DA & QMG IV Corps discussing roads, and road arrangements in Corps area. Arranging attendance of witnesses for Court of Inquiry being assembled on 18th inst by 4th Corps to investigate cause of large number of gas casualties in FONQUEVILLERS on the 11th inst.	
AUTHIE	19/5/18		Visit to Corps and 112th Infantry Brigade at Louvencourt inspecting billets, and arranging details regarding amalgamation of 6th Bedfords and 1/1st HERTS	

T2134. Wt. W708 - 776. 500000. 4/15. Sir J. C. & S.

Instructions regarding War Diaries and Intelligence Summaries are contained in F. S. Regs., Part II. and the Staff Manual respectively. Title pages will be prepared in manuscript.

WAR DIARY
or
INTELLIGENCE SUMMARY.
(Erase heading not required.)

Administrative Staff 37th Divn
H.Q. 37

Army Form C. 2118.

Place	Date	Hour	Summary of Events and Information	Remarks and references to Appendices
BERTHE	20/3/18		Q Conference at Corps H.Q. Conference at Div H.Q. GOC present. Discussing training whilst Div remains in reserve, also called for suggestions for Div Horse Show	
"	23/3/18		A.Q. Conference Div H.Q. discussing method of carrying additional Lewis Guns; also transport for trench mortar batteries – Question of extra regimentally employed men also discussed. Lieut. Col. N.H.A. Hunter D.S.O. appointed AQMG at G.H.Q. Lt Col Reid DSO AA&QMG New Zealand Division appointed AA&QMG 37th Div.	
" "	24/3/18		Lt Col Hunter proceeded to take up appointment. Lt Col Reid assumed duties AA&QMG 37th Div –	
" "	25/3/18		Army Commander visited troops of 111th Inf Bde training	
" "	26/3/18		Committee meeting to discuss conditions for Div Horse Show. Lt Col G.H. Humphrys presided.	
" "	27/3/18		Engaged in arranging for despatch of surplus of 6th Bedford R. [illegible] from WARLINCOURT on 28th. Reorganization now completed.	

Instructions regarding War Diaries and Intelligence Summaries are contained in F. S. Regs., Part II. and the Staff Manual respectively. Title pages will be prepared in manuscript.

WAR DIARY
or
INTELLIGENCE SUMMARY.
(Erase heading not required.)

Administrative Staff
H.Q. 37th Division

Army Form C. 2118.

Place	Date	Hour	Summary of Events and Information	Remarks and references to Appendices
AUTHIE	28/5/18		134 Fd Coy held sports at AUTHIE. Div Commander was present in the afternoon.	
Authie	29/5/18		Engaged in preparation of provisional programme for Divisional Transport competition to be held on 4 5 6 7th June also sub allotment of leave vacancies 5 per day for Div including special cases.	
Authie	30/5/18		Orders received that Division would be in GHQ Reserve and must be held in readiness to move at 8 hrs notice.	
	31/5/18		Visit to Traffic at BERNAVILLE ascertaining details separately entraining stations etc in event of orders being [illegible]. DOULLENS and Mondicourt allotted. Preparation of Administrative instructions.	

[illegible] Major
DAAG 37th Division

T2134. Wt. W708–776. 500000. 4/15. Sir J. C. & S.

Instructions regarding War Diaries and Intelligence Summaries are contained in F. S. Regs., Part II. and the Staff Manual respectively. Title pages will be prepared in manuscript.

17

WAR DIARY
or
INTELLIGENCE SUMMARY.
(Erase heading not required.)

Administrative Staff
HQ 37th Division

Army Form C. 2118.

Vol 35

Place	Date	Hour	Summary of Events and Information	Remarks and references to Appendices
AUTHIE	1/6/16		Divisional Artillery withdrawn from the line where [illegible] under 62nd Division. Orders received that 37th Div will replace 42nd Div at POSNY [illegible]	
AUTHIE	2/6/16		37th Signal Coy Sports. Div Commander was present.	
			Engaged in reconnoitring ground for Divisional Transport competition to take place on 4.5.6 & 7th June	
AUTHIE	3/6/16		Engaged in preparation of ground for Transport competition arranging final details	
			Visit from representative of E.F. Canteens, discuss present policy as regards stocking Div and Regtl Canteens	
AUTHIE	4/6/16		Division transport competition commenced 10 AM.	
			Orders received about 12 noon for Division to be held in readiness to embuss on 5th inst. Engaged in arranging details of embussing with officer from GHQ Bus company	
			All transport and Div Artillery moved to staging area Div Artillery to CANAPLES and HALLOY Infantry Transport to HAVERNAS	
			Div Train and M.V.S. to . R.A. HQ moved to HAVERNAS	

T2134. Wt. W708–776. 500000. 4/15. Sir J. C. & S.

Instructions regarding War Diaries and Intelligence Summaries are contained in F. S. Regs., Part II. and the Staff Manual respectively. Title pages will be prepared in manuscript.

WAR DIARY
or
INTELLIGENCE SUMMARY.
(*Erase heading not required.*)

Army Form C. 2118.

Place	Date	Hour	Summary of Events and Information	Remarks and references to Appendices
5/6/18	AUTHIE		Engaged in reconnaissance of CAVILLON area. Dismounted personnel of Div moved by bus. Infantry Brigades accommodated as follows. 63rd Inf Bde PICQUIGNY area. 111th Inf Bde to BOVELLES area, 112th Inf Bde to OISSY area. Div Artillery moved to REINCOURT, LE MESGE, SOUES. Div HQ to CAVILLON. Transport of Infantry Fd Coy etc moved from CANAPLES area and rejoined units.	
6/6/18	CAVILLON		Visits to three Bde HQ. and round billeting area. Application made to 4th Army Q for water tank lorries. All units other than Artillery experiencing difficulty as regards water supply. Reconnoitring bathing facilities in the area.	
7/6/18	CAVILLON		Visit to Army Q. and visit from Staff Captain 4th Army A. Discussing returns required, travelling boards for reclassification of A personnel.	
8/6/18			Engaged in preparation of scheme for [illegible] to move by bus or train.	

T2134. Wt. W708–776. 500000. 4/15. Sir J. C. & S.

Instructions regarding War Diaries and Intelligence Summaries are contained in F. S. Regs., Part II. and the Staff Manual respectively. Title pages will be prepared in manuscript.

WAR DIARY
or
INTELLIGENCE SUMMARY.
(Erase heading not required.)

Army Form C. 2118.

Place	Date	Hour	Summary of Events and Information	Remarks and references to Appendices
CAVILLON	9/6/18		Received orders during evening for dismounted personnel of Division to be ready to embus at 10am 10th for CONTY area under 1st French Army.	
WAILLY	10/6/18		Div H.Q. and H.Q. R.A. moved to WAILLY, Infantry Brigades by bus 63rd to LOEUILLY area 111th to HEBECOURT, RUMIGNY. 112th to ESSERTAUX - LE BOSQUEL LAWARDE. Divl Artillery to NAMPTY - PROUZEL BACOUEL. Engaged in reconnoitring areas allotted billets and to 1st French Army to obtain particulars of accommodation	
" "	11/6/18		Arranging details in connection with water supply which in most cases is inadequate. Applied to 22nd Corps for Water cart lorries and 120 trench shelters to accommodate personnel of batteries ordered to move forward	

2353 Wt. W2544/1454 700,000 5/15 D. D. & L. A.D.S.S./Forms/C. 2118.

Instructions regarding War Diaries and Intelligence Summaries are contained in F. S. Regs., Part II. and the Staff Manual respectively. Title pages will be prepared in manuscript.

WAR DIARY
or
INTELLIGENCE SUMMARY.
(Erase heading not required.)

Army Form C. 2118.

Place	Date	Hour	Summary of Events and Information	Remarks and references to Appendices
Wailly	12/6/18		Reconnoitring accommodation in ORESMAUX and ST SAUFLIEU for 2 battns 63rd Inf Bde - Somersets and Lincolns moved to the above villages	
WAILLY	13/6/18		112th Inf Bde group moved to SAINS en AMIENOIS ST FUSCIEN HEBECOURT VERS - Engaged in reconnoitring area and allotting accommodation. Artillery moved into Reserve positions	
WAILLY.	14/6/18		Div Commander held conference discussed readjustment of Brigade areas, decided to move Brigades	
	15/6/18		Infantry Brigades moved as follows 111th Sains en Amienois and HEBECOURT 63rd Inf Bde ST SAUFLIEU and RUMIGNY 112th Infantry Brigade ST FUSCIEN SURY and HEBECOURT	

2353 Wt. W2544/1454 700,000 5/15 D. D. & L. A.D.S.S./Forms/C. 2118.

Instructions regarding War Diaries and Intelligence Summaries are contained in F. S. Regs., Part II. and the Staff Manual respectively. Title pages will be prepared in manuscript.

WAR DIARY
or
INTELLIGENCE SUMMARY.
(Erase heading not required.)

Army Form C. 2118.

Place	Date	Hour	Summary of Events and Information	Remarks and references to Appendices
WAILLY.	16/6/18.		Rear waggon lines of 123rd Bde moved from NAMPTY to VERS(?)RE engaged in water reconnaissance in Bryalle area & ascertaining additional troughing required. Visit to 31st French Corps—	
WAILLY	17/6/18		Orders received that Division is to be prepared to entrain on 19th inst for return to 4th Corps. Visit to Traffic to ascertain details. No 3 Coy train held sports. Advanced Div HQ established at St FUSCIEN.	
WAILLY	18/6/18		Orders received for mounted personnel and transport of Division to move to 4th Corps on 20th inst staying on night of 20/21st in Picquigny - VIGNACOURT - ST SAUVEUR area— Dismounted personnel to move on 21st by train entraining Longueau - SALEUX - Prouzel, and detraining at Mondicourt AUTHIEULE and DOULLENS.	

2353 Wt. W2544/1454 700,000 5/15 D. D. & L. A.D.S.S./Forms/C. 2118.

Instructions regarding War Diaries and Intelligence Summaries are contained in F. S. Regs., Part II. and the Staff Manual respectively. Title pages will be prepared in manuscript.

WAR DIARY
or
INTELLIGENCE SUMMARY.
(Erase heading not required.)

Army Form C. 2118.

Place	Date	Hour	Summary of Events and Information	Remarks and references to Appendices
WAILLY	19/6/18		Attended conference 4th Corps HQ held to decide how Division was to be accommodated on arrival. It was decided to allot accommodation as shown in attached Table Appendix "A". Visit from Staff Officer of 3rd French Division which is relieving 37th Division in reserve. Arranging details regarding handing over of accommodation.	
Wailly.	20/6/18		Transport and Artillery commenced march to 4th Corps area. Arranging final details with traffic for entrainment of dismounted personnel. Billeting parties despatched by lorry to new area in 4th Corps.	
PAS.	21/6/18		D.H.Q. moved and opened at PAS. Division arrived in 4th Corps area and accommodated as shown in appendix A. Engaged in supervising detrainment of troops.	

2353 Wt. W2544/1454 700,000 5/15 D. D. & L. A.D.S.S./Forms/C. 2118.

Instructions regarding War Diaries and Intelligence Summaries are contained in F. S. Regs., Part II. and the Staff Manual respectively. Title pages will be prepared in manuscript.

WAR DIARY
or
INTELLIGENCE SUMMARY.
(Erase heading not required.)

Army Form C. 2118.

Place	Date	Hour	Summary of Events and Information	Remarks and references to Appendices
PAS	22/6/18		Orders received that 37 Division is to relieve 62nd Division in left sector of Corps front. Relief to be completed by 10 AM on 26th inst. Divisional Commander held a conference at Div HQ.	
" "	23/6/18		Visit to 62nd Division arranging administrative details of relief, issued administrative instructions. Major Anderson DSO MC GSO2 37 Division slightly wounded near Gommecourt evacuated to 3rd CCS DOULLENS. Div Commander visited New Zealand Division horse show.	
" "	24/6/18		Engaged in preparation of rolls of category A men recommended for reclassification by travelling inspector of drafts.	
" "	25/6/18		Div HQ moved to HENU. 63rd and 111th Infantry Brigades relieving Brigades of 62nd Division in the line. 112th Inf Bde relieved Bde in support with HQ at SOUASTRE. Div Arty relief completed.	

Instructions regarding War Diaries and Intelligence Summaries are contained in F. S. Regs., Part II. and the Staff Manual respectively. Title pages will be prepared in manuscript.

WAR DIARY
or
INTELLIGENCE SUMMARY.
(Erase heading not required.)

Army Form C. 2118.

H.Q. 37th Divn
Administrative Staff.

Place	Date	Hour	Summary of Events and Information	Remarks and references to Appendices
~~P.D.S.~~ HENU	26/6/18		Visit to various transport lines to ascertain if bomb proof protection has been erected. Visit to Reception Camp ORVILLE arranging supply of clean clothes for baths there	
	27/6/18		Corps boxing competition commenced at MARIEUX	
	28/6/18		Finals of Corps Boxing. Army Conference at DOULLENS to discuss policy regarding distribution of canteen stores in Army and L of C areas.	
	29/6/18		Special performance of Barn Owls at P.D.S. Div Commander attended. G.O.C. New Zealand Division and Staff invited.	
	30/6/18		4th Corps H.A. Horse show. Divisional Commander attended	

D Dennis Major
DAAG

A5834 Wt. W4973/M687 750,000 8/16 D. D. & L. Ltd. Forms/C.2118/13.

CONFIDENTIAL

Volume XXXVI

37th Division.

Administrative Staff War Diary.

July 1918.

Instructions regarding War Diaries and Intelligence Summaries are contained in F. S. Regs., Part II. and the Staff Manual respectively. Title pages will be prepared in manuscript.

WAR DIARY
or
INTELLIGENCE SUMMARY.
(Erase heading not required.)

Army Form C. 2118.

HEADQUARTERS * No. .... Date .... 37th DIVISION

Place	Date	Hour	Summary of Events and Information	Remarks and references to Appendices
			(a) CASUALTIES, SICK EVACUATIONS & REINFORCEMENTS are shewn by units in Appendix I	
			(b) STAFF APPOINTMENTS of the Division are shewn in Appendix II.	
			(c) Copies of the WEEKLY FIGHTING STRENGTH Returns are attached as Appendix III.	
			(d) Copies of DIVISIONAL ROUTINE ORDERS are attached as Appendix IV.	
			(e) IMMEDIATE HONOURS & REWARDS are shown in in the order in which they were published in DIVISIONAL ROUTINE ORDERS. Appendix IV	
			(f) SELF INFLICTED AND ACCIDENTAL CASUALTIES.	
			A table showing the number of Self-Inflicted Wounds and Accidental Casualties which have occurred during the month is attached Appendix V.	
			(g) COURTS MARTIAL.	
			A table showing the number and the particulars of F.G.Cs. M. assembled during the month is attached Appendix VI.	
			No G.C.M. was convened during the month of July.	

Instructions regarding War Diaries and Intelligence Summaries are contained in F. S. Regs., Part II. and the Staff Manual respectively. Title pages will be prepared in manuscript.

WAR DIARY
or
INTELLIGENCE SUMMARY.
(*Erase heading not required.*)

Army Form C. 2118.

HEADQUARTERS No. ... Date ... 37th DIVISION

Place	Date	Hour	Summary of Events and Information	Remarks and references to Appendices
			PIPE LIGHTERS. Owing to the cost of matches for the Armies in FRANCE and the amount of tonnage required therefore an opinion was called for as to the practicability of issuing each man with a petrol pipe lighter instead of two boxes of matches per week. The idea was concurred in although it was pointed out that the issue of petrol in such small quantities to men in forward areas would present difficulties.	
			TRANSPORT & PACKING OF LEWIS GUNS. Experiments were carried out in packing Lewis Guns in a Limber as a result of a Circular letter on the subject from G.H.Q. A method suggested by the 8th S.L.I. was shown to representatives of IV Corps and Third Army and was approved and may be adopted generally.	
			WINTER ACCOMMODATION. The Village of SOUASTRE was reconnoitred and arrangements made that as far as possible the inhabitants should be helped with men and materials to put all barns in good repair for billeting troops during the winter.	
			E.F.C. SUPPLIES. A new system of distribution of Canteen supplies began on the 29th under which each Division received a proportion of the total amount allotted to the Army. Units were in turn allotted a proportion of the Divisional allotment, and no purchases on behalf of Units were allowed from the E.F.C. The Scheme has not been in force long enough to judge results.	
			COARSE SALT. Difficulty experienced in obtaining a sufficient supply owing to the shortage of transportation.	
			TRANSPORT. Machine Gun Battalion issued with 2 extra Water Carts to complete establishment to 4 per Battalion.	
			H.G. Reed Lieut. Colonel. for Major General. Commanding 37th Division.	
			22/8/18.	

A5834 Wt. W4973/M687 750,000 8/16 D. D. & L. Ltd. Forms/C.2118/13.

Office Copy

37th **DIVISION.** **SECRET** "C."

STRENGTH RETURN MADE UP TO 12 NOON, SATURDAY July 27th 1918 July 27th 1918.

UNIT.	(i.) Fighting strength for previous week, compiled in accordance with A.G.'s instructions.		(ii.) Increase during week, due to drafts, etc., taken on strength of Unit.		(iii.) Totals from (i.) and (ii.)		(iv.) Decrease during week—casualties, etc., deducted from strength of Unit.		"A." Strength, excluding Attached.		"B." Not present with the Unit and not at the disposal of C.O. included in column "A."		"A" minus "B." Available fighting strength, including Personnel of Battalion Transport and Quartermaster's Stores.		REMARKS. (Brief notes regarding (ii.), (iv.) and "B," etc.)
	Officers.	O.R.	Officers.	O.R.	Officers.	O.R.	Officers.	O.R.	Officers.	O.R.	Officers.	O.R.	Officers.	O.R.	
63rd Infantry Brigade															
8th Lincolns.	37	952	2	20	39	972	1	21	38	951	8	120	30	831	
8th Somersets.	37	894	2	2	39	896	1	16	38	880	11	165	27	715	
4th Middlesex.	37	916	3	12	40	928	2	48	38	880	9	108	29	772	
Total Brigade.	111	2762	7	34	118	2796	4	85	114	2711	28	393	86	2318	
111th Infantry Brigade.															
10th R.Fusiliers.	37	867	-	39	37	906	3	74	34	832	6	111	28	721	
13th K.R.R.C.	37	884	2	44	39	928	-	27	39	901	7	112	32	789	
13th Rifle Bde.	39	916	6	24	45	940	1	25	44	915	14	141	30	774	
Total Brigade.	113	2667	8	107	121	2774	4	126	117	2648	27	364	90	2284	
112th Infantry Brigade.															
13th R.Fusiliers.	42	855	1	34	43	889	1	16	42	873	12	128	30	745	
1/1st Herts.	40	960	2	6	42	966	3	7	39	959	11	180	28	779	
1st Essex.	43	908	-	38	43	946	1	10	42	936	12	123	30	813	
Total Brigade.	125	2723	3	78	128	2801	5	33	123	2768	35	431	88	2337	
9th Nth. Staffs.(Pnrs.)	32	825	-	23	32	848	-	13	32	835	7	71	25	764	
TOTAL DIVISION.	381	8977	18	242	399	9219	13	257	386	8962	97	1259	289	7703	
37th Bn. M.G. Corps.	44	879	1	4	45	883	1	31	44	852	3	59	41	793	
TOTALS															

H.G. Ruddlewick(?)

Major General
Commanding 37th Division.

PRINTED IN FRANCE BY ARMY PRINTING AND STATIONERY SERVICES.

PRESS B. E2317. 2000. 6-18.

37th **DIVISION.** "C."

STRENGTH RETURN MADE UP TO 12 NOON, SATURDAY July 20th 1918. July 20th 1918.

UNIT.	(i.) Fighting strength for previous week, compiled in accordance with A.G.'s instructions.		(ii.) Increase during week, due to drafts, etc., taken on strength of Unit.		(iii.) Totals from (i.) and (ii.)		(iv.) Decrease during week—casualties, etc., deducted from strength of Unit.		"A." Strength, excluding Attached.		"B." Not present with the Unit and not at the disposal of C.O. included in column "A."		"A" minus "B." Available fighting strength, including Personnel of Battalion Transport and Quartermaster's Stores.		REMARKS. (Brief notes regarding (ii.), (iv.) and "B," etc.)
	Officers.	O.R.	Officers.	O.R.	Officers.	O.R.	Officers.	O.R.	Officers.	O.R.	Officers.	O.R.	Officers.	O.R.	
63rd Infatry Brigade.															
8th Lincolns.	39	924	1	41	40	965	3	13	37	952	10	115	27	837	
8th Somersets.	39	857	-	45	39	902	2	8	37	894	11	145	26	749	
4th Middlesex.	37	843	1	90	38	933	1	17	37	916	8	106	29	810	
Total Brigade.	115	2624	2	176	117	2800	6	38	111	2762	29	366	82	2396	
111th Infantry Brigade.															
10th R.Fusiliers.	37	844	1	43	38	887	1	20	37	867	3	110	34	757	
13th K.R.R.C.	38	881	1	24	39	905	2	21	37	884	8	83	29	801	
13th Rifle Bde.	39	912	-	26	39	938	-	22	39	916	13	136	26	780	
Total Brigade.	114	2637	2	93	116	2730	3	63	113	2667	24	329	89	2338	
112th Infantry Brigade.															
13th R.Fusiliers.	44	816	1	55	45	871	3	16	42	855	13	120	29	735	
1/1st Herts.	40	990	1	21	41	1011	1	51	40	960	10	165	30	795	
1st Essex.	43	867	1	53	44	920	1	12	43	908	11	157	32	751	
Total Brigade.	127	2673	3	129	130	2802	5	79	125	2723	34	442	91	2281	
9th Nth. Staffs (Pnrs.)	31	821	1	21	32	842	-	17	32	825	9	72	23	753	
TOTAL DIVISION.	387	8755	8	419	395	9174	14	197	381	8977	96	1209	285	7768	
37th Bn. M. G. Corps.	46	879	-	12	46	891	2	12	44	879	2	46	42	833	
TOTALS															

H. A. G. Reid
Lieut Colonel
for
Major General
Commanding 37th Division.

PRINTED IN FRANCE BY ARMY PRINTING AND STATIONERY SERVICES.

PRESS B. E2317. 2000. 6-18.

Appendix III

SECRET

37th DIVISION. "C."

STRENGTH RETURN MADE UP TO 12 NOON, SATURDAY July 6th 1918. July 6th 1918.

UNIT.	(i.) Fighting strength for previous week, compiled in accordance with A.G.'s instructions.		(ii.) Increase during week, due to drafts, etc., taken on strength of Unit.		(iii.) Totals from (i.) and (ii.)		(iv.) Decrease during week—casualties, etc., deducted from strength of Unit.		"A." Strength, excluding Attached.		"B." Not present with the Unit and not at the disposal of C.O. included in column "A."		"A" minus "B." Available fighting strength, including Personnel of Battalion Transport and Quartermaster's Stores.		REMARKS. (Brief notes regarding (ii.), (iv.) and "B," etc.)
	Officers.	O.R.	Officers.	O.R.	Officers.	O.R.	Officers.	O.R.	Officers.	O.R.	Officers.	O.R.	Officers.	O.R.	
63rd Infantry Brigade.															
8th Lincolns.	37	896	-	1	37	897	-	18	37	879	15	109	22	770	
8th Somerset L.I.	36	890	-	2	36	892	1	26	35	866	13	123	22	743	
4th Middlesex.	37	954	-	-	37	954	1	90	36	864	13	146	23	718	
Total Brigade.	110	2740	-	3	110	2743	2	134	108	2609	41	378	67	2231	
111th Infantry Brigade.															
10th R.Fusrs.	36	863	4	-	40	863	2	13	38	850	6	105	32	745	
13th K.R.R.C.	38	877	-	19	38	896	-	24	38	872	10	137	28	735	
13th Rifle Bde.	43	894	-	12	43	906	3	18	40	888	12	108	28	780	
Total Brigade.	117	2634	4	31	121	2665	5	55	116	2610	28	350	88	2260	
112th Infantry Brigade.															
13th R.Fusrs.	41	824	-	3	41	827	1	3	40	824	11	113	29	711	
1/1st Herts.	49	1021	3	-	52	1021	11	22	41	999	16	205	25	794	
1st Essex.	41	899	5	5	46	904	4	19	42	885	10	132	32	753	
Total Brigade.	131	2744	8	8	139	2752	16	44	123	2708	37	450	86	2258	
9th Nth Staffs (Pnrs)	31	860	1	9	32	869	1	34	31	835	3	111	28	724	
Total Division.	389	8978	13	51	402	9029	24	267	378	8762	109	1289	269	7473	
37th Bn.M.G.Corps.	47	913	1	6	48	919	1	30	47	889	-	21	47	868	
TOTALS															

A. C. Reed Lt Col
for Major General.
Commanding 37th Division.

PRINTED IN FRANCE BY ARMY PRINTING AND STATIONERY SERVICES.

PRESS B. E2317. 2000. 6-18.

Office Copy

SECRET

"C."

37th **DIVISION.**

STRENGTH RETURN MADE UP TO 12 NOON, SATURDAY July 13th 1918. July 13th 1918.

UNIT.	(i.) Fighting strength for previous week, compiled in accordance with A.G.'s instructions.		(ii.) Increase during week, due to drafts, etc., taken on strength of Unit.		(iii.) Totals from (i.) and (ii.)		(iv.) Decrease during week—casualties, etc., deducted from strength of Unit.		"A." Strength, excluding Attached.		"B." Not present with the Unit and not at the disposal of C.O. included in column "A."		"A" minus "B." Available fighting strength, including Personnel of Battalion Transport and Quartermaster's Stores.		REMARKS. (Brief notes regarding (ii.), (iv.) and "B," etc.)
	Officers.	O.R.	Officers.	O.R.	Officers.	O.R.	Officers.	O.R.	Officers.	O.R.	Officers.	O.R.	Officers.	O.R.	
63rd Infantry Brigade															
8th Lincolns.	37	879	3	77	40	956	1	32	39	924	15	126	24	798	924
8th Somersets.	35	866	4	16	39	882	-	25	39	857	13	109	26	748	884
4th Middlesex.	36	864	1	25	37	889	-	46	37	843	10	107	27	736	40
Total Brigade.	108	2609	8	118	116	2727	1	103	115	2624	38	342	77	2282	
111th Infantry Brigade.															
10th R.Fusiliers.	38	850	1	2	39	852	2	8	37	844	4	118	33	726	
13th K.R.R.C.	38	872	2	36	40	908	2	27	38	881	9	73	29	808	
13th Rifle Bde.	40	888	1	52	41	940	2	28	39	912	13	129	26	783	
Total Brigade.	116	2610	4	90	120	2700	6	63	114	2637	26	320	88	2317	
112th Infantry Brigade.															
13th R.Fusiliers.	40	824	4	4	44	828	-	12	44	816	14	148	30	668	
1/1st Herts.	41	999	-	9	41	1008	1	18	40	990	17	229	23	761	
1st Essex.	42	885	1	27	43	912	-	45	43	867	10	154	33	713	
Total Brigade.	123	2708	5	40	128	2748	1	75	127	2673	41	531	86	2142	
9th Nth. Staffs (Pnrs.)	31	835	-	19	31	854	-	33	31	821	9	65	22	756	
TOTAL DIVISION.	378	8762	17	267	395	9029	8	274	387	8755	114	1258	273	7497	
37th Bn. M.G. Corps.	47	889	-	2	47	891	1	12	46	879	2	46	44	833	
TOTALS															

H.G.C.

Major General
Commanding 37th Division.

PRINTED IN FRANCE BY ARMY PRINTING AND STATIONERY SERVICES.

PRESS B. E2317. 2000. 6-18.

Appendix H

ACCOMMODATION ALLOTTED TO 37th DIVISION IN IV CORPS AREA.

Div. H.Q. ...	...	PAS.
H.Q., Div.Arty..	...	"
H.Q., Div.Engnrs.	...	"
Employment Coy.	...	"
H.Q.,M.G.Battn. & 1 Coy.		"

Divl. Arty. ...)	...	(SARTON, ORVILLE,
No.1 Coy.Train..)	...	(CAUMESNIL.

63rd Infantry Brigade Group.

Brigade H.Q. ...	...	COUIN.
'A' Battalion...	...	"
'B' " ...	...	"
'C' " ...	...	"
M.G.Coy. ...	...	"
Field Ambulance.	...	HENU(accommodation to be vacated by N.Z. Field Ambce.)
Field Coy. RE...	...	FAMECHON.
Train Company...	...	COUIN.

Town Major COUIN will hand over 195 tents to supplement accommodation at COUIN.

111th Infantry Brigade Group.

Brigade H.Q. ..	...	HENU.
'A' Battalion..	...	"
'B' " ..	...	"
'C' " ..	...	THIEVRES.
M.G.Coy.. ...	...	HENU.
Field Ambulance	...	THIEVRES.
Field Coy. RE..	...	FAMECHON.
Train Company..	...	HENU.

Town Major HENU will hand over 95 tents to supplement accommodation at HENU.

112th Infantry Brigade Group.

Brigade H.Q. ...	...	AUTHIEULE.
'A' Battalion...	...	"
'B' " ...	...	AMPLIER.
'C' " ...	...	TERRAMESNIL.
M.G.Coy. ...	...	"
Field Ambulance..	...	"
Field Coy. RE...	...	AUTHIEULE.
Train Coy. ...	...	"

Pioneer Battalion ... DOULLENS.

Mobile Vet.Sect. ... FAMECHON.

Div. Reception Camp.... ORVILLE.

SECRET

Vol 37

W A R   D I A R Y.   AUGUST. 1918.

ADMINISTRATOVE BRANCH.

37th DIVISION.

Instructions regarding War Diaries and Intelligence Summaries are contained in F. S. Regs., Part II. and the Staff Manual respectively. Title pages will be prepared in manuscript.

WAR DIARY
or
INTELLIGENCE SUMMARY.
(Erase heading not required.)

HEADQUARTERS No. ... Date ... 37th DIVISION

Army Form C. 2118.

Place	Date	Hour	Summary of Events and Information	Remarks and references to Appendices
			(a) CASUALTIES, SICK EVACUATIONS & REINFORCEMENTS are shewn by units in	Appendix I.
			(b) Copies of the WEEKLY FIGHTING STRENGTH Returns are attached	Appendix II.
			(c) Copies of DIVISIONAL ROUTINE ORDERS are attached	Appendix III.
			(d) IMMEDIATE HONOURS & REWARDS are shewn in the order in which they are published in Divisional Routine Orders.	Appendix IV.
			(e) SELF INFLICTED AND ACCIDENTAL CASUALTIES.	
			A table shewing the Self-Inflicted Wounds and Accidental Casualties which have occured during the month is attached.	Appendix V
			(g) COURTS MARTIAL.	
			A table shewing the number and the particulars of F.G.Cs.M. assembled during the month is attached.	Appendix VI.
			No. G.C.M. was convened during the month of August.	

D. D. & L., London, E.C.
(A8c04) Wt W1771/M2031 750,000 5/17 Sch. 52 Forms/C2118/14

APPENDIX I

August 1st - 31st 1918.

37th DIVISION.

1 9 1 8.	CASUALTIES. Killed. O.	Killed. O.R.	Wounded. O.	Wounded. O.R.	Missing. O.	Missing. O.R.	Sick Evacuations. Off.	Sick Evacuations. O.R's.	Reinforcements. Off.	Reinforcements. O.R's.
August 1st	-	-	-	4	-	-	-	12	1	-
2nd	-	1	-	5	-	-	-	19	1	119
3rd	-	-	-	14	-	-	3	8	-	47
4th	-	-	-	3	-	-	2	21	12	72
5th	-	4	1	13	-	1	2	14	1	-
6th	1	1	-	4	-	-	1	8	4	10
7th	-	-	-	7	-	-	1	9	-	30
8th	-	-	-	7	-	-	-	14	6	26
9th	-	2	-	6	-	-	1	16	1	2
10th	-	4	1	9	-	-	-	8	3	44
11th	-	1	-	8	-	-	-	3	1	28
12th	-	3	-	12	-	-	-	3	2	12
13th	-	-	1	11	-	-	1	4	3	17
14th	-	2	-	6	-	1	-	10	1	-
15th	-	5	-	17	-	1	1	6	2	-
16th	-	1	-	9	-	-	2	11	-	4
17th	-	1	1	15	-	-	-	17	1	45
18th	-	-	-	8	-	-	2	18	-	-
19th	-	-	-	17	-	-	-	24	1	99
20th)	-	-	-	-	-	-	-	12	-	31
21st)	2	27	10	155	-	-	1	8	1	12
22nd)	-	-	-	-	-	-	2	21	4	8
23rd)	-	-	-	-	-	-	-	9	-	24
24th)	7	170	-	655	-	26	3	16	2	1
25th)	-	-	-	-	-	-	1	5	(-	-
26th)	-	-	-	-	-	-	1	14	(-	-
27th)	12	195	35	1154	-	11	-	7	(-	-
28th)	-	-	-	-	-	-	-	11	(25	1748
29th	-	1	-	4	-	-	1	8	(-	-
30th	-	1	1	11	-	-	-	7	(-	-
31st	-	-	1	13	-	-	2	15	(-	-
TOTAL.	22	419	51	2167	-	40	27	358	73	2379

Office Copy

37th DIVISION.

SECRET "C."

STRENGTH RETURN MADE UP TO 12 NOON, SATURDAY August 3rd 1918. Aug. 3rd 1918.

UNIT.	(i.) Fighting strength for previous week, compiled in accordance with A.G.'s instructions.		(ii.) Increase during week, due to drafts, etc., taken on strength of Unit.		(iii.) Totals from (i.) and (ii.)		(iv.) Decrease during week—casualties, etc., deducted from strength of Unit.		"A." Strength, excluding Attached.		"B." Not present with the Unit and not at the disposal of C.O. included in column "A."		"A" minus "B." Available fighting strength, including Personnel of Battalion Transport and Quartermaster's Stores.		REMARKS. (Brief notes regarding (ii.), (iv.) and "B," etc.)
	Officers.	O.R.	Officers.	O.R.	Officers.	O.R.	Officers.	O.R.	Officers.	O.R.	Officers.	O.R.	Officers.	O.R.	APPENDIX II
63rd Infantry Brigade.															
8th Lincolns.	38	951	1	14	39	965	1	14	38	951	13	135	25	816	
8th Somersets.	38	880	1	-	39	880	2	11	37	869	8	150	29	719	
4th Middlesex.	38	880	4	62	42	942	2	6	40	936	6	107	34	829	
Total Brigade.	114	2711	6	76	120	2787	5	31	115	2756	27	392	88	2364	
111th Infantry Brigade.															
10th R. Fusiliers.	34	832	-	85	34	917	-	26	34	891	10	128	24	763	
13th K.R.R.C.	39	901	-	43	39	944	-	13	39	931	12	120	27	811	
13th Rifle Bde.	44	915	1	24	45	939	-	20	45	919	17	150	28	769	
Total Brigade.	117	2648	1	152	118	2800	-	59	118	2741	39	398	79	2343	
112th Infantry Brigade.															
13th R.Fusiliers.	42	873	1	76	43	949	3	18	40	931	12	118	28	813	
1/1st Herts.	39	959	-	17	39	976	1	8	38	968	13	171	25	797	
1st Essex.	42	936	-	32	42	968	1	41	41	927	14	121	27	806	
Total Brigade.	123	2768	1	125	124	2893	5	67	119	2826	39	410	80	2416	
9th Nth. Staffs.(Pnrs.)	32	835	-	11	32	846	-	14	32	832	8	75	24	757	
TOTAL DIVISION.	386	8962	8	364	394	9326	10	171	384	9155	113	1275	271	7880	
37th Bn. M. G. Corps.	44	852	-	34	44	886	1	8	43	878	2	49	41	829	
TOTALS															

H. G. Reed [signature]

for Major General
Commanding 37th Division.

PRINTED IN FRANCE BY ARMY PRINTING AND STATIONERY SERVICES.

PRESS B. E2317. 2000. 6-18.

Office Copy

SECRET

"C."

37th DIVISION.

STRENGTH RETURN MADE UP TO 12 NOON, SATURDAY August 10th 1918. Aug. 10th 1918.

UNIT.	(i.) Fighting strength for previous week, compiled in accordance with A.G.'s instructions.		(ii.) Increase during week, due to drafts, etc., taken on strength of Unit.		(iii.) Totals from (i.) and (ii.)		(iv.) Decrease during week—casualties, etc., deducted from strength of Unit.		"A." Strength, excluding Attached.		"B." Not present with the Unit and not at the disposal of C.O. included in column "A."		"A" minus "B." Available fighting strength, including Personnel of Battalion Transport and Quartermaster's Stores.		REMARKS. (Brief notes regarding (ii.), (iv.) and "B," etc.)
	Officers.	O.R.	Officers.	O.R.	Officers.	O.R.	Officers.	O.R.	Officers.	O.R.	Officers.	O.R.	Officers.	O.R.	
63rd Infantry Brigade.															
8th Lincolns.	38	951	1	1	39	952	-	9	39	943	14	134	25	809	
8th Somersets.	37	869	-	47	37	916	1	39	36	877	10	135	26	742	
4th Middlesex.	40	936	4	31	44	967	-	32	44	935	11	109	33	826	
Total Brigade.	115	2756	5	79	120	2835	1	80	119	2755	35	378	84	2377	
111th Infantry Brigade.															
10th R.Fusiliers.	34	891	5	38	39	929	-	9	39	920	10	117	29	803	
13th K.R.R.C.	39	931	1	3	40	934	1	20	39	914	11	120	28	794	
13th Rifle Bde.	45	919	8	70	53	989	-	34	53	955	18	141	35	814	
Total Brigade.	118	2741	14	111	132	2852	1	63	131	2789	39	378	92	2411	
112th Infantry Brigade.															
13th R.Fusiliers.	40	931	3	13	43	944	-	7	43	937	17	125	26	812	
1/1st Herts.	38	968	1	11	39	979	2	19	37	960	12	138	25	822	
1st Essex.	41	927	1	1	42	928	-	12	42	916	13	142	29	774	
Total Brigade.	119	2826	5	25	124	2851	2	38	122	2813	42	405	80	2408	
9th Nth. Staffs. (Pnrs.)	32	832	-	5	32	837	1	5	31	832	9	59	22	773	
TOTAL DIVISION.	384	9155	24	220	408	9375	5	186	403	9189	125	1220	278	7969	
37th Bn. M.G. Corps.	43	878	5	20	48	898	1	6	47	892	4	57	43	835	
TOTALS															

H. Reddie
for Major General
Commanding 37th Division.

PRINTED IN FRANCE BY ARMY PRINTING AND STATIONERY SERVICES.

PRESS B. E2317. 2000. 6-18.

Office Copy

37th **DIVISION.** SECRET "C."

STRENGTH RETURN MADE UP TO 12 NOON, SATURDAY August 17th 1918. August 17th 1918.

UNIT.	(i.) Fighting strength for previous week, compiled in accordance with A.G.'s instructions.		(ii.) Increase during week, due to drafts, etc., taken on strength of Unit.		(iii.) Totals from (i.) and (ii.)		(iv.) Decrease during week—casualties, etc., deducted from strength of Unit.		"A." Strength, excluding Attached.		"B." Not present with the Unit and not at the disposal of C.O. included in column "A."		"A" minus "B." Available fighting strength, including Personnel of Battalion Transport and Quartermaster's Stores.		REMARKS. (Brief notes regarding (ii.), (iv.) and "B," etc.)
	Officers.	O.R.	Officers.	O.R.	Officers.	O.R.	Officers.	O.R.	Officers.	O.R.	Officers.	O.R.	Officers.	O.R.	
63rd Infantry Brigade.															
8th Lincolns.	39	943	3	4	42	947	-	15	42	932	11	114	31	818	
8th Somersets.	36	877	-	28	36	905	2	34	34	871	10	93	24	778	
4th Middlesex.	44	935	-	30	44	965	-	27	44	938	15	79	29	859	
Total Brigade.	119	2755	3	62	122	2817	2	76	120	2741	36	286	84	2455	
111th Infantry Brigade.															
10th R.Fusiliers.	39	920	4	14	43	934	-	2	43	932	10	142	33	790	
13th K.R.R.C.	39	914	2	24	41	938	-	12	41	926	13	123	28	803	
13th Rifle Bde.	53	955	-	33	53	988	-	5	53	983	20	156	33	827	
Total Brigade.	131	2789	6	71	137	2860	-	19	137	2841	43	421	94	2420	
112th Infantry Brigade.															
13th R.Fusiliers.	43	937	1	7	44	944	-	13	44	931	18	138	26	793	
1/1st Herts.	37	960	-	2	37	962	-	21	37	941	12	146	25	795	
1st Essex.	42	916	1	38	43	954	-	27	43	927	12	136	31	791	
Total Brigade.	122	2813	2	47	124	2860	-	61	124	2799	42	420	82	2379	
9th Nth. Staffs.(Pnrs.)	31	832	1	22	32	854	-	6	32	848	10	69	22	779	
TOTAL DIVISION.	403	9189	12	202	415	9391	2	162	413	9229	131	1196	282	8033	
37th Bn. M.G.Corps.	47	892	1	3	48	895	2	8	46	887	9	83	37	804	
TOTALS															

M

for Major General
Commanding 37th Division.

PRINTED IN FRANCE BY ARMY PRINTING AND STATIONERY SERVICES.

PRESS B. E2317. 2000. 6-18.

37th DIVISION.

WEEKLY FIGHTING STRENGTH RETURN UP TO 12 NOON SATURDAY 24/8/18.

(a) Casualties reported in List No.1. dated 22-8-18 have been deducted.

(b) No figures are available to compile the return for the 111th Infantry Brigade.

(c) The following estimated casualties are subsequent to List No. 1 mentioned above, and have not been deducted.

63rd Inf.Bde.	Off.	O.R.
8th Lincolns.	5	100
8th Somersets.	5	100
4th Middlesex	5	100

111th Inf.Bde.	Off.	O.R.
10th R.Fus.	6	250
13th K.R.R.C.	6	150
13th Rif.Bde	3	250

112th Inf.Bde.	Off.	O.R.
13th R.Fus.	6	150
1st Essex	12	250
1/1st Herts	10	325

37th Bn.M.G.Corps.	
Off.	O.R.
1	34.

(d) Est/imated Casualties mentioned in para (c) have already been reported in this office wires Nos E.C. 2,3 & 4.

(e) Strength Return for 111th Infantry Brigade will be forwarded as soon as possible.

37th DIVISION. "B."

STRENGTH RETURN MADE UP TO 12 NOON SATURDAY August 24th 1918 ....1918.

UNIT.	(i.) Fighting strength for previous week, compiled in accordance with A.Gs. instructions.		(ii.) Increase during week, due to drafts, etc., taken on strength of unit.		(iii.) Totals from (i.) and (ii.)		(iv.) Decrease during week—casualties, etc., deducted from strength of unit.		"A" Strength, excluding Attached.		"B" Not present with the Unit and not at the disposal of C.O. included in column "A."		"A" minus "B" Available Fighting Strength including Personnel of Battalion Transport and Quartermaster's Stores.		REMARKS. (Brief notes regarding (ii.), (iv.) and "B," etc.)
	Officers.	O.R.	Officers.	O.R.	Officers.	O.R.	Officers.	O.R.	Officers.	O.R.	Officers.	O.R.	Officers.	O.R.	
63rd Infantry Brigade.															
8th Lincolns.	42	932	-	1	42	933	-	18	42	915	15	141	27	774	
8th Somersets.	34	871	1	53	35	924	1	47	34	877	11	118	23	759	
4th Middlesex.	44	938	-	19	44	957	3	64	41	873	14	77	27	796	
Total Brigade.	120	2741	1	73	121	2814	4	149	117	2665	40	336	77	2329	
111th Infantry Brigade.															
10th R.Fusiliers.	43	932													
13th K.R.R.C.	41	926													
13th Rifle Bde.	53	983													
Total Brigade.	137	2841													
112th Infantry Brigade.															
13th R.Fusiliers.	44	931	-	-	44	931	2	29	42	902	18	116	24	786	
1st Essex.	43	927	-	-	43	927	-	20	43	907	10	88	33	819	
1/1st Herts.	37	941	-	12	37	953	1	15	36	938	13	111	23	827	
Total Brigade.	124	2799	-	12	124	2811	3	64	121	2747	41	315	80	2432	
9th N.th Staffs (Pnrs)	38	848	1	2	38	850	-	23	38	827	12	80	21	747	
Total Division.															
37th Bn. M.G.Corps.	46	897	-	6	46	903	-	27	46	866	11	112	35	754	
TOTALS															

[signature] Major a/DAAG
for Major General.
Commanding 37th Division.

3rd Field Survey Co., R.E. 2759 13-3-18.

"B."

37th DIVISION.

STRENGTH RETURN MADE UP TO 12 NOON SATURDAY ....August 24th........ ....1918.

UNIT.	(i.) Fighting strength for previous week, compiled in accordance with A.Gs. instructions.		(ii.) Increase during week, due to drafts, etc., taken on strength of unit.		(iii.) Totals from (i.) and (ii.)		(iv.) Decrease during week—casualties, etc., deducted from strength of unit.		"A" Strength, excluding Attached.		"B" Not present with the Unit and not at the disposal of C.O. included in column "A."		"A" minus "B" Available Fighting Strength including Personnel of Battalion Transport and Quartermaster's Stores.		REMARKS. (Brief notes regarding (ii.), (iv.) and "B," etc.)
	Officers.	O.R.	Officers.	O.R.	Officers.	O.R.	Officers.	O.R.	Officers.	O.R.	Officers.	O.R.	Officers.	O.R.	
<u>111th Infantry Brigade.</u>							<u>Approx-imate.</u>								
10th Royal Fusrs.	43	932	-	6	43	938	2	174	41	764	10	144	31	620	Estimated Casualty Wire No. E.C. 3 of 24th Aug.
13th K.R.R.C.	41	926	-	37	41	963	10	147	31	816	15	134	16	682	
13th Rifle Bde.	53	983	-	13	53	996	4	155	49	841	18	169	31	672	
Total Brigade.	137	2841	-	56	137	2897	16	476	121	2421	43	447	78	1974	
TOTALS															

[signature] Major for DAAG

Major General.
Commanding 37th Division.

3rd Field Survey Co., R.E. 2759 13-3-18.

Office Copy

"B."

37th DIVISION.

STRENGTH RETURN MADE UP TO 12 NOON SATURDAY August 31st 1918.

Aug. 31st 1918.

UNIT.	(i.) Fighting strength for previous week, compiled in accordance with A.Gs. instructions.		(ii.) Increase during week, due to drafts, etc., taken on strength of unit.		(iii.) Totals from (i.) and (ii.)		(iv.) Decrease during week—casualties, etc., deducted from strength of unit.		"A" Strength, excluding Attached.		"B" Not present with the Unit and not at the disposal of C.O. included in column "A."		"A" minus "B" Available Fighting Strength including Personnel of Battalion Transport and Quartermaster's Stores.		REMARKS. (Brief notes regarding (ii.), (iv.) and "B," etc.)
	Officers.	O.R.	Officers.	O.R.	Officers.	O.R.	Officers.	O.R.	Officers.	O.R.	Officers.	O.R.	Officers.	O.R.	
63rd Infantry Brigade.															
8th Lincolns.	42	915	-	68	42	983	5	180	37	803	15	152	22	651	
8th Somersets.	34	877	3	150	37	1027	6	149	31	878	14	128	17	750	
4th Middlesex.	41	873	5	106	46	979	9	217	37	762	15	76	22	686	
Total Brigade.	117	2665	8	324	125	2989	20	546	105	2443	44	356	61	2087	
111th Infantry Brigade.															
10th R.Fusiliers.	41	764	1	102	42	866	9	83	33	783	9	140	24	643	
13th K.R.R.C.	31	816	10	173	41	989	6	247	35	742	11	115	24	627	
13th Rifle Bde.	49	841	4	401	53	1242	8	221	45	1021	19	97	26	924	
Total Brigade.	121	2421	15	676	136	3097	23	551	113	2546	39	352	74	2194	
112th Infantry Brigade.															
13th R.Fusiliers.	42	902	-	109	42	1011	8	218	34	793	16	126	18	667	
1st Essex.	43	907	-	251	43	1158	14	296	29	862	9	89	20	773	
1/1st Herts.	36	938	-	305	36	1243	9	198	27	1045	11	116	16	929	
Total Brigade.	121	2747	-	665	121	3412	31	712	90	2700	36	331	54	2369	
9th Nth. Staffs (Pnrs.)	33	827	1	27	34	854	1	11	33	843	11	68	22	775	
TOTAL DIVISION.	392	8660	24	1692	416	10352	75	1820	341	8532	130	1107	211	7425	
37th Bn. M.G. Corps.	46	866	1	56	47	922	4	57	43	865	11	128	32	737	
TOTALS															

Major General.
Commanding 37th Division.

3rd Field Survey Co., R.E. 2759 13-3-18.

SECRET

Vol 38

W A R D I A R Y. SEPTEMBER 1918.

ADMINISTRATIVE BRANCH.

37th DIVISION.

Instructions regarding War Diaries and Intelligence Summaries are contained in F. S. Regs., Part II. and the Staff Manual respectively. Title pages will be prepared in manuscript.

WAR DIARY
or
INTELLIGENCE SUMMARY.
(Erase heading not required.)

Army Form C. 2118.

Place	Date	Hour	Summary of Events and Information	Remarks and references to Appendices
			(a) CASUALTIES, SICK EVACUATIONS & REINFORCEMENTS are shewn by units in	Appendix I.
			(b) Copies of the WEEKLY FIGHTING STRENGTH Returns are attached	Appendix II.
			(c) Copies of DIVISIONAL ROUTINE ORDERS are attached.	Appendix III.
			(d) IMMEDIATE HONOURS & REWARDS are shewn in the order in which they are p ublished in Divisional Routine Orders.	Appendix IV.
			(c) SELF INFLICTED AND ACCIDENTAL CASUALTIES.	
			A table shewing the Self-Inflicted Woundes and Accidental Csaialties which have occured during the month is attached.	Appendix V.
			(g) COURTS MARTIAL.	
			A table shewing the number and the particulars of F.G.Cs.M. assembled during the month is attached.	Appendix VI.
			No. G.C.M. was convened during the month of September.	

D. D. & L., London, E.C.
(A8c04) Wt W1771/M2031 750,000 5/17 Sch. 52 Forms/C2118/14

APPENDIX I

Sept. 1st - 30th 1918.

37th DIVISION.

1918.		CASUALTIES. Killed.		Wounded.		Missing.		Sick Evacuations.		REinforcementa.	
		O.	O.R.	O.	O.R.	O.	O.R.	Off.	O.R's.	Off.	O.R's.
Sept.	1st	-	-	-	1	-	-	-	10	-	26
	2nd	-	2	1	13	-	-	1	10	-	39
	3rd	-	-	-	-	-	-	2	15	4	25
	4th	-	18	6	145	-	10	3	28	-	1
	5th	-	-	-	12	-	-	1	15	2	190
	6th	-	2	2	25	-	-	-	16	1	58
	7th	-	4	-	15	-	-	1	20	2	19
	8th	1	-	1	26	-	-	-	14	3	37
	9th	-	5	1	25	-	-	1	15	4	132
	10th	-	4	-	18	-	-	1	15	1	13
	11th	-	-	-	-	-	-	-	7	5	35
	12th	-	-	-	-	-	-	-	11	4	158
	13th	4	66	5	248	-	39	1	15	3	73
	14th	-	-	-	-	-	-	-	9	1	22
	15th	-	-	-	-	-	-	-	11	1	55
	16th	-	12	-	88	-	30	1	15	2	99
	17th	-	1	-	17	-	-	2	19	1	71
	18th	-	1	4	43	-	-	1	15	3	108
	19th	-	14	3	96	-	30	-	12	1	118
	20th	1	3	1	45	-	-	-	15	2	20
	21st	-	2	1	14	-	-	-	12	3	49
	22nd	-	4	1	25	-	-	-	9	-	26
	23rd	-	1	-	1	-	-	1	10	1	9
	24th	-	-	-	5	-	-	1	6	1	26
	25th	-	-	-	-	-	-	-	10	1	7
	26th	-	-	-	-	-	-	1	10	-	-
	27th	-	-	-	5	-	-	-	11	-	2
	28th	-	-	-	-	-	-	2	18	-	5
	29th	-	-	-	9	-	-	1	15	5	-
	30th	-	-	-	-	-	-	-	14	11	108
		6	139	26	876	-	109	21	402	62	1531

Office Copy.

APPENDIX II

"B."

37th. DIVISION.

STRENGTH RETURN MADE UP TO 12 NOON SATURDAY September 7th. 1918. Sept. 7th. 1918.

UNIT.	(i.) Fighting strength for previous week, compiled in accordance with A.Gs. instructions.		(ii.) Increase during week, due to drafts, etc., taken on strength of unit.		(iii.) Totals from (i.) and (ii.)		(iv.) Decrease during week—casualties, etc., deducted from strength of unit.		"A" Strength, excluding Attached.		"B" Not present with the Unit and not at the disposal of C.O. included in column "A."		"A" minus "B" Available Fighting Strength including Personnel of Battalion Transport and Quartermaster's Stores.		REMARKS. (Brief notes regarding (ii.), (iv.) and "B," etc.)
	Officers.	O.R.	Officers.	O.R.	Officers.	O.R.	Officers.	O.R.	Officers.	O.R.	Officers.	O.R.	Officers.	O.R.	
63rd Infantry Brigade.															
8th Lincolns.	37	803	3	131	40	934	1	15	39	919	14	129	25	790	
8th Somersets.	31	878	7	18	38	896	-	12	38	884	12	126	26	758	
4th Middlesex.	37	762	-	16	37	778	1	11	36	767	14	80	22	687	
TOTAL BRIGADE.	105	2443	10	165	115	2608	2	38	113	2570	40	335	73	2235	
111th Infantry Brigade,															
10th R.Fusiliers.	33	783	1	30	34	813	-	6	34	807	8	139	26	668	
13th K.R,R,C.	35	742	4	214	39	956	-	25	39	931	10	117	29	814	
13th Rifle Bde.	45	1021	1	19	46	1040	3	33	43	1007	19	184	24	823	
TOTAL BRIGADE.	113	2546	6	263	119	2809	3	64	116	2745	37	440	79	2305	
112th Infatry Brigade.															
13th R.Fusiliers.	34	793	1	5	35	798	3	111	32	687	12	119	20	568	
1st Essex.	29	862	-	20	29	882	-	6	29	876	8	88	21	788	
1/1st Herts.	27	1045	1	46	28	1091	2	102	26	989	8	#103	18	886	# 143. O.R. shown by unit at Composite Bn. but not included in Col. B. of this return.
TOTAL BRIGADE.	90	2700	2	71	92	2771	5	219	87	2552	28	310	59	2242	
9th Nth. Staffs.(Pnrs.)	33	843	3	-	36	843	-	8	36	835	10	80	26	755	
TOTAL DIVISION.	341	8532	21	499	362	9031	10	329	352	8702	115	1165	237	7537	
37th Bn. M.G. Corps.	43	865	4	24	47	889	1	15	46	874	9	126	37	748	
TOTALS															

[signature]
Major General.
Commanding 37th Division.

3rd Field Survey Co., R.E. 2759 13-3-18.

Office Copy

"B."

37th DIVISION.

STRENGTH RETURN MADE UP TO 12 NOON SATURDAY September 14th. 1918 ..... Sept. 14th ..... 1918.

UNIT.	(i.) Fighting strength for previous week, compiled in accordance with A.Gs. instructions.		(ii.) Increase during week, due to drafts, etc., taken on strength of unit		(iii.) Totals from (i.) and (ii.)		(iv.) Decrease during week—casualties, etc., deducted from strength of unit.		"A" Strength, excluding Attached.		"B" Not present with the Unit and not at the disposal of C.O. included in column "A."		"A" minus "B" Available Fighting Strength including Personnel of Battalion Transport and Quartermaster's Stores.		REMARKS. (Brief notes regarding (ii.), (iv.) and "B," etc.)
	Officers.	O.R.	Officers.	O.R.	Officers.	O.R.	Officers.	O.R.	Officers.	O.R.	Officers.	O.R.	Officers.	O.R.	
63rd Infantry Brigade.															
8th Lincolns.	39	919	-	7	39	926	3	67	36	859	12	115	24	744	
8th Somersets.	38	884	-	30	38	914	4	104	34	810	9	100	25	710	
4th Middlesex.	36	767	2	132	38	899	2	51	36	848	13	83	23	765	
TOTAL BRIGADE.	113	2570	2	169	115	2739	9	222	106	2517	34	298	72	2219	
111th Infantry Brigade.															
10th R.Fusiliers.	34	807	1	13	35	820	-	7	35	813	10	131	25	682	
13th K.R.R.C.	39	931	3	15	42	946	6	258	36	688	7	114	29	574	
13th Rifle Bde.	43	1007	-	20	43	1027	4	217	39	810	19	106	20	704	
TOTAL BRIGADE.	116	2745	4	48	120	2793	10	482	110	2311	36	351	74	1960	
112th Infantry Brigade.															
13th R.Fusiliers.	32	687	1	158	33	845	1	21	32	824	10	94	22	730	
1st Essex.	29	876	13	58	42	934	1	16	41	918	8	75	33	843	
1/1st Herts.	26	989	9	15	35	1004	1	76	34	928	6	94	28	834	
TOTAL BRIGADE.	87	2552	23	231	110	2783	3	113	107	2670	24	263	83	2407	
9th N.Staffs (Pnrs)	36	835	-	20	36	855	2	13	34	842	10	72	24	770	
TOTAL DIVISION.	352	8702	29	468	381	9170	24	830	357	8340	104	984	253	7356	
37th Bn. M.G.Corps.	46	874	2	2	48	876	1	35	47	841	9	96	38	745	
TOTALS															

[illegible signature]

Major General.
Commanding 37th Division,

3rd Field Survey Co., R.E. 2759 13-3-18.

SECRET

"B."

37TH DIVISION.

STRENGTH RETURN MADE UP TO 12 NOON SATURDAY September 21st .... 1918.

UNIT.	(i.) Fighting strength for previous week, compiled in accordance with A.Gs. instructions.		(ii.) Increase during week, due to drafts, etc., taken on strength of unit.		(iii.) Totals from (i.) and (ii.)		(iv.) Decrease during week—casualties, etc., deducted from strength of unit.		"A" Strength, excluding Attached.		"B" Not present with the Unit and not at the disposal of C.O. included in column "A."		"A" minus "B" Available Fighting Strength including Personnel of Battalion Transport and Quartermaster's Stores.		REMARKS. (Brief notes regarding (ii.), (iv.) and "B," etc.)
	Officers.	O.R.	Officers.	O.R.	Officers.	O.R.	Officers.	O.R.	Officers.	O.R.	Officers.	O.R.	Officers.	O.R.	
63rd Infantry Brigade.															
8th Lincolns.	36	859	-	48	36	907	1	9	35	898	12	119	23	779	
8th Somerset L.I.	34	810	2	4	36	814	2	10	34	804	10	115	24	689	
4th Middlesex.	36	848	2	15	38	863	2	32	36	831	10	108	26	723	
Total Brigade.	106	2517	4	67	110	2584	5	51	105	2533	32	342	73	2191	
111th Infantry Brigade.															
10th Royal Fusrs.	35	813	11	150	46	963	4	138	42	825	8	113	34	712	
13th K.R.R.C.	36	688	3	242	39	930	5	12	34	918	7	110	27	~~873~~ 808	The difference of 65 OR of 13th KRR deducted in the decrease col for 28/9/18
13th Rifle Bde.	39	810	-	98	39	908	2	32	37	876	16	105	21	771	
Total Brigade.	110	2311	14	490	124	~~2866~~ 2801	11	182	113	~~2684~~ 2619	31	328	82	~~2356~~ 2291	
112th Infantry Brigade.															
13th Royal Fusrs.	32	824	8	16	40	840	2	59	38	781	11	100	27	681	
1st Essex.	41	918	2	5	43	923	2	82	41	841	12	76	29	765	
1/1st Herts.	34	928	-	62	34	990	2	90	32	900	7	99	25	801	
Total Brigade.	107	2670	10	83	117	2753	6	231	111	2522	30	275	81	2247	
9th N.Staffs(Pnrs).	34	842	1	14	35	856	2	48	33	808	10	70	23	738	
TOTAL DIVISION.	357	8340	29	~~719~~ 654	386	~~9059~~ 8994	24	512	362	~~8547~~ 8482	103	1015	259	7467	
37th Bn. M.G.Corps.	47	841	-	28	47	869	-	15	47	854	8	79	39	775	
TOTALS															

Major General.
Commdg. 37th Division.

3rd Field Survey Co., R.E. 2759 13-3-18.

"B."

37th DIVISION.

STRENGTH RETURN MADE UP TO 12 NOON SATURDAY September 28th ... Sept. 28th 1918.

UNIT.	(i.) Fighting strength for previous week, compiled in accordance with A.Gs. instructions.		(ii.) Increase during week, due to drafts, etc., taken on strength of unit.		(iii.) Totals from (i.) and (ii.)		(iv.) Decrease during week—casualties, etc., deducted from strength of unit.		"A" Strength, excluding Attached.		"B" Not present with the Unit and not at the disposal of C.O. included in column "A."		"A" minus "B" Available Fighting Strength including Personnel of Battalion Transport and Quartermaster's Stores.		REMARKS. (Brief notes regarding (ii.), (iv.) and "B," etc.) …tets advised not included in Col. A		Leaving … left today	
	Officers.	O.R.	Officers.	O.R.	Officers.	O.R.	Officers.	O.R.	Officers.	O.R.	Officers.	O.R.	Officers.	O.R.	O.	O.R.	O.	OR.
63rd Infantry Brigade.																		
8th Lincolns.	35	898	-	51	35	949	-	35	36	914	12	132	23	782	-	-	-	-
8th Somerset L.I.	34	804	-	19	34	823	4	62	30	761	8	128	22	633	-	-	-	9
4th Middlesex.	36	831	1	40	37	871	2	37	35	834	10	114	25	720	1	69	-	-
Total Brigade.	105	2533	1	110	106	2643	6	134	100	2509	30	374	70	2135	1	69	-	9
111th Infantry Brigade.																		
10th R.Fusiliers.	42	825	-	11	42	836	-	5	42	835	8	123	34	720	2	-	-	-
13th K.R.R.C.	34	983	3	4	37	987	-	69	37	918	10	109	27	809	-	-	1	9
13th Rifle Bde.	37	876	-	27	37	903	1	26	36	877	13	124	23	753			2	12
Total Brigade.	113	2684	3	42	116	2726	1	98	115	2628	31	346	84	2282	2	-	3	21
112th Infantry Brigade.																		
13th R.Fusiliers.	38	781	1	14	39	795	-	15	39	780	11	90	28	690	4	-	-	-
1st Essex Regt.	41	841	2	24	43	865	1	35	42	830	9	77	33	753	-	-	-	-
1/1st Herts. Regt.	32	900	1	64	33	964	2	33	31	931	8	105	23	826	-	-	-	-
Total Brigade.	111	2522	4	102	115	2624	3	83	112	2541	28	272	84	2269	4	-	-	-
9th N.Staffs.(Pnrs).	33	808	2	8	35	816	-	11	35	805	10	91	25	714	-	-	-	-
TOTAL DIVISION.	360	8547	10	262	372	8809	10	326	362	8483	99	1083	263	7400	7	69	3	30
37th Bn. M.G.Corps.	47	854	1	52	48	906	1	6	47	900	9	69	38	831	-	-	-	-
TOTALS																		

Brigadier General
Commdg. 37th Division.

3rd Field Survey Co., R.E. 2759 13-3-18.

www.ingramcontent.com/pod-product-compliance
Lightning Source LLC
Chambersburg PA
CBHW080907230426
43664CB00016B/2743